TOUCHED

The Jerry Sandusky Story

BY
JERRY SANDUSKY
AND KIP RICHEAL

SPORTS PUBLISHING INC.
WWW.SPORTSPUBLISHINGINC.COM

Director of production: Susan M. McKinney
Dustjacket and photo insert design: Jeff Higgerson

ISBN: 1-58261-270-6
Library of Congress Number: 00-101305

SPORTS PUBLISHING INC.
804 N. Neil
Champaign, IL 61820
www.sportspublishinginc.com

Printed in the United States.

I would like to dedicate this book to all the people who have touched my life: parents; family; teachers; coaches; friends; along with the volunteers, staff and kids from The Second Mile. You will touch my life forever.

—J.S.

My efforts in this book are dedicated to some very special people whom I will remember for as long as I live. First, my late brother, James, who passed away December 4, 1999, after a lengthy illness. I miss him asking me if the baseball team I coach picked up a win. I miss the happiness he showed when I answered yes, and I even miss the "What happened?" questions every coach faces when I had to answer no. Jimmy never said much, but I know he told everyone he knew about my personal accomplishments. I know he was proud of me and I'm sure he is proud to read these words. I am grateful for his eternal support.

Secondly, my efforts are dedicated to Stacy, Brianna, Celena, and Jessica Rae. Your love and support gave me the inspiration I needed to see this book to its completion.

—K.R.

Contents

Acknowledgments

My greatest thanks in seeing this book through to its finish go out to: Ron Bracken, sports editor of the *Centre Daily Times* newspaper in State College; the Penn State Sports Information office, especially Jeff Nelson and Budd Thalman; Phil Grosz, editor of *Blue-White Illustrated* magazine; Maria Carpico of the *Pittsburgh Post-Gazette*; and Logan Cramer for his photographic efforts. Special thanks to two very special friends who taught me so much about coaching: the late Bob Phillips, who was as kind and cordial a person as anyone would ever want to meet, and J.T. White, who worked with the defense like no other. Thanks, guys, for always being there for me. Thanks also to the many great fans of Penn State football.

Special thanks to Dick Vermeil for contributing the foreword to this book, as well as his services in the past for The Second Mile. Special thanks to Kip Richeal, my co-author and good friend who helped me formulate my thoughts and ideas into what you are about to read. We became friends when Kip was a student manager at Penn State in the early 1980s. I have always been impressed with his desire for life. Despite a disability, he has never let it keep him down. I kidded him about being on the nine-year plan at Penn State, but Kip overcame surgery to obtain his degree and he sweated through many great wins and heartbreaking losses with me. I consider Kip to be a great part of the Penn State family, and an even bigger part of my own family.

—J.S.

Many thanks go to my parents and family for their genuine love and support in all of my efforts; to my friends, Jim and Toni Riggio, Joe Young, Steve Ford, and Joe Baran, for helping with research and for being such loyal Penn State fans; to my cousin, Scott Steckman, who took some great photographs for us. Thanks also to former Penn State football players, Lance Mehl, Jack Ham, Matt Millen, Ed O'Neil, Kyle Brady and Greg Buttle for spending their time to support Jerry's efforts in this book. Thanks also to Amy Pullman for her computer help in pulling the book together. Also, special thanks to Mike Pearson, Susan McKinney, Amanda Romine, Vicki Marini, Jeff Higgerson and the rest of the staff at Sports Publishing for their great assistance and undying patience. You are truly appreciated.

—K.R.

Foreword

I have recently called a halt to a 48-year football career that began in 1952 as a sophomore in high school and ended January 31, 2000, with a victory in Super Bowl XXXIV. Needless to say, the past 48 years have been a very wonderful and rewarding experience for me. What made those 48 years so enriching is the quality people I've come into contact with due to the game of football.

I would be hard pressed to find another profession that exposes a person to so many who can be placed into the "special" category. The coaches, coaches wives, players and administrators are, in my opinion, in a league of their own. Now, when a person can rise to the top of a group of people like this, he has to be an outstanding person.

That is what this book is all about. Jerry Sandusky is a man who has risen to the upper echelon of the coaching profession, both as a football coach and a humanitarian.

I first met Jerry following my arrival in Philadelphia to coach the Eagles football team in 1976. State College, Pennsylvania is just a three-hour drive from the Philadelphia area, so my staff and I would travel to the Penn State campus each spring to work out any Penn State players who would be eligible for the upcoming draft. Jerry was usually involved in helping to coordinate this routine.

Coach Sandusky is one of those guys who take a little getting used to in terms of getting to know. He could be laid back, witty, and self-effacing all at the same the time. You were never sure if he was putting you on or telling you the truth. Once you got to know him, however, you realized you had better listen, because Jerry was going to be very honest and straightforward.

When Jerry said a player could, couldn't, or might be able to play in the NFL, he was right on. He always knew so much more about the kids than just how they played football, especially if he coached the kid himself. It was obvious Jerry really cared about a kid way beyond how he played the game, and the more one is around him, the more one realizes that the players feel the same way about Jerry.

I have witnessed and heard many warm exchanges between Jerry and his kids. What I didn't realize until later on was that his kids were not only football players. He was coaching a totally different team along with his group of Nittany Lions -- the team from The Second Mile.

Jerry has invested a lot of time in building an organization that was designed to help youngsters in need of a support system. The Second Mile organization was designed to fill as many of these needs as possible. They were dedicating their first Second Mile home by the time I really got to know what Jerry Sandusky was all about. The home provided a family life experience for only a few kids at that time, but it was a beginning and this was when I realized that Jerry Sandusky was truly something special. Not only was he a father raising his own family and a defensive coordinator coaching a second family, he took on the responsibility of trying to provide leadership and support to a third group, his Second Mile family. Since the initiation of this program, The Second Mile has become a statewide institution that helps youngsters in need of a support system they aren't otherwise receiving from direct family members.

After leaving the coaching profession my first time around, I spent 14 years broadcasting college and professional football games. This again provided me with opportunities to be around Coach Sandusky. Sportscaster Brent Musberger and I were assigned to announce many of Penn State's big games over the years. We would always get into town on a Thursday so we could watch practice and meet with the coaches.

Jerry's coordinator meeting was always a highlight for Brent and myself. The meetings were always a combination of concern for the opponent, his game plan and, of course, his humor. It was when he talked about specific kids that you could really read his sincere interest in the people who played football for him. He loved them.

This book will be a special read for anyone who respects people who are unselfish and give a little piece of themselves to everyone with whom they come in contact. I think Jerry can be best described by saying he very well could be the Will Rogers of the coaching profession. Enjoy, because this man, Jerry Sandusky, is an original piece of work!

Dick Vermeil, Head Coach
St. Louis Rams, Super Bowl XXXIV Champions

Introduction

How do I acknowledge the subject of this book? I am more than proud to call Jerry Sandusky my friend. Meet him and you will immediately know he is a story-teller. One of the best. Jerry and I have shared many great adventures in our lives. More often than not, there is Jerry's version of the story, and then there is what really happened. There is no doubt in my mind that Jerry's versions are far more interesting.

When I was a freshman at Penn State, I became a student equipment manager with the football team. Based on seniority, the managers got to choose which coach they would spend the season working with. I soon learned how popular Jerry Sandusky was, because he was usually the first or second coach chosen in our meetings. I dealt more with administrative issues as a manager, things such as paperwork and making sure players were in meetings and at meals, so I worked with all the coaches in one way or another. I could not do the heavy work because of a disability, but I appreciated being part of the team.

My first real contact with Jerry Sandusky came from a rather odd question he posed to me: "How much do you weigh, young man?" I was puzzled, because I knew he wasn't interested in me as a linebacker, but I told him I weighed about 95 pounds. "Get up on that scale," he ordered. I did and the locker room scale topped out at 96.

"Not bad," Jerry said, trying to sound as mean as possible, "but you still have some work to do." Sensing my confusion, Jerry stared at me and continued. "We gotta get you up to 100 pounds before you're ready to fight me."

Fight him? I barely knew him. "When you get to 100 pounds, it's gonna be you and me in the center of the locker room in a boxing match. Then I'll show you who the real boss is. It'll be you and me eyeball-to-belly button." The last remark was made in reference to my five-foot height, but I smiled and let it go. Suddenly, about a dozen players became my friend and they stood by me every day on that scale to see if I could reach my goal. It took me until my senior year, amazingly, but it had become such an important issue to Jerry and me, that practically the whole locker room cheered when the number 101 was announced.

I stepped off the scale, took hold of my walking cane and calmly made my way to the center of the locker room. With all eyes on me, I stopped, turned to Jerry with fists up and said, "Let's go!" So, we had our famed title bout—eyeball-to-belly button—and to the delight of the audience, I laid Jerry out with a swift (and well-rehearsed) right hook.

One other memorable experience from our Penn State experience together was an incident we shared at the 1979 Liberty Bowl in Memphis, Tennessee. We were playing Tulane University, and a few days before the game, both teams were invited to a luncheon sponsored by the Liberty Bowl committee. I was seated at Jerry's table and, being a journalism major, I listened intently to famed ABC sportscaster Keith Jackson give a speech about competitive spirit and what fine institutions both teams represented.

I clapped like everyone else when Mr. Jackson completed his speech and I nudged Jerry with my elbow. "You know him, don't you, Jer?" I asked. I figured with Jerry being such a self-proclaimed big shot, he would know all the sportscasters who had ever covered Penn State football.

"Well, sure," Jerry stammered. "I sort of know him." Maybe he figured he could escape without me saying anything more, but I pressed on.

"How about walking up there with me and introducing me?" I pleaded. Jerry didn't seem too excited.

"Oh, they don't want to be bothered," he answered. Keith Jackson was seated next to his broadcast partner for the upcoming game, Ara Parseghian, who was the famous Notre Dame football coach for many years. As nice as it would be to meet Coach

Parseghian, my biggest thrill would be to meet an icon in the same profession that I was seeking back then. Jerry may have felt sorry for me, or he may have felt he had to save face, but he told me to follow him, and we headed to the main table.

Fortunately, Keith Jackson and Ara Parseghian were seated at the end of the table, and we would not have to step over people to reach them. I kept my mouth shut so Jerry could do the talking, and he approached the two men in a rather confident manner.

"Excuse me, Keith, I'm Jerry Sandusky, one of the Penn State coaches." They shook hands, and Keith Jackson showed Jerry great respect by calling him "Coach" and asking him how things were going. I was sure they had met a few times before. Coach Parseghian was equally cordial with Jerry, and I was nervous as Jerry told Keith Jackson of my journalistic background and how interested I was to meet him. And Keith Jackson was a pro and a gentleman all the way. He didn't let me down one bit. "Nice to meet you, Kip," he said, "How do you enjoy Penn State football?"

As we walked away from the main table, I was highly impressed with meeting one of my broadcasting idols in person, as well as Jerry's influential position. Of course, Jerry was beaming, knowing that he had made it through this episode somehow, perhaps letting the thought into his head that maybe Keith Jackson actually did remember him.

Three years later, we were playing Georgia in the Sugar Bowl for the national championship. On the day before the game, our team had a light practice inside the New Orleans Superdome, where the game was to be played. I was walking beside Jerry on one side of the field and I noticed on the other sideline none other than Keith Jackson strolling around, practically by himself.

I brought this to Jerry's attention and I said, "Remember when you introduced me to him at the Liberty Bowl?" Jerry smiled at the thought and said, "Let's go over there and say hi to him." I wasn't sure if I wanted to do that because I didn't expect him to remember me for one thing, plus I pointed out to Jerry that maybe he didn't want to be bothered.

"Nonsense," Jerry said. "He'll want to talk to us. We're his buddies." With that, we were on our way across the Superdome floor in a straight trajectory for Keith Jackson. This time, Jerry was brimming with confidence, knowing he would surely be remembered. As we reached Mr. Jackson, Jerry confidently extended his right hand and put his left hand on the broadcaster's shoulder.

"Keith, it's good to see you again," Jerry said, as though he were attending a class reunion. "How have you been? I guess you're doing the game tomorrow." As the seconds went by, I stood quietly and watched the bewildered look on Keith Jackson's face. I figure he noticed that Jerry was wearing a shirt similar to some of the other Penn State coaches who were out on the field and that was what might have triggered his memory. Finally, he spoke in a rather cautious manner.

"Oh, hello Coach," Mr. Jackson said as he returned the handshake. "How are you?" Jerry was humbled, I could tell by the look on his face. I didn't think anything could bring him lower until what happened next. It had been three years, but as Keith Jackson shook hands with Jerry, he noticed a smaller figure out of the corner of his eye.

When he turned, his eyes lit up and a smile crossed his face from ear to ear. "Hello, Kip!" he exclaimed loudly. "How are you?" Jerry went through the rest of the day not knowing how he could concentrate on stopping Herschel Walker, Georgia's All-American running back. I had humbled him once more.

As I said, a story involving Jerry Sandusky can be told the way things really happened, or it can be told in Jer's way. Keep in mind that Jerry's version is usually more interesting. I have shared many other experiences with Jerry, but these were a couple of my favorites. I will let you, the reader, decide who was really telling the story.

I am very proud to call Jerry Sandusky my friend, and I was deeply honored when he asked me to help him with this project several years ago. We have gathered many stories and experiences to share, which we hope you will find interesting. In and out of football, Jerry is an outstanding individual. If you like football, you will like this book, and if you cherish everything life has to offer, you will enjoy it even more.

Kip Richeal, July 2000

A Family Perspective

It is truly an honor for me to write an introduction to this book. My goal in this short segment is to paint a portrait of what my life has been like growing up with the man some people know as "Coach," others as Mr. Sandusky, and most just as plain old Jer. I simply call him Dad.

My father's career with the Penn State football team, as well as his role as founder of The Second Mile, has taken my family on a journey through one exciting adventure after another over the years.

The 1999 season was an emotional roller coaster for me because I knew it would be the last season of Penn State football, at least in the same manner that I had grown up with. I supported my dad's decision to retire at the end of the season wholeheartedly, but I couldn't help being filled with so many overwhelming feelings as the season wound down. From a family standpoint, we could stroll down memory lane forever and never get tired of the walk. The following are just a few of my memories of what it was like to grow up, not only as a Penn State football insider, but also as a Sandusky insider.

It was cold and dark in the early morning hours and pretty much all of us had been through a restless night of sleep. Our minds were racing and our stomachs were churning with the excitement of what was ahead. We packed like sardines into one car after a last-minute check of plugs, wires, etc., in our home and then we were on our way. As we approached the parking lot of the Penn State football practice complex, we could see the charter buses and smell that old familiar exhaust.

It was a sight that few families got to experience in State College, but for us and a few proud others, it had become an annual ritual. As we unpacked the car and approached the buses, we could hear the roll call taking place: "PATERNO! . . .Here!; ANDERSON! . . . All here!; SANDUSKY!" I loved to hear our name called because I couldn't wait to yell, "HERE!" loud enough for all of State College to hear. We were all present and accounted for and after the last few names were called, we were safely aboard the buses and ready to go. As the final door closed with a thud and the brakes gave a light howl from the pressure being released, we were ready to continue on another journey—one which we referred to as "BOWL TRIP!" I will certainly miss those wonderful experiences, but the memories I have experienced will stay with me forever.

There was an incident when I was a senior in high school; an age, of course, when I was trying very hard to impress all the good-looking football players. I was wearing old clothes as I maneuvered our riding mower around the lawn. Generally, I enjoyed doing this. It was often relaxing and I used to belt out my favorite song, "Amazing Grace," loud enough for the neighbors to hear.

On this particular day, however, the mower was clogging a lot. I was already hot from the sun and becoming frustrated with the situation. I needed to empty the grass-catcher bags, but they wouldn't come off the mower. I shook, pushed, and pulled, but it wouldn't budge. In the meantime, the mower took on a mind of its own. From my pushing and pulling, it jumped into gear by itself, lurched forward and headed up the hill, straight for our house and the gutter that led from the roof to the ground.

I frantically ran after it, not really sure what my plan would be if I happened to catch it. As I crested the top of the small hill, I could see my dad coming out of the front door and, unfortunately, into the path of the mower. He was with three big guys, and I have since blocked out the memories beyond my cresting of the hill, but I am thankful that Brian Gelzheiser, Craig Fayak and Kyle Brady were there to step into the path of the out-of-control mower. I was afraid they would think I was a complete idiot, but maybe they think I just experience a lot of the same crazy episodes they had grown accustomed to with my dad.

Much like my father, my football stories could go on forever, but I also remember many great times in my youth when my dad worked so diligently to get The Second Mile up and running, never really sure what road blocks he would encounter along the way.

Even as a small child, my family members and I were the first real volunteers of this incredible organization. I remember going into a very hot White Building gymnasium on the Penn State campus when I was young to help sell a book called *Developing Linebackers the Penn State Way*. which was written by my dad. We stuffed fliers and envelopes in the back seat of our car during family trips, much like an assembly line, for him to get this book in print and in the book stores. He used the proceeds from sales of the book to get The Second Mile started, and we couldn't think of a better way to do so. We were always proud of the things he did for kids.

Because I grew up surrounded by The Second Mile and the people involved, I failed to truly see its magnitude and importance in high school. I accompanied my dad and a few others on a short fund-raising trip one time, and it was on this trip that I first saw a video The Second Mile had created and it made me cry. It touched me deeply and made me realize how important it is to reach out to those the rest of the world had given up on.

It is my hope that this brief portrait of my life's experiences, and that of my family's, will show the reader how greatly we have all been touched by so many people over the span of so many years. To all of you, we are truly grateful. There are people from The Second Mile and Penn State football that I will think of and remember for the rest of my life. Although my dad's final chapter closed with the passing of the 1999 football season, what he and the rest of our family have experienced will never end. As for The Second Mile, the chapters are still unfolding each day and who knows what adventures lie ahead.

Please don't hurry through this book. Sit back, relax, and learn about the life of an incredible man who has touched the lives of so many, although his first thoughts are of those who have greatly touched his life at some point in time. Be prepared to laugh out loud, but also keep a box of tissues nearby because you are liable to release a tear or two.

My brothers, E.J., Ray, Jeff, Jon, and Matt, and I thank the friends and family of Penn State football and The Second Mile, and we thank you, the reader, for taking the time to learn about the greatest man we have ever known: our father, Jerry Sandusky.

Kara Sandusky Werner
July, 2000

The Authors . . .

JERRY SANDUSKY retired as defensive coordinator of the Penn State University football team following the 1999 season. He spent 32 years at Penn State, all as an assistant to legendary head coach Joe Paterno, including the last 23 as defensive coordinator. Sandusky is the founder of The Second Mile, a charitable foundation that has touched the lives of more than 100,000 children. Sandusky is the author of a previous book, entitled *Developing Linebackers the Penn State Way*. He and his wife, Dottie, are the parents of six children.

KIP RICHEAL is a 1987 graduate of Penn State University and a former student equipment manager with the Nittany Lion football team. Richeal is the author of two previous books: *Pittsburgh Pirates: Still Walking Tall* and *Welcome to the Big Ten: Penn State's Inaugural Season*. He resides in Beaver Falls, Pennsylvania.

Front and back cover photographs by Craig Houtz
Dust jacket design by Jeff Higgerson

1

A Point of Light

ON THIS FRIDAY MORNING, NOVEMBER 9, 1990, I was preparing, as I do every Friday at 7 a.m., to meet with John Reidell, Jack Raykovitz and Katherine Genovese, who were serving on the Board of Directors for The Second Mile: an organization for children who are at risk or have special needs. I am the founder and chairman of this special organization.

The Second Mile had just received a letter the day before from President George Bush's office recognizing the organization as the 294th Point of Light. While this wasn't earth-shattering news to most folks, it was greatly significant to all of The Second Mile volunteers, contributors and children.

In the letter, President Bush conveyed his "delight" in learning of our "outstanding work on behalf of the community." He added that "our generosity and willingness to work with others merit the highest praise."

"Since taking office as president," the letter continued. *"I have urged all Americans to make community service central to their lives and work. Judging by your active engagement in helping others, it is clear that you understand this obligation.*

"We must not allow ourselves to be measured by the sum of our possessions or the size of our bank accounts. The true measure of any individual is found in the way he or she treats others — and the person who regards others with love, respect and charity holds a priceless treasure in his heart. With that in mind, I have often noted that from now on in America, any definition of a

successful life must include serving others. Your efforts provide a shining example of this standard..."

At the time we received the letter, The Second Mile was an organization offering support to over 51,000 children who required adult guidance, encouragement and role models. There were eight programs that included prevention, early intervention and community-based efforts.

The major purpose of this meeting was to prepare for a small press conference to be held in The Second Mile offices around 9 a.m. Jack, the organization's executive director, handed me a typed message that he suggested I present at the press conference. The statement had been prepared by he and Katherine, and as is their usual way, it was thoroughly well-organized and eloquent.

I studied the message carefully and shook my head. "I can't say this," I told them.

"Jer, you have to," Jack responded. "It is *extremely* important that we deliver our message to the public."

"No, I can't do it this way," I told him once again. "It just isn't me. It won't come out naturally, and I don't want to sound like I'm just *reading* it."

"You must!" Jack and Katherine both insisted. "Tell ya what," I said as I scanned the information once more. "Since we have some time before the press conference, I'll go back to my office, try to put this thing into my own words and still say what you want me to say."

Before anyone could disagree, I was out the door and on my way to the Greenberg Sports Complex on the campus of Penn State University, where I was the defensive coordinator for the Nittany Lion football team.

I reviewed Jack and Katherine's presentation in my office — adding a little of my own flavor here and there — and then slipped across the street to the team's locker room, where I ran into Penn State's long-time equipment manager, Tim Shope, and his assistant, Brad "Spider" Caldwell.

Shopey and Spider are Penn State's version of *The Odd Couple* in that one gets his message across by barking orders to just about anyone who crosses his path, while the other goes about his business in a mild-mannered fashion.

Brad Caldwell is the "Clark Kent" of this outfit. He is the quiet and subdued member of the equipment staff, but the tasks he performs are monumental — definitely in the same league as Superman. He began his Penn State career as a student manager in 1983 and stayed on after his graduation four years later when there was an opening for the assistant's position. I can't picture Brad being anywhere else because, ever since he came on as a student manager, it hasn't been difficult to spot the love in his eyes that he holds for Penn State football.

The feeling has been mutual from the players and coaches, who almost immediately tagged the "Spider" nickname on Brad in his first year. He acquired the name from a scoliosis condition which gives him the appearance of a man with long arms and long skinny legs. But that appearance shouldn't be misconstrued because Brad is as strong as an ox, and any doubts as to whether he can fulfill the requirements of his position have long since passed.

The toughest lessons Brad Caldwell might have ever endured at Penn State have no doubt come from Tim Shope. Shopey replaced a man named John Nolan as Penn State's head equipment manager just before the beginning of the 1979 football season. John was a member of Penn State's first Cotton Bowl team in 1947. Back then, the Nittany Lions played a knock-down, drag-out style of football that carried them to a 9-0-1 record, including a hard-fought 13-13 Cotton Bowl tie with a highly-touted Southern Methodist University team. Working as John Nolan's assistant, Shopey learned that same resilient and hard-nosed approach to the game, and he has held a competitive edge ever since.

Shopey is a former serviceman who started his career at Penn State in the maintenance department. He loves his farm and lives for the rodeo, which is quite evident by the way he sometimes practices his lasso tricks on the many laundry baskets he strategically places throughout the locker room.

Every preseason, Penn State head coach Joe Paterno holds a full-squad meeting where *everyone* is required to attend. This mandatory gathering includes players, coaches, trainers and equipment staff, and one of the many topics discussed is the expected camaraderie between all members of the team. Coach Paterno reminds the players that the student managers are not there to act as personal servants to them, and the managers should be accorded the same respect the player would hope to receive in return.

There have been many times when this formula has been tested, and Shopey — with his unmistakable bark — has always made sure the person who dared to challenge either him or his crew got a refresher course in the meaning of respect.

Some would say there are many differences in Tim Shope and Brad Caldwell, and that might be true. But as a pair, they possess one definite common bond. That is to do their part to keep Penn State football at its peak of excellence at all times — and at all measures.

When I came across my two friends, I talked them into acting as a makeshift audience while I rattled off a practice run of the Second Mile speech, *a la Jer*. They listened intently, both shrugging their shoulders and squirming in their seats. When I closed it out, Shopey was the first to offer a remark.

"Uh, that's a fine talk there, Jer," he said in his own inimitable style. "Yeah, Jer," Spider agreed. "I thought it was pretty good, especially the part at the end."

The words from my two locker-room pals assured me that I didn't need to seek advice from the university's English department. I shook their hands as I thanked them and then headed back to the Second Mile office for the press conference.

There were two television stations and several members of the newspaper and radio media in attendance. The event also included Pennsylvania State Senator Doyle Corman, who was on hand to present the presidential recognition.

John Reidell, board president of The Second Mile, spoke first: "The work of The Second Mile with kids exemplifies the most positive aspects of volunteerism and its societal impact. The organization provides opportunities for kids, which offer a 'hand up' rather than a 'handout', and challenges them to maximize the benefits of those opportunities. While honored by this award, the real satisfaction comes from seeing the efforts the kids put forth and the resultant changes in their behavior and feelings about themselves."

Katherine Genovese followed and remarked how pleased she was to have The Second Mile recognized as a model organization and speculated on the opportunities the honor would provide for the organization to recognize the hundreds of volunteers who work on behalf of the kids to make The Second Mile possible.

Jack Raykovitz then pointed out: "The Second Mile's early intervention and prevention programs were of particular interest to the 'Point of Light' committee, as these programs offered the skills, values and confidence needed to make positive choices and improve their lives."

Now it was my turn. I could see the anxious — and perhaps nervous — looks on the faces of our board members as I ambled up to the podium. I sensed that every eye and ear was fixed on me as I noticed the faint, whirring sounds of the several cameras that were triggered at my attention.

"We are proud to receive this award from the White House," I began. "It is very meaningful to us because this award recognizes all of the people who have made The Second Mile possible: hundreds of volunteers, thousands of contributors, board members and staff. People who were determined to do something worthwhile. People who have steered an organization in eight years from a point where we had two programs serving 35 kids to a level that now features eight programs touching 51,000 children.

"It is also very meaningful because it recognizes the children who are a part of our program. They are special, and hopefully this award will make them feel that way. The kids; the volunteers; the people. They are The Second Mile, and we are grateful that our president has recognized them."

I concluded my presentation with a "thank-you," and the staff breathed a collective sigh of relief as I stepped away from the platform. I hadn't embarrassed them after all. Or so they thought.

"Wait a minute," I said as I reached back toward the microphone. Jack and Katherine looked at each other with a knowing sense of helplessness. The lights from the TV cameras flicked on again, and the small audience was back in my grasp. The Second Mile board members were shielding their eyes and staring at the floor, not sure if they wanted their association with me to be mentioned in public. But I was determined to complete my message the way *I* wanted it to be completed.

"That was The Second Mile talking," I continued. "This is Jer!" I held up the award in triumph. "It's about time, George! This is long overdue!!!"

The room buzzed from the potential stir I had created. Jack and Katherine first grimaced, then scurried to see if *(hoping)* the cameras had missed my conclusion. During all the commotion, I simply sat back, smiled and wondered if the people who would watch this film would notice just how touched I really was.

2

Tylerdale

HERE I WAS, A GROWN MAN AND A COACH for a nationally respected football institution, and I had reverted back to the days of my mischievous youth. I had always professed that someday I would reap the benefits of maturity, but my lifestyle just wouldn't let me. There were so many things I had done in my life — so many of them crazy and outlandish. But I have always had fun, and one thing is for certain: My time on this earth has always been unique. At the times when I found myself searching for maturity, I usually came up with insanity. That's the way it is in the life of Gerald Arthur Sandusky.

This unusual life began in Washington, Pennsylvania: a third-class city with a population of approximately 26,000 people. I used to — and still often do — say that Washington, D.C., might be the capital of the United States, but Washington, Pennsylvania, is the capital of the *world*.

Actually, Washington is a very diverse community located about 30 miles south of Pittsburgh. My friends and I never quite knew what diversity was, but we grew up enjoying the many different people who came from what seemed like every ethnic background imaginable. There were blacks and whites, along with people from Italian, Irish and Polish descent, and the town was divided into wards.

East Washington was an exclusive area, while the Fifth and Sixth Wards were predominantly black. The Seventh and Eighth Wards were more of a white, Anglo-Saxon Protestant community. Washington and Jefferson College bordered East Washington and Sixth Ward, while

Tylerdale and the scenic Goat Hill (formally known as Angora Heights) consisted mostly of Italians, Poles and blacks.

Tylerdale was where I grew up. I spent most of my early years in a small, two-story wooden house etched firmly in a back alley. It was here that I learned the meaning of competition with friends like Butch Horn, Johnny Kazarick, John Liptak, Ron Kubovcik and Benny Lucas. Together, we played the many childhood games of tag and hide and seek. We also wrestled and played sandlot basketball and baseball, which we played with a homemade sock ball. Our basketball games usually ended when the ball rolled into Leo Zaney's yard. Old Leo had his moments when he seemed like a regular tyrant to the neighborhood kids, and he thought nothing of calling the police to chase away the kids that he considered trespassers. I used to look at some of those cops and wonder if they were the same ones that chased my dad off many a street corner in his youth.

I was never one to have my face plastered on the "Ten Most Wanted" list at the Washington County Post Office, but as a teenager, I experienced my share of run-ins with the law. Looking back, my dad and some of his antics might have served as fuel for the inspiration of my *mischievous* youth.

During many hot and humid summer nights, Art Sandusky and his friends gathered on some street corner in town and whiled away the hours trying to solve the world's problems. Usually, the gang became loud and boisterous, and one of the town's residents finally resorted to calling the police. As routine would have it, the officers would arrive, the kids would separate, and the cops would take off in pursuit.

One particular night when the world seemed to be lacking in major dilemmas, my dad and his friends decided to have some fun with the local authorities. Figuring they would have no problem raising enough ruckus to warrant a call for the police, the gang planned their course for the imminent chase. It would be the usual route through the yards and over the hedges, but this time there would be a clothesline strung about ankle-high across the end of their path with a *special* surprise waiting just beyond.

It wasn't long before the boys had provoked someone into calling the police and like clockwork, the large police cruiser came strolling around the corner just as the sky was turning dark. With a quick motion, one of the officers jumped from the car and spotted the kids just as they took off on their designated paths. They avoided the clothesline they had strung across the end of their rendezvous point and watched with delight as the stunned officer tripped the same line perfectly.

S-p-l-a-t-t!!! The bewildered officer went head-first into the perfectly arranged pile of manure: two wheelbarrows full to be exact. The nice thing in our town, though, was that incidents like this usually had a little give-and-take. That was the case between this policeman and my father's gang of friends (although not right away) as everyone declared a truce. Sometimes, indulging in pranks such as this even created a mutual respect between both police and perpetrator.

My friends and I acted in much the same manner when it came to amusement in our teenage years. We hung out on street corners and did our best to create a stir when otherwise all was quiet. Things were different during those times, as kids could have fun and not be forced to take life so seriously. At the same time, we were still careful not to hurt anybody or do anything to get into serious trouble. Some of our favorite times were spent down by the railroad tracks, where just a short distance across were the steel mills, coal mines, tin mill and glass factory that supplied the workforce in our town. The street leading to the mills had a bar on just about every corner, and it amazed me to see the number of men that ended their graveyard shift at eight o'clock on a Saturday morning by going into one of those bars and not coming out again until dusk. Their ventures usually led to a wasted day and a spent pay check.

Mr. Helitski was a factory worker who bounced from bar to bar, and my friends and I got a kick out of watching him stagger down the alley to end his evening. If he didn't make it to his house, he thought nothing of sleeping it off right there in the alley. We loved that man, and we really appreciated the way he always stopped and chatted with us.

Well, sometimes it was a chat. Usually when Mr. Helitski had too much to drink, he challenged one of us to a fight. We politely declined, realizing he was in no shape for such an encounter, and instead we prodded him into telling one of his old stories, which was something that was always more enjoyable.

One time, I asked old Mr. Helitski about his son, Abby, who was attending what was then known as Slippery Rock State College. I said: "How's Abby making out at the college, Mr. Helitski?"

"Ah, Abby do real good," he answered in his distinguished Polish accent. "He doing good work at that Sliding Stone school."

Mr. Helitski favored us with a certain gleam in his eye every time we mentioned his son's name. Despite his drinking problem, he shared his love and sincerity with everyone he came in contact with, and I believe that was what made Mr. Helitski someone very special to the people of Tylerdale.

Fishing was always a highlight in Tylerdale. It was certainly one of my dad's treasured hobbies, and if I wasn't tagging along to one of his favorite fishing holes, I was searching for a nearby lake or pond with my friends.

One day, my friend Joe Johnson and I wanted to fish at a spot that we looked at as *a place where no man had ever gone before.* There was a little pond outside Andy Brother's Tire Company that we knew was filled with carp. The factory had a fence around it, and the signs posted there clearly stated that trespassers were unwelcome. In the past, we had noticed the factory workers feeding bread to the fish, so with our penchant for inviting trouble, Joe and I looked at the ominous NO TRESPASSING sign as the ultimate challenge.

Knowing what ecstacy it would be to bag one of Mr. Andy's fish, Joe and I set out with our fishing equipment — and an ample supply of bread — in hand. We sneaked across the railroad tracks and underneath the trestle with the determination of Davy Crockett and Daniel Boone. As we studied our course of action, we could see the factory through the diamond-shaped holes of the cyclone fence we would have to climb and the pond that was our mission just a few yards away.

We weren't about to turn back now, so I turned to Joe and said: "There it is. Let's hit it." We scaled the six-foot fence with no trouble and sprinted to the factory, staying as close to the building as possible so we wouldn't be spotted by any potential security guards.

We set up our position near a wall along the banks of the pond — hopefully out of sight — and we baited our hooks with the bread we had brought from home. Joe set his fishing pole along the ground about 10 yards from the wall, while I sat with my back to the wall and kept a sharp eye on the line in my hands. Within two minutes, Joe Johnson's pole was being dragged into the water, while at the same time, I started to feel a tug on my own line.

My fish splashed frantically as I struggled to reel it in, and Joe barely managed to grab hold of his own rod and reel before it was wrested into the murky water. Our lines had become entangled as we tried to bring our catches to the shore. We were certain that the guards (if there were any) would hear the commotion and come running for us.

I was able to bring my fish — about a 16-inch carp — to land, but Joe's slipped away. We decided that fate had been tempted enough for one day, so together we ran for the fence, stopping for only a moment so I could hand the still-hopping fish to Joe. The slimy creature wriggled free from Joe's grasp after just a few steps, but it flip-flopped along behind us, bobbing on the nylon thread like a yo-yo, with the hook still planted firmly in its mouth. Its dead eyes stared at us, as if pleading for an end to this bumpy ride. There was no time for either of us to stop.

With my heart pounding, I reached the fence with the fish still tagging along behind me. Joe and I threw our gear over the cyclone meshing and I remember the dull *thud* the fish made as it landed on the other side. We climbed the fence once again and made a hasty retreat, not looking back until we were under the trestle, across the train tracks and at the top of the hill from where we had started. It was then, and only then, that we felt we could hold our heads up high.

Andy Brother's had been conquered! Joe Johnson and I both agreed on that. We felt that we were ready for the Fisherman's Hall of Fame. Until, that is, we made a somewhat unpleasant discovery. It wasn't the police that destroyed our adventure. Not even the factory security (which we still weren't sure even existed). The reason there would be no bronze statuettes of our likenesses lay right at the end of my fishing line.

What was once a proud and beautiful 16-inch carp was now just a bony skeleton. Our fish could not stand up to the climbing and running and dragging we had so unwittingly subjected it to. I held the skeleton up to the sunlight and realized I could probably have pulled a better trophy out of a garbage can.

It was an exhilarating and unforgettable experience for Joe Johnson and myself that day, but we were dejected because there was no evidence to prove that we had raided the forbidden pond beyond the factory — and had conquered it.

Fishing was mostly a time of relaxation to my dad, although that was seldom the case when I and a group of friends decided to tag along. One time, a group of friends and I went to a nearby lake with my dad and my grandfather. We did everything to unintentionally disrupt this otherwise peaceful day, including casting my grandfather's cap right off his head and into the water.

Mercifully, we left the older men alone (mostly because we were bored) and decided to walk up the path to see what other adventures could be had in these woods. We came across an open cornfield and decided to whet our appetites on the sweet fruits that were near full growth there. We picked several ears of corn but became confused as to how we would cook it. We found an old bucket, but that proved to be of no use because of the several large holes torn in the sides.

We started to build a fire, and I remembered an old lesson I had learned in school. "Wait a minute," I said to my friends. "I remember reading about the Indians and how they used to pack mud on the corn before cooking it."

My idea was met with a wave of enthusiasm, so we proceeded to shuck the corn and cake the bare ears with mud. We realized later that, at best, this might have been a great Polish idea. But the bitter discovery of biting into an ear of corn with mud-lined kernels only proved it as an idea the Indians would not have sought credit for.

We put out the fire and left this *old Indian custom* in the ruins of the ashes, deciding we'd be better off just sticking with the customs of our own times.

3

Art and Evie

WHEN I WAS A CHILD, I played the games an only child plays when friends are scarce in the neighborhood. The games that involve imagination and invisible friends with fictional names. I loved to play baseball by myself, which wasn't as difficult as it sounds.

I was the pitcher. I was the batter. I was the announcer on the radio. I was the noise of the crowd. I loved the game, and I studied it until I knew every player's name on every team. My favorites were Stan Musial of the St. Louis Cardinals and anybody who played for the Pittsburgh Pirates.

My driveway was often my baseball diamond as I clicked my tongue to the roof of my mouth to emulate the sound of the bat making contact with the imaginary ball. The louder the click, the mightier the hit. It was this fantasy game, believe it or not, that taught me one of the greatest lessons I would ever learn in my young life.

I was preparing myself for another exciting Sandusky Fantasy League matchup — this one, as fate would have it on this unusually cool July evening in Pittsburgh, a showdown between the Pirates and the Cardinals. *"There's Jerry Sandusky,"* I imagined Bob Prince telling the vast Pittsburgh radio audience, *"the eight-year-old fireballer from nearby Tylerdale, warming up down there in the Pirate bullpen. He's coming into this game with a 19-2 record, and what a day this would be for him if he could pick up his 20th win right here in front of the hometown crowd."*

I recall that I *was* holding the Cardinals in check that day, and the crowd was roaring its approval as imaginary Pittsburgh home runs flew out of old Forbes Field at an alarming rate. My wooden Louisville Slugger (the one part of my game that wasn't imaginary) was experiencing a workout like it had never experienced before.

"Kiss it good-bye!" Prince shouted from his press box seat high above the roof of the garage, as he described another Pirate homer.

My mom and dad weren't a part of the sold-out crowd for this particular game because they were busy working at the ice-cream stand they owned and operated just down the street. The stand was within walking distance, which meant the family car was left parked in the driveway. That wasn't such a problem. In fact, automobiles often provide the perfect backstop when playing imaginary baseball. But as the excitement of the game grew with every breathtaking pitch, I failed to notice that I was edging ever so closer to the car. The realization came to me right about the time I heard the smash of the driver's side headlight and locked my eyes on the shards of broken glass that were splattered across the driveway.

"Oh no," I repeated over and over to myself. "What am I gonna do?" I was still gripping the baseball bat firmly, wondering how I could avoid the almost certain punishment I would face from my parents.

I thought of sweeping away the evidence with the broom from the garage. After all, there weren't any witnesses *(except for the roughly 35,000 who were jammed into old Forbes Field and saw the mighty swing that smashed my dad's headlight. They might squeal on me just because they were tired of waiting for the game to resume).* That idea wouldn't work because, glass or no glass, a broken headlight stays broken when you're only eight years old and not mechanically inclined to fix it.

As much as I labored and agonized over the situation, I realized there was no easy way out. There was no alternative but to tell my parents.

The problem weighed even heavier on my shoulders as I walked the few blocks to my parents' ice-cream stand. *How was I going to tell them? Where would I begin?*

At last, I made it. I was at the ice-cream stand, and I was, at least for a little while, relieved to find no customers hanging around the counter. The less people that knew of my imaginary baseball fiasco the better.

My parents looked somewhat puzzled as I stumbled for the right words. I was unconsciously kicking at the ground trying to think of how I could tell my dad I had destroyed the family's only means of transportation.

Finally, I just blurted it out. "Mom, Dad. I broke the headlight on the car." The burden eased just a little when I let the words roll off of my tongue, but the feeling of guilt was still holding firm.

"What?" they asked in unison. I remember wondering how they could remain so calm.

I cleared my throat and spoke a little louder, feeling slightly more confident. "I said, I broke the headlight on the car."

My parents looked at each other for just a moment and then turned their attention back to me.

"How did you do it, son?" my dad asked me, still as calm as I had ever seen him.

"I was playing baseball in the driveway," I said as I wiped away a tear that began rolling down my cheek, "and I accidentally hit it with the bat. I didn't mean to do it, and I . . . I'm really sorry."

The 15 seconds of utter silence that followed seemed almost certainly like 15 minutes.

"Listen son," my dad finally said. "It's okay. I can appreciate the fact that you were able to face us with the truth like you did. As long as we're honest with each other, we shouldn't expect anything bad to happen."

He followed his words with a hug, and my mom joined in. For a few precious moments, the world was all right again. That moment as an eight-year-old with my mother and father made a tremendous impact on my life. I learned that day that it took far more courage to tell the truth sometimes than it did to make up a lie. And by telling the truth, I found I could gain a far greater amount of respect. The moment solidified the foundation of an everlasting relationship. I had always trusted my parents, but confessing about the broken headlight and witnessing their pardoning reaction told me that *they* trusted *me*. The experience instilled in me a faith in humanity, and for the rest of that evening, it was a wonderful feeling.

Art and Evie Sandusky have always been my shining light. They've given me guidance and direction in an often difficult world, making themselves available during times of trouble or sorrow, while beaming in the shadows during my moments of triumph.

Art was the youngest of four children. He grew up in an era of depression during the 1930s, when America was facing its toughest challenge, and his mother and father did everything they could to survive. His parents were Polish immigrants who never had much and wasted very little. His father worked 12 hours a day, six days a week in the local tin mill, while his mother performed odd jobs such as sewing and food-canning to make ends meet.

Evelyn Mae Lee came from a small coal-mining community in southwestern Pennsylvania. Her father worked in the mine and her mother took care of the home. Evie was the only girl out of seven children, so she learned the meaning of survival at an early age.

Both of my parents were sports-minded in their early days. My dad was an excellent athlete in high school, where he competed in football, basketball, baseball and track. He entertained several athletic scholarship offers for college, but World War II intervened, and, instead, he was off to the service. He never took up golf until he was in his 40s, yet he somehow managed to become extremely good at the game. I had played golf quite a bit before my dad ever started, but I couldn't beat him.

My mom could probably have been an outstanding athlete herself, but she grew up in an era where women's sports weren't as emphasized as they are today. Still, she competed against her brothers on the sandlots, playing whatever sport was in season. She also got her workouts by swimming in a nearby creek and climbing a rugged old slate dump that was just down the hill from where she lived.

It was Evie's love for sports and activity that brought her and my father together. She was a teenager when her family moved to Washington, Pennsylvania, where they lived in a house that was situated about three houses away from the Sandusky residence. She was playing baseball with her brothers one day when she caught Art's eye. It was a mutual feeling of love at first sight, and it wasn't long before the two of them were going out on dates and playing football, basketball and baseball together. They went to the movies once in a while, but most of the time a *big* date was a relaxing evening spent just sitting together and talking on the back porch. They used to flick the porch lights on and off to each other at the end of every date. It was their romantic way of saying good night.

Evie had to quit high school during her junior year because of the escalating need to help her family. Financially, things were difficult in western Pennsylvania, so she took a job in the packing department of the local glass factory and stayed there until quite some time after her marriage to Art.

Art and Evie were married July 25, 1942. That day began a union that would last through eternity, because that's the kind of love and determination they had for each other. Though the times remained tough, my parents channeled their combined energies into everything they did. My dad worked as a conductor for the Pittsburgh Trolley Company and my mom kept the house when she wasn't at the glass factory. They operated the ice-cream stand together, opening daily at one or two in the afternoon and closing at around 10 or 11 that night — or whenever the last customer went home. There was no staff; just one of my parents running the counter during the day and both of them at night.

Art's Ice Cream Stand was well known by the people of the community, and my parents loved it when locals stopped by for a visit. They were known for their generosity and it was not uncommon for them to give away various food items. That was their way, just as it was their way to forget about someone's unpaid tab. I remember a guy named Joe Popeck who always walked by the stand on warm summer evenings and gave my dad a friendly yell. "Hey Art," he would say in his broken Polish accent. "How 'bout *I-ceam* cone?" That was the way he said it, never correctly pronouncing the *r*. My parents usually obliged him, and I watched Joe Popeck eat that ice cream cone like he hadn't eaten in days.

My parents were never trained in the business world, but they did a good job with what they had to work with. The ice cream business was decent but not satisfying, and what little profits there were usually went toward paying the bills. My parents did, however, save enough to buy the house they had always dreamed of owning.

The house we were living in at the time was actually the upstairs of my grandparents' home. While this living arrangement was nice, my parents dreamed of a place they could call their own. Not any specific house. Just a house that they could consider "Home Sweet Home."

Their wish came true one day at an auction. They bid on a house in Houston, Pennsylvania, just a few miles down the road from Washington, and their bid came through. The house was just what they had been looking for. There were two bedrooms and a bath upstairs and a living room, dining room and kitchen downstairs. Nothing fancy. Just a place they could say they acquired on their own, and one they could be proud of.

They continued to operate the ice cream stand, and my dad maintained his job at the trolley company. They worked together during every spare moment to fix up their new home in a way that would make them most comfortable.

Not long after my parents had purchased the house in Houston, a group of concerned Tylerdale citizens approached my father about the closing of the Brownson House Recreation Center. The Brownson House was opened around 1920 by Judge Roy Brownson. It was originally an office building for the local mine, but when business began to slow down, the town residents decided the building would serve its greatest use as an outlet for children from the Tylerdale area. A place where kids could go for recreation; an outlet to keep the kids out of trouble. My dad spent much of his youth on the playgrounds of the Brownson House himself.

Unfortunately, the Brownson House was forced to close its doors in the early 1950s because of the lack of discipline shown by a handful of kids in town who abused the good fortune that was handed to them on a silver platter. The place became overrun with juvenile delinquents who enjoyed the destruction they brought with them. They broke many of the recreational tools provided to them and showed not an ounce of respect to the town's dignitaries who trusted them.

The Brownson House needed a disciplinarian; someone who could relate to the interests and desires of a growing teenager. The people of Tylerdale came to my dad and asked him to keep the recreation center's doors open because they knew he had a way with kids. He was an excellent motivator, whether dealing with sports or schoolwork. He knew when to be serious with kids and when to have fun with them. He was an intense competitor, and that was probably the biggest reason the people of Tylerdale wanted him to be the director of the recreational center. They knew he wouldn't back down to the few kids who constantly felt the need to make trouble.

Art decided to accept the position, and the town council agreed to reopen the recreation center on a six-month trial basis. The salary was low — approximately $100.00 a month — but still my father found the position was one he couldn't resist because of the opportunity to be with people and, more importantly, to work with the kids.

He quit his job at the trolley company because he had the confidence to rebuild the Brownson House to the status of respectability that it once had. The job was supposed to be eight hours a day, but his time often ran over with the cleaning and painting that needed to be done along with the plumbing and electrical work. There was also the time that needed to be spent with the kids who dropped in at the center. But through it all, Art had his Evie, who helped him with the chores and still had time for the ice-cream stand and me.

It wasn't long before my parents sold their dream house in Houston and moved into the Brownson House. I think the biggest reason they moved back to Tylerdale (aside from the recreation center) was because they never wanted to forget their roots. Tylerdale was their home; the place where all their friends lived. In Tylerdale, Art was just Art, and Evie was just Evie. They were considerate to their neighbors, and they taught me the meaning of respect toward all people — young or old; rich or poor; black or white.

My dad never asked anyone to give more than he was willing to give of himself. If he asked someone to lend a hand with work, he would surely be working right along side that person. It was common to see him painting houses, digging ditches, dragging the baseball fields, and cutting grass. The people relied on him, and he hated to disappoint them.

He was tough in his younger days but not in the way to make himself a brute or a bully. He didn't go looking for trouble, but he didn't back down when the odds were against him. His leadership qualities stood out during the sensitive moments in his life and also during critical times. He worked with the neighborhood kids in athletics, and during the summer of 1955, he took the Washington Pennsylvania Pony League baseball team all the way through the loser's bracket to win the Pony League World Series. That moment gave him the reputation of being a great coach in Tylerdale because his fire and determination wouldn't let that team quit even though the odds were stacked tremendously against them.

To Art and Evie, honoring family was a way of life. They never turned their backs on a family in need, and they made it clear to everyone that theirs was a house of sharing. Their time was never restricted when it came to the care and attention of children. They did not tolerate drinking in their house because they figured a person could enjoy life and have fun in so many other ways than by resorting to alcohol. That was the message they worked so diligently to instill in the young people that frequented the recreation center.

Evie often went out of her way to prepare food for people, and even though the recreation center was normally closed on Sunday, its doors were usually open because my parents couldn't see the justice in locking the kids outside.

Holidays were special in the Sandusky household because it was a time to share with friends and family and to reach out to the poor with fruit baskets and turkeys. I always got a special feeling when I helped my dad deliver the food packages to those who might not have had anything otherwise.

Preparation usually began in mid-November for the Christmas party that was held every year at the recreation center. We packed candy in boxes and gathered presents throughout the community and wrapped them for the hundreds of children that came to the event.

There was always plenty of food, and everyone sang Christmas carols and watched holiday movies. Then came the highlight of the evening: a visit from Santa Claus, who passed out the gifts and spent hours talking and playing with the kids.

More than all the candy. More than all the food and presents. There was love. Love between the people of a small, industrious community who found the time to associate with each other and enjoy the good things that holidays were meant to bring.

I truly believe that being a mother is the highest honor any woman can achieve. Women should be proud of all their accomplishments. Trophies and titles come and go, but children are with us for a lifetime. Women develop an automatic pride for their children, and if there is one constant in this world, it is a mother's love for her child. My mother has shared her love with me through all kinds of stormy weather, and I tried, on one particular Mother's Day, to make my feelings known for her by writing a very special poem:

> *Today is special, it's Mother's Day;*
> *I honor the one who has helped me along the way.*
> *Most of the time she's behind the scene;*
> *She's a pillar of strength on which I lean.*
>
> *To Dad, she is a guiding force;*
> *She does her job with no remorse.*
> *Mom is taken for granted the most;*
> *You won't hear her brag or boast.*
>
> *Today I remember what she has done;*
> *My mom is special, she's number one.*
> *She's been a wonderful gift to me;*
> *For the rest of the world, she's a legacy.*
>
> *She's prepared me for life by the Golden Rule;*
> *My mom, for sure, is nobody's fool.*
> *She cleans the house both day and night;*
> *Everything around her is shiny and bright.*

When we're not around, she prepares a meal;
She fixes our wounds and helps us heal.
There is never a challenge for her that's too great.
Mom keeps on giving, to that there's no debate.

Each new task is approached with a smile;
If you need an ear, she'll listen for a while.
With love and patience, she's done it all;
She makes it easy to feel 10 feet tall.

Today, I say thanks for all that you've been;
You've helped me to handle a loss and a win.
Thanks, thanks for just being you;
You're a symbol of caring through and through.

I called that poem "Happy Mother's Day," but really, it was to honor her for every Mother's Day and every *other* day that we had been through together. She is a very special part of me and my love for her will live through the ages.

Just as Evie is special to me, so was Art. Without him, I would have known a far less notable meaning of sportsmanship and I may never have discovered the true importance of loving thy neighbor. I did not consider poetry one of my strong points, but when I thought of my parents, the writing came easy. This is one I simply called "DAD:"

I'm not sure what a dad is supposed to be;
But I do know what my dad means to me.
It is very difficult to explain;
Yet so real to me just the same.

First, he is the leader of my family;
That has especially meant a lot to me.
Quite an example, this guy has been;
He's shown me love and guidance and discipline.
He's been there for me every single day;
There are not a lot of words he's had to say.
The person he's been is quite enough;
My dad is really strong; he's awfully tough.

I guess he's not as perfect as I make him appear to be;
However, he's the best dad one could ever give to me.
Dad has never expected much in return;
When I need him, he's there to express concern.

His courage is what I admire;
It is unlike him to ever tire.
He keeps on giving, making the sacrifice;
To say "that's enough" would never suffice.

God gave me a rock on which to stand;
One who is ever-present, with an outstretched hand.
Being a part of him, I will always be glad;
I'm so proud and grateful that he's my dad.

There have been many outstanding people that have crossed the path of my life, but none will compare to my parents. There will be no strength greater than that of my father and no beauty deeper than that of my mother.

It would seem nearly impossible for me to match the quality and sincerity that they have upheld, but if I can do half as good a job as they have, I will consider myself the most fortunate man on Earth.

4

Grandparents

THE PRECARIOUS TIMES OF A YOUNG MAN'S LIFE often include his relationship with Mom and Dad's mom and dad. In most cases, there are not just two but *four* grandparents to know, understand and learn from.

I was fortunate—very fortunate—to have been blessed with lessons and guidance from four of the best. There was a mixture in the relationships I had with my grandparents. Over the years, I grew close to all of them, but it seemed like I needed a special bond with each one before that relationship solidified.

I grew close to my dad's parents at a very young age, probably because we lived in the upstairs of the back-alley, two-story wooden house that belonged to them. They were always there for me, and more often than not, they spoiled me the way that grandparents are so accustomed to doing.

Edward and Josephine Sendecki immigrated to the United States from Poland and settled in the small, quiet town of East Vandergrift, Pennsylvania. The last name is different because of interpretation, which is how my father's name was settled as "Sandusky."

To me, Edward and Josephine were simply known as "Jaja" and "Bucka." Jaja used to always refer to me as his "favorite little boy," and

Bucka might have been the reason I was a little bit on the plump side as a youngster because of her passion for cooking my favorite meals. She made unique delicacies such as yard mush, duck soup, beet soup and pierogies. I think I also hold the unofficial world record for eating cottage cheese pancakes.

Bucka loved to cook, and when she and Jaja moved to Washington, Pennsylvania, they opened a bakery, which they operated for six years before it was destroyed by fire. Jaja took work in the local tin mill and proved there what a strong and relentless worker he could be.

He spent many long and arduous hours at his job but still found time for family and friends. Sunday was his day of relaxation, which he accomplished by attending church in the morning and playing cards on the back porch in the afternoon. He loved to chase me around in the back yard, and he was never too old to toss a baseball with me.

On certain Sunday evenings, Jaja would go over to the Pulaski Club and meet with a few of his friends. It was here that the older Polish men of the community could get together and have a few drinks while discussing old times. My grandfather didn't participate in the drinking very much, probably because he feared the consequences of facing Bucka when he got home. She never cared for alcohol, and she wasn't afraid to speak her mind if Jaja came home intoxicated.

Instead, Jaja usually indulged in a game of pinochle. The men would gamble, but the stakes weren't exactly astronomical. The games were usually 35 cents a hand, and a tough night at the card table normally meant a loss of 70 cents or so.

My grandparents didn't travel very often — none of us really did. Upon their migration from Poland to Pennsylvania, Bucka and Jaja settled in Washington and became comfortable there. There was, however, the family vacation we took to Southern California.

It was the summer of 1959, and my parents and grandparents were geared for the trip to Los Angeles to see my Uncle Ed. It was a vacation that everyone had planned and saved for many years to enjoy. I'll never forget my anticipation before we left because I was 15 years old, and I was about to set my eyes on so many of the fascinating wonders our United States had to offer. And I was traveling with my favorite people in the whole world.

Bucka and Jaja were a joy to travel with because I was able to witness their old-fashioned ways, and I watched with amusement their uneasiness over the long trip in the automobile. Bucka loved to eat while she traveled. She ate hard candy most of the time in the car, and if she wasn't eating, she was sleeping. She constantly tried to push the candy on to my grandfather, but Jaja was adamant in his refusal. Instead, he enjoyed filling the car with the soft aroma of his 25-cent cigars. The greatest laugh on the trip was watching Jaja stuff a lit cigar in Bucka's mouth while she was taking one of her several daily naps. He loved to give her a hard time, and fortunately, she was a good-natured woman who could laugh at most of his antics. Their ways of communication amazed me. If ever a couple could read each other like a book, it was those two.

The ride was long and difficult, but my father never seemed to tire of the constant highway driving. We crossed the lengthy stretches of Interstate 70 through Columbus, Indianapolis, St. Louis and Kansas City, and my eyes were wide as I compared the uniqueness of every major city as well as the smaller points of interest. As we rolled through Kansas, I learned firsthand just how long and flat this Midwest territory really was.

We swept through Denver, Colorado, and began our climb up the winding slopes of the great Rocky Mountains. I would never have believed the steepness and beauty of those mountains if I hadn't seen them with my own eyes.

Another memory that stands out about the Rockies was the fear that overcame my grandmother at the sight of the tremendous drop that would await any car that made a wrong turn on those steep and narrow roads. Despite my parents' reassurances that everyone was perfectly safe, Bucka refused to sit on the side of the car that was closest to the guardrail. She said she wouldn't feel safe until Jaja traded seats with her. It was amusing, but I believe the fear I saw in her eyes was truly genuine.

Even though Kansas was long and flat, and Colorado was very mountainous, the longest part of our trip west came when we traveled through Utah. We were still in the Rockies, but we were on our way down, and the descent, for whatever reason, seemed somewhat boring. My dad was even beginning to feel the tedium of the trip as we were being swept in by the heat and desolation that seemed to hang over the family car.

We had spent about five hours on the road that day when my dad spotted a quiet and beautiful lake. The sky was a perfect blue over us, and the tall, green pine trees flashed a mirror image of themselves over the calm waters that were currently being enjoyed by a couple of playful ducks.

We were currently traveling on Interstate 15, which we met up with somewhere in Utah and would eventually take us through Nevada, all the way into Southern California. The lake, with its picture-postcard reflection, had my father mesmerized, and as he cast one look at my grandfather, I knew they both had a fishing expedition on their minds.

My dad pulled off the highway, and he and Jaja proceeded to search the car for their fishing equipment, ignoring the reminders from the women that none of them had their fishing license with them. The two men stepped over the guardrail and walked the 200 yards or so to the banks of the lake.

"You two is-a crazy," Bucka hollered after them in her thick Polish accent. "You gonna get arrested." They were still within earshot, but neither my dad or Jaja acknowledged her.

Twenty minutes or so had passed before a green truck arrived with two uniformed officials in tow. I knew we were in trouble when I spotted the license plate which had U.S. GOVERNMENT written boldly across the bottom. I'm sure my mom was glad she kept me in the car with her and Bucka, rather than let me go to the lake with the men like I had wanted to.

The official-looking gentlemen got out of their truck and didn't say a word to us. Instead, they calmly strolled to the lake and returned seven minutes later (Bucka was counting right down to the last minute) with my father and grandfather walking slowly in front of them. Both hung their heads low as they made their way to the car. Jaja opened the back door, and before Bucka could say anything, he said: "Give me one candy."

"I'm-a gonna give you candy, all right," she snapped right back as she shook her fist at him. "I also knock-a you head."

The green government truck pulled away, and my dad — still having not spoken — followed close behind. The truck led us to a small town, and we came to a stop in front of the office of the local justice of the peace. Once again, my mother, Bucka and I stayed in the car while Jaja and my dad took care of their legal matters inside the small office building. It took them a little more than an hour, and, although we were allowed to leave, Dad and Jaja were being relatively quiet about what had taken place inside. Perhaps another hour or two went by before my dad finally explained that they were assessed a $50 fine for fishing in the state of Utah without a license.

It was a modest fine, but I could tell that Dad and Jaja's lengthy silent treatment was mainly due to the fact they didn't want to admit the women were right about fishing without a license. Once the smoke had cleared on that subject, however, everyone's attention turned to the excitement of reaching California.

Once we cleared the Utah state line, it seemed as though the ride took no time at all. We spent a lot of time visiting with relatives and touring the many wondrous attractions that Southern California had to offer. I learned so much about lifestyles in an area that seemed worlds away from what I was accustomed to back in tiny Washington, Pennsylvania.

The highlight of the trip was supposed to be a deep-sea fishing expedition that my Uncle Ed had arranged for us in San Diego. The way he had carried on about it, we figured we were going to stay on some elegant luxury liner, but by the time we had arrived, our extravagant vessel had shrunk to a 24-foot fishing boat.

We arrived at the dock at approximately 11 p.m. to board our *yacht* and our scheduled departure time was for three in the morning. Bucka was probably the wisest person of the bunch because of her decision to stay at home with Uncle Ed's family. That left Mom, Dad, Uncle Ed, Jaja and myself to take our chances with seasickness while tackling the perils of the great Pacific.

The boat had a hole that connected the deck to the sleeping quarters below. The small staircase spiraled downward to a cabin with about 10 bunk beds scattered throughout the very tiny quarters. This room — with the bunks stacked on top of each other — was to be our haven on this fishing trip, and we had to share it with several other adventurous fishermen. It had an odor of stale seaweed, but my uncle and I figured we'd put up with it and try to get some sleep before the boat left its port.

I developed a fun relationship with Uncle Ed during our stay in California. He seemed to understand what it was like to be 15 in a world *(my world)* that was mostly filled with adults. He laughed and joked with me and made me feel like a part of the crowd.

We were pretty tired, what with the two-hour trip down the coast and the time it took to board, so we were relatively quiet as we climbed into our separate bunks. After a short time, however, I began to laugh as I thought of our *luxurious accommodations.* My nose was only four inches or so from the bunk above me, and I couldn't resist the urge to tease my uncle about this *luxury liner.* Soon we were both laughing, which became somewhat of a nuisance to the other fishermen who were trying to get their sleep.

"Must be eastern fishermen," one old salt chirped to another. That only made us laugh even harder.

Our carrying on subsided after a short while, but no one in our party was really able to sleep. We were much too excited about fishing for the first time in the deep blue waters of the Pacific Ocean. My heart thumped even harder as I heard the boat's engine kick in right at 3 a.m. The crew set sail for some prime fishing sites, and soon, all of us (including the cranky fishermen) were up on the deck watching the moon cast its beaming light over the calm and clear waters.

Pretty soon it was 5 a.m., and everyone on board had their lines cast in hopes of landing some great treasure. The boat was resting comfortably, and the day had started out quite serene. It was the perfect atmosphere for fishing until a group of seals decided to congregate near our site. They must have thought it was playtime or something because of the way they splashed and frolicked in the ocean. There was nothing the captain could do except sail to another location. The seals might have been having fun, but they also succeeded in scaring away the fish.

The captain started the engine once again and steered us to an area near a rock island. It seemed like a nice place to fish, but soon the winds began to pick up, and the once calm seas had all of a sudden become very choppy.

The boat rocked back and forth and gave everyone the feeling that if they didn't hang on to something, they were liable to fall overboard. The rapidly developing storm didn't bother my grandfather. He barely noticed the wind fluttering underneath his rain jacket as he continually tried to cast his line into the sea.

Sometimes, when I'm uncomfortable, I laugh. It might be at a thought or maybe from someone's actions, but I find my discomfort in a situation is best suppressed when I laugh. I don't mean to say that I laugh at everything that is sad, and I never aim laughter at any one individual. Sometimes, my laughing is misinterpreted. It appears that I have no feelings for people or their problems. But that is not the case. Laughing is just my way of tending to what might or might not develop into a touchy situation.

At the moment when the storm, got worse and everyone was clutching the ship's railing, I found myself laughing. To us, this was a perilous situation. Amateurs at sea, with the wind and rain raging all around us. But there was my grandfather, still holding on to that vision of snaring his trophy. Jaja probably felt I was laughing at him, and in truth, maybe I was. But at the moment we were rocking back and forth on this fishing boat, I started to think of the last 12 hours or so, and it made me laugh.

First, there was the discovery of the not-so-luxurious luxury liner. Then the grouchy fishermen that were our shipmates and finally, the seals that aided in the escape of our aquatic targets. These bizarre events had me now laughing uncontrollably, while at the same time I was feeling sicker than a dog.

The rhythmic waves of the ocean were getting inside everyone's stomach as the passengers struggled to maintain a firm stance on the deck.

My mother was the first to succumb to the boat's lurching. Her face turned a bright shade of pale as she rushed to the ship's lower half with her hands held tightly over her mouth. It wasn't long before I followed her, and we were both resting on the bunks downstairs when Uncle Ed joined us about 20 minutes later with the most nauseated look on his face I had ever seen.

We asked him how my father and grandfather were doing, and he told us that both of their faces were turning green, but their lines were still in the water. I remember thinking that the fish would probably take shelter from the storm before Dad and Jaja would.

Near the end of the cruise, everyone was miserable. And even though it was only a day-long expedition that just *seemed* to last forever, I was never more happy in my young life than when I spotted the familiar dock site we had left from just one night before. At last, we were on dry land!

The times I spent with my mother's parents were never as close in my young life as with Bucka and Jaja. I was always a bit intimidated around Grandpap because, of all things, his hearing aid. The device compelled him to talk extremely loud when he spoke to anyone, and I just couldn't get comfortable around him because his voice boomed as though it was coming from an amplifier.

Like most men during the depression years, Grandpap struggled to help his family make ends meet. He was an electrician in the coal mine, and he raised his family in a house with a dirt basement and an outdoor toilet. But families back then joined hands during adversity and built their foundations on love and togetherness.

The responsibility of keeping everything together fell into Grammie's hands. She was the rock that raised seven children without the modern conveniences that fill so many homes today. She washed the clothes on an antique scrub board, and the water she used came from an old iron pump in the backyard. She made her children's clothes by hand and saw to it that they were educated as well as could be expected.

I remember how much she was like Bucka in one respect because of her love for cooking. She made delicious baked hams and succulent pumpkin pies. And Grammie, also like Bucka, loved to watch me eat. It was rare that I disappointed either of them.

Grammie was always a busy person. She was constantly involved in this activity or that, and I never took the time that I later wished I had to get to know her as well. I regret that I only got to *really* know her after Grandpap had passed away. At that time, she moved into a low-income apartment complex, and I began to stay with her more frequently. I suppose this was to keep her company, but I also began to discover all the wonderful things about her that I had missed out on for so many years.

I found that she, like most everyone in my family, was a tough competitor. Grammie used to challenge me to every card game she knew, while checkers was just about her favorite pastime. She helped me to understand the intelligence in crossword puzzles, and I taught her how to box. I would hold my fists up in the natural boxer's stance, and she would laugh and do the same.

As Grammie aged, she became somewhat of a troublemaker in her apartment complex, and little did I know that she would ultimately take my boxing lessons to heart.

Grammie was never satisfied in that building, and she was always searching for ways to voice her displeasure to the apartment complex staff. She once left her water running until it leaked into the apartment below hers, and she thought nothing of barging into staff meetings, where she would plop herself down at the table and just start humming.

Just as she liked to cook, Grammie also loved to eat. Meals were provided to the residents of this complex — three squares a day. But the meals were at very precise times throughout the day, and residents were allowed only one serving per meal. One day, Grammie decided to go through the serving line a second time, but the lady in charge quickly recognized her and told her she had been through the line once already.

"I'm not leaving," Grammie told the woman stubbornly. "I live here, and that gives me every right to eat here."

The cafeteria worker went to fetch the manager, while Grammie proceeded through the line and back to her table with a second helping. When the manager arrived, he approached her calmly from behind and tapped her on the shoulder.

That was all it took.

Mistaking his gesture for a cold slap on the back, Grammie turned in one motion and sent the apartment manager reeling with a strong right hook. This, she would later say, was from the boxing lessons I had given her, when all I really meant was to have a little fun with her.

The apartment manager didn't see the humor in my grandmother's actions, and he promptly evicted her from the residence. The most logical solution for my mom and dad was to have Grammie move in with us.

When I was all grown up and coaching football at Penn State, Grammie could hardly wait for the next trip to State College with my mom and dad. She enjoyed the three-and-a-half-hour ride and the beautiful Pennsylvania scenery that always accompanied them through the winding two-lane highway of Route 22.

She loved my family, and they always enjoyed her many visits. I used to get her mad when she visited because I always asked her where she and Grandpap were married.

"In Jacob's Creek," she would answer proudly.

I was aware that Jacob's Creek was a very small coal-mining town, but I always frustrated her by asking how they could have possibly been married in a creek.

Becoming disgusted, she would answer: "I didn't say we got married *in* the creek."

This prattle would go on and on until I thought she had been through enough aggravation for one day. She was very sporting about all my jokes and teasing. Her sense of humor that I had missed so much of as a child was one of her strongest attributes.

1982 was an exciting year for Penn State football. We enjoyed a successful regular season and topped it off with a Sugar Bowl victory over the University of Georgia and the first national championship in school history.

When our plane landed at Harrisburg International Airport in Pennsylvania, there were thousands of people waiting at the gates, dressed from head to toe in blue and white, clamoring for the opportunity to see their Penn State heroes.

The two-hour bus ride after we left the airport seemed like one long victory parade as thousands more jammed the road sides waving banners and hoisting signs proclaiming: "WE'RE NUMBER 1!" I never expected such a strong reception. It continued on until the buses finally pulled into State College around 1 a.m.

I thought the celebrations were over until I turned onto the street that leads to our driveway. Right then, my family immediately spotted the lights on in the house and the numerous congratulatory signs posted all around the neighborhood. We were greeted by many of our friends and neighbors inside, and they were gushing with pride at the thought of a Penn State national championship.

It didn't take long to spot my mom and dad in the crowd. They had driven all the way from Tylerdale that day, and I was delighted to see that they hadn't forgotten to bring Grammie for the celebration. I knew she would be happy for her grandson, who was enjoying the moment of success that every college football coach dreams about.

The party lasted for a couple of hours and I found myself answering the same questions over and over: *How do you feel?; What was it like in New Orleans?* I took the questions in stride and secretly hoped these wonderful feelings would never end. Grammie didn't say much through the entire evening. She, too, seemed to be basking in the limelight that was shining on the Sandusky household, and I felt she had every right to. She was forever loyal to Penn State — and to her family.

My eyes met hers a few times, and her smile let me know that she was proud. I could see she was growing tired and soon she headed upstairs to sleep away the night's jubilant celebration. The people who decorated our house had taped signs and newspaper clippings on practically every wall, and I noticed that Grammie had stopped to admire one of the headlines. She had a strangely puzzled look on her face.

"What does this mean?" she asked to no one in particular. "Hmmph! How can they say we're no one?"

I came closer and laughed out loud when I saw the headline she was reading. The headline of the *Centre Daily Times* championship edition revealed a bold salutation to Penn State with the words "WE'RE NO. ONE" pasted at the top.

I explained it to her and then joked with everyone about how Penn State went from being *number* one to *no* one in a span of about five minutes.

The trait I'll never forget about Grammie is her singing. She had quite a few of what she considered to be her favorite songs, but together we had a favorite that we always sang as a duet.

One night, while she was visiting with us in State College, I decided to take Grammie for a little ride. The radio was off, but that didn't stop the melody as Grammie slid over on the front seat close to me and nestled her head on my shoulder. She started a chorus of "Let Me Call You Sweetheart," our favorite song, and I took that as my cue to join in.

We were probably a sight to those who noticed us, but to this day, if I find myself driving down that same street alone, I start to hum the tune that became so special between myself and the grandmother that I wished I had discovered so much earlier in life. I will cherish the memories and I'll always consider Grammie my very special sweetheart.

5

Art's Boy

MY FATHER PROBABLY SPOKE THE MOST TRUTHFUL WORDS about me that had ever been spoken. It happened when I was very young — probably still in grade school. "Jer," he said, "you could mess up a free lunch."

How right he was. Wherever I went, it seemed like trouble was sure to follow. Not the kind of trouble that would land me in jail. Just the mischievous kind of trouble. The kind that might leave me with a bloodied nose or a reprimand from a teacher. These were the perils I faced as a youngster. I did so because I thrived on testing the limits of others, and I enjoyed taking chances in danger.

I had a personal law — "Jer's Law" — that I stuck to when I was growing up and I still abide by that law today. I allowed myself to be mischievous, but I didn't let it get to the point that someone would be intentionally hurt. I also vowed that I would never be disrespectful to teachers, and I swore I would tell the truth if I was ever caught doing something wrong.

That law has certainly been tested through the years, and just because it is a law doesn't mean it has kept me out of trouble. On the contrary, I was known to lead others into my mischievous pranks, and even though I looked at it as good-natured fun, there were quite a few who would be quick to disagree.

Eighth grade was an important time in my life. It was a step up to the big time; a time to start thinking about being a man. It was my first year in high school, where I would face many new and interesting challenges in front of many new and interesting faces. Washington High School was just a little more than a mile from the Brownson House. It was an easy walk, and my friends and I did it several times a day. We walked to school in the morning and walked home for lunch. Then it was back to school and home again after the final bell. The walks were usually uneventful, but then came one afternoon experience that changed all that.

It was a cold and blustery winter day. The snow was coming down in huge crystal shapes and rapidly filling the streets with its hazardous driving effects. School was dismissed early, much to the delight of the students, and my friends and I were having a great time heaving snowballs at each other.

As we packed the snow and built up our ammunition, we noticed a boy by the name of Mitchell walking about 20 yards ahead of us. Mitchell was a senior: tall and lanky and seemingly twice the size of any of us. As Mitchell walked along with his girlfriend, we knew we couldn't pass up the chance to have a bit of fun. I tossed a snowball in his direction, and it barely missed grazing his shoulder. Mitchell turned and looked at us and muttered something about cutting it out. Nobody paid much attention to him and continued instead with the assault.

Mitchell and his girlfriend continued forward, moving just a slight bit faster. I didn't know if he was actually afraid or if he just didn't want to waste his time with a bunch of puny eighth-graders.

Finally, one of the snowballs connected. It came from the direction of one of my friends and hit Mitchell's girlfriend right in the back. She was not our primary target, but that seemed of little interest to Mitchell. He finally turned in our direction and stomped through the snowflakes toward our small army.

Mitchell was 6'3" and even bigger looking up close. I learned that firsthand as it was me that Mitchell sucker punched in the nose instead of the actual thrower.

"If you ever do that again, you'll get it a lot worse," Mitchell said. Steam was pouring from his nostrils. Blood was streaming from mine. Right then, I knew we could rule out the possibility of Mitchell being afraid of us.

He collected his fist from the bridge of my nose and turned with a swagger back to his girlfriend. He shrugged his shoulders and gave her a look that said: *I didn't wanna do it, but the kid forced me to.*

My dad had always taught me to be competitive, and I was infuriated that I let Mitchell have the first whack at me. The next day, I gathered my friends, and we all agreed to get even with Mitchell after school.

We developed a plan where everybody would have a shot at him. One of us would charge him; another would grab his legs; another would jump him from behind. The smallest of our group was the lookout. It was his job to warn us of any authoritative-looking people approaching (not to mention, we needed someone to hold our books). We met after school and waited for Mitchell, confident we'd get our revenge.

We spotted him two blocks ahead, and once again, he was walking ever so close to his girlfriend. We followed them all the way to her house, being careful to stay out of sight, and when they went in, we stopped across the street to finalize our plans.

"Hey, Mitchell!" we began to shout. "Come out here, Mitchell!"

There was no response from inside the house, but we continued to call him. Finally, the front door opened, and we saw his hulking figure step out onto the porch.

"What do you guys want?" Mitchell growled. I could see the steam billowing from his nostrils again.

The members of our *tough* gang sort of looked at each other without even moving. Immediately I had an inclination that the plan was falling apart. Someone had to do something. *Say* something.

"Nothing," I answered with a gulp. "We just wanted to make sure you were all right."

Mitchell shook his head disgustedly and walked back into the house. Another waste of time. I sarcastically thanked each of my friends for their bravery, and as we walked back toward town, each kid was telling how he thought the other was supposed to do one thing, while he did the other.

Mischief followed me *in* the school as well as out of it because, while I enjoyed school, I hated the actual schoolwork. Each day was a challenge filled with many practical jokes and very few dull moments. And though I pulled many pranks in school, the rules of "Jer's Law" stayed in my mind and were never violated.

I had a chemistry teacher who was not only nice but a pretty good sport, considering he had to put up with me every day. We called him Chemist Dunn, and he constantly had us moving from the classroom to the lab working on this experiment or that.

Chemist Dunn had an old-fashioned black phone mounted on the wall in his classroom, and I think he liked the idea of being able to take calls right in his room instead of having to go all the way to the school office. One day, my class was in the lab, but I managed to sneak back to the classroom, where I decided to pull a prank on Chemist Dunn.

I took the earpiece of his precious phone and rubbed charcoal all around the edges. I managed to sneak back into the lab right before he told everyone to go back to the classroom. There were still about 10 minutes of class time, left so I went to the front of the classroom and acted as if I was going to sharpen my pencil. When Chemist Dunn had his head turned, I snuck out the door and hurried back to the lab, where Chemist Dunn also had a phone set up. I dialed the extension for our classroom, and when Chemist Dunn answered, I quietly returned the phone to the wall.

As I moved swiftly back into the hallway, I could already hear the laughter from the classroom. I saw it for myself when I slipped in the backdoor. Chemist Dunn walked back to his desk figuring someone had dialed a wrong extension, but little did he know that he had a big black ring of charcoal circling his ear. The bell rang to end class and soon everyone in the hallway was getting a chuckle out of it. Poor Chemist Dunn. He walked down the hall wondering what everyone was laughing at and why they were looking at him.

Chemistry wasn't the only class I goofed around in. I labored through Spanish, hating everything about it. My teacher, Miss Marino, was especially proud of a new lab in our school, which featured Spanish audio tapes and corresponding worksheets. The lab was designed so a student could sit in a booth and practice with the tapes and worksheets while the teacher could monitor the progress of the student from another booth.

I was in the lab one particular afternoon near the end of the current unit we were working on. I didn't understand a word the guy on the tape was saying. It was Spanish, but for all I knew, it could have been any language. We were required to answer certain questions at the end of the tape, but feeling rather bored with the whole thing, I leaned over to my friend in the next booth and said: "This is the dumbest thing I've ever heard. If she thinks I can answer this stuff, she's crazy."

Of course, Miss Marino just happened to be listening to me at the time and she pronounced her Spanish words quite clearly through my headset: "Señor Sandusky, come here so I can show you just how crazy I am."

Soon after that experience, I was required to give a three-minute presentation on Spanish art in front of the class — in Spanish. I think my speech established a record for the least amount of information given in a three-minute period.

I carried a book to the front of the room with me. It had a picture of King Ferdinand and his dog in it and as I reached the front of the room, I slowly and deliberately opened the book to the page with the picture.

"This is a report on Spanish art," I announced to the class in Spanish. I then held the book with the picture facing open above my head. First, I turned to my right, then to the left. Everyone was sure to see the picture as I took my time. I lowered the book to waist level and pointed at King Ferdinand.

"This is King Ferdinand," I said. I then moved my finger just off to the side at the king's waist. "This is his dog."

I casually closed the book, held it at my side very nobly and said: "This concludes my presentation on Spanish art."

Miss Marino just hung her head and muttered to herself over and over: "Oh my, Señor Sandusky. What am I going to do with you?" As I expected, my name was not mentioned for student of the month honors.

One of my most distinguishable characteristics in my youth was my inability to know when to quit. Somehow, some way, I seemed to always to take things one step too far.

There was a time in school when a friend and I decided to mix some chemicals together and put them in a waste can. We debated for a while as to who would light the can, and I finally agreed to do it. *I wasn't afraid,* or at least I thought so at the time. I stuck my head right inside that waste can and lit it. Naturally, with all the chemicals, there was a minor explosion. The hospital said I had suffered only some minor burns on my face, but it could have been a lot worse.

There were times when I was a little bit older when my friends and I would borrow the truck from the recreation center and go swimming over at the nearby camp grounds. I used to feel we could drive that truck just a little bit further into the stream, and sure enough, we would end up being stuck in a ditch near a creek bed.

Fortunately, the people at the nearby YMCA camp wouldn't get upset with us for interrupting them, and they were actually very helpful in getting us out of our predicaments.

Tylerdale was like a big family. There were arguments and sometimes fights. But underneath, the people were loyal. They were giving of
themselves and would stick their necks out to help a neighbor, knowing
the same courtesy would be extended in return.

That's the way it is with people like the Hughes family. Robert was
a daredevil who swayed from the highest trees in town and could walk on
his hands almost as well as his feet. And Jack Hughes, who loved to fight.
When he came to a basketball game, we found ourselves counting the
minutes until he exploded into a battle. Often, it was with the biggest
person in the gym, and Jack usually came out on the short end. But he
didn't care. In fact, he made fighting his life by becoming a Green Beret.

Fighting was also a way of life for the Gaulteri family. Most of them
channeled their energy into organized boxing, but Frank, whom we all
knew as "Chico," was different from the rest. Chico was crippled from
birth, so life forced him to be different, but nevertheless, he was a competitor. When he could only crawl, he was ornery enough to club my dad
over the head with a lead pipe. And when he was older and able to walk,
he was always off getting into a card game somewhere. Chico hated to
lose, so he usually found a reason to fight when the cards didn't fall his
way. Two hours later, however, his card-playing companion would end up
being his best friend. That's just the way it was with Chico Gaulteri.

When we were young, probably in our late teens, my friends and I
used to end many evenings congregated outside of Osso's Pizza Stand. It
was here that we formed the Tylerdale Recreation Club, which consisted
of David Schieck (whom we called Schiecko), Benny Lucas (Benny Biceps), Ron Kubovcik (The Jessop Jester), Paul Pchinow (Pauly Bird),
Johnny Kazarik and me. We spent a lot of our time at the Brownson
House playground, where many of the younger kids would challenge the
TRC to the various water balloon battles, wrestling matches, and constant harassment we enjoyed in those years of growing up.

One day, I decided to issue the challenge. It was to a group of younger
kids for a water balloon battle to be held at the Clark Elementary School
playground that evening. It was a hot and humid summer day as Benny,
Jessop Jester, Johnny and I loaded my dad's truck with three large boxes of
water balloons. Each box was loaded to the top.

We studied the Clark School playground and strategically placed our balloons at various locations. We utilized fire escapes and hidden walkways. We didn't miss a trick. TRC was ready for the little runts. As promised, the enemy showed up at 9 p.m., and while nobody remembers exactly how many kids they had, their army seemed like 100.

Benny Biceps was a junior at Washington and Jefferson College, the Jessop Jester was a sophomore at the University of Pittsburgh, Johnny was a high school senior, and I was a sophomore at Penn State. On this day, however, we were simply all wet. The younger kids came at us from all directions. They got us with their balloons, and if that wasn't bad enough, they took over our locations and attacked us with our *own* firepower. The TRC was destroyed in a massacre. Some tough club!

The devastating loss we suffered that day did not stop me from tossing out challenges. There was a group that hung around the neighboring town of Canonsburg, and I had always felt this group thought they were pretty tough. Once again, it was I who came up with the brilliant idea of hitting this group in their hometown with an arsenal like they had never seen before.

This time we went in Benny's car, a 1957 sedan, the make I can't recall. And we loaded up with the same group — the one that was humiliated by a group of young kids just a few days earlier.

Washington and Canonsburg provided great competition in just about every sport, so we knew, or had the feeling, we would be in for a huge confrontation. As we reached the town, Johnny decided to send an early message by tossing a balloon out the right side of the car, over the roof and into a group of people moving about on the other side of the road. Naturally, his throw fell short and splatted on the windshield of a car traveling in the opposite direction. We heard some horns blow and, without our knowledge, the driver behind us had jotted down Benny's license plate number.

We were seemingly off to a bad start, and we let Johnny know just how foolish his stunt could have been. We disregarded the consequences for now and continued our venture into the Burg, as the townspeople so affectionately referred to their home.

We made a left onto an isolated street, and a smile crossed my face as I saw the group of 15 or so that would be our quest for this evening. "This is gonna be fun," I said as we approached the corner. Some of the so-called tough guys wore cutoff T-shirts, and they all seemed to walk with a swagger. I rolled down my window and got the festivities underway.

"Hey buddy, come here," I said to no one in particular. One of the bigger ones took the bait and proceeded toward Benny's car.

"W-H-O-O-S-H, W-H-O-O-S-H." The hotshot barely took three steps before he was walloped with a pair of water balloons. They came flying from all directions at the bewildered group, and we could hear them screaming for our butts as Benny pulled away in a screech of tire.

In my mind, once was not enough for these guys, so despite Benny's urgings that we head for home, I suggested we make one more go around to dispense of the many water balloons still in our possession. Johnny and the Jessop Jester weren't too excited with my proposition, but soon everyone agreed, and we circled around for another confrontation.

The gang was still at the corner — as if they had expected us to return — and I was more than happy to let them know we were back by firing another missile in their direction. We attacked with another barrage of water balloons, and the car stuttered — almost stalled — as Benny pressed the accelerator to the floor. Five or six of their gang gave chase on foot, and when they nearly caught us, even I was in agreement that this second attack was too close for our comfort, and we should set our sights for home.

As we made our way toward the town limits, we noticed a police car traveling in the opposite direction. We kept one eye on the car as it passed us, and sure enough, he turned around right in the middle of the street. Seconds later, we were spotted by those ominous flashing lights, and we could do nothing but pull over to the side of the road. The officer's eyes widened as he approached the car and peered in the window to see a box once full of water balloons but now soaked with about an inch of just plain water.

"Get in the back," the officer said matter-of-factly to me. I obliged, and the cop directed Benny downtown as he took my place in the front seat. The other officer followed in the police cruiser, and we were greeted by a gruff-looking desk sergeant as we arrived at the police station.

"Bring 'em over here!" the sergeant barked to show his authority. He gave us a good tongue-lashing and informed us that our stunt was simply ridiculous. The sergeant even fabricated the story about the car Johnny had plugged, saying the windshield had been broken. We were subjected to about five more minutes of condemnation before the sergeant gave his final decision.

"LOCK 'EM UP!" he said for the whole building to hear. He had an awful-looking grin on his face.

Johnny let out a stream of vomit at the sergeant's words, and when he was finished, he turned to me with a look of terror.

"What am I gonna do?" he asked me. Johnny was always a worrier. "My mother always said that good people do one thing wrong, and they get caught. What am I gonna do, Jer?"

This wasn't the time for me to worry about comforting John. "What are *you* gonna do?" I said to him. "What do you think *I'm* gonna do?!?"

Before I could finish, Benny was asking the desk sergeant if that old crime show thing in the movies is true about getting one phone call before they lock you up.

"Yeah, you can have one phone call," the sergeant growled to him.

After some discussion, Benny decided to call his uncle, who was a justice of the peace. Thank goodness we reached him at home, and he agreed to come to the police station. I was sitting on a bench across from the desk corner when I heard another policeman report a call about a group of youths who had formed a human chain across a downtown street stopping all traffic. He told the sergeant that a car was on the way to bring this group in. I immediately realized what group he was talking about.

"Great," I said, thinking of the gang we had blasted with the water balloons. "If they bring those guys to jail, we'll never get outta here alive."

Somehow we dodged a bullet, however, when a report came back that the group had scattered and traffic was back to normal.

Benny's uncle arrived 20 minutes later, and after a lengthy discussion with the desk sergeant, it was agreed that we'd be released on the grounds that we return two nights later for a hearing. There was mostly silence on the way home, but the members of TRC agreed that we would not tell our parents until — or unless — it was absolutely necessary.

We met the next night at Osso's to discuss our situation and once again, the discussion revolved around Johnny. It seems he was scheduled to have a baseball game the same night as the hearing, and how could he explain his absence to his parents, who were sure to be at the game?

"Sorry, Mom and Dad. I can't make the game...I have to go to a court hearing to explain why I bombed a car's windshield with water balloons, not to mention half the kids in Canonsburg."

No, he couldn't tell them that. We had another dilemma on our hands, and it was up to me to fix it.

"Here's what we do," I said. "We'll get the truck and hose, go out to the park and water down the baseball field. We'll make history. The first artificially rained out baseball game."

Benny, who had some of my flaky tendencies, thought the idea was great. The only person who didn't go along with us was the Jessop Jester, although Johnny was a bit apprehensive too. The three of us got a long garden hose, loaded it into the truck and headed for the city park. Along the way, Johnny decided the risk for further trouble was too great, so Benny and I told him to drop us off at the park and come back for us in about one hour. Benny and I jumped out at the park with our equipment, and as Johnny drove away, I yelled back at him.

"Relax," I said. "We'll have that game rained out in no time."

We carried the hose down a hill to the waterline situated near the field. Immediately, we encountered problems as we couldn't get the hose connected to the line. We thought we'd try the restroom to see if there was a line to be found there, all the while keeping a careful eye on any unfamiliar passing cars through the park.

As luck would have it, the restroom was locked. We spotted a small opening near the roof, and the temptation of climbing the wall and trying to crawl through was tremendous. But as another vehicle passed through, we knew that might not be such a smashing idea. After all, we didn't want a "breaking and entering" rap hanging over our heads.

Benny and I were discouraged as we walked back toward the field, but that was soon forgotten when we spotted the headlights of another car coming right toward us. Thinking for sure it was the police this time, I dropped the hose, and we scrambled for the woods. We watched the vehicle's silhouette as it moved toward the restroom. As it slowly rolled under the light, we were relieved to see that it wasn't really the police at all. Just good old nervous Johnny. We watched him as he parked and walked around the area where we had been. He froze for just a moment when he noticed the hose lying where I had dropped it a few minutes earlier.

Good grief, Johnny's first thoughts were. *The police must've come and took them off to jail.*

At first, Johnny thought he should go to the town jail to see if we *had* been taken in, but fear got the better of him, and he decided to return to the park to make sure he didn't miss us the first time around.

Meanwhile, Benny and I decided saturating the field was not the answer. We agreed that our best move would be to simply go to the Canonsburg Police Station the next day to see if the date of the hearing could be changed.

The officer we spoke to the next day was very friendly, and after listening to our dilemma, he found it to be no problem to have the hearing postponed to the following evening. He even offered us advice, saying it would be wise for us all to get together and have just one person accept the blame. That way, the fine would be less, and everyone could divide the cost. We met that night and drew straws to see who would take the blame. Guess who drew the shortest one.

As trifle as it might seem now, the whole experience bordered on the traumatic for Johnny Kazarik. During those few days, he lost five pounds and gained very little sleep. The night before the big hearing, he was pacing his living room at around three in the morning. His mother was awakened by the sound of his foot steps and asked him if anything was wrong.

"No," he answered with a quiver in his voice. She waited for a while and poured herself a cup of coffee before asking him again. This time, Johnny couldn't hold it in. He let the whole incident spill, and pretty soon the whole community would know of the TRC's bout with the law.

We met at Osso's the next evening at around 6:20 p.m. and left in Benny's car for the hearing. With the incident now open to all the parents — something we did not yet realize — my dad was soon right behind us. When we arrived at the Canonsburg Municipal Building, we were greeted by the arresting officer, the clerk of courts and the mayor.

"This is the real thing," I said in a lowered voice as we were asked to take our seats. Almost as quickly as we were seated, the court clerk asked us to stand before the mayor. That was when I locked eyes with my dad, who was seated just over my shoulder.

"How did you find out about this?" I leaned over and whispered to him. When he told us he heard it from Johnny's mother, we all shot an icy glare in Johnny's direction.

The mayor reviewed the charges brought before us. He discussed the car bombing and the artillery fire into the congregation on the street corner.

"Do you have anything to say for yourselves?" he asked us with a somewhat perturbed glare.

"Oh Mr. Mayor," Johnny pleaded, "I did a foolish thing, and I swear I'll never do anything like that again. We're all very sorry."

What baloney, I thought to myself, trying to hold back the laughter. Leave it to Johnny to say something like that.

No one else had anything to say, so the mayor continued with the proceedings. "What is your plea?" he asked.

Remembering the scientific method of drawing straws we used, my friends all pleaded not guilty. When it was my turn I stood tall and faced the mayor eye to eye.

"Guilty!" I said emphatically. "I did it!"

The mayor didn't feel the dramatic moment quite like I did. He simply accepted our pleas and said he would return with a decision shortly.

When I look back on it, I guess I was happy to see my dad in the courtroom after all. He spoke with the arresting officer and the mayor during the short break and explained that we weren't really bad people and had meant no harm to any specific individuals. He was concerned that the arrests would go on permanent record and be held against us later in our lives.

The conference between my dad, the mayor and the officer helped us tremendously as the mayor — after what seemed like an eternity — decided to reprimand us with a $25 fine, and not a word of the situation would appear on our records.

The four of us split the fine, and as I gave my dad a look of thanks, I realized this was just another of the many experiences in a young man's life that showed how special a father's love can be. It made me glad that people in the Tylerdale community thought of me as *Art's boy*.

We even realized that Johnny might have done the right thing by telling the story to his mother. Maybe this little incident would teach us a lesson. But then again...

It was around the same time one year later that the TRC was again dreaming of ways to pass the time. We often spent our summer afternoons at the Washington Park swimming pool, with 10 to 20 kids piling into the back of my dad's pick-up truck. The younger kids all looked up to us and wanted to be around us all the time.

Benny Lucas had just graduated from Washington and Jefferson, where he majored in philosophy and also became an outstanding wrestler. Johnny Kazarik was attending Franklin & Marshall College, and Schiecko and myself had just completed our junior years at Penn State. Pauly Bird was home for the weekend from his summer classes at California (Pennsylvania) State College. He was a rather bright guy, but his grades were struggling a little at the time because he had transferred from John Carroll University in Ohio.

It was a Sunday evening, and we made our usual jaunt over to Osso's Pizza Stand. Pauly was acting a little peculiar for some reason, and we all thought it was really strange when he told us he was going to charge after Chico Gaulteri, who was standing by himself about 20 feet away.

It didn't really seem like much of a contest. Pauly Bird, who played football and wrestled in high school, tackling Chico Gaulteri, who was tough, but still disabled.

Our first impression was that Pauly was merely going to scare Chico, but with a banzai-type scream, Pauly charged with a full head of steam and hit Chico with a bone-crunching, flying tackle. Why? None of us have ever known. How Chico ever got up from the tackle also remains a mystery.

Pauly was always a nice guy, but every once in a while, he seemed to skip a beat and do something crazy. Believe it or not, Pauly Bird Pchinow later became a Pennsylvania State police officer.

After the incident with Chico that evening, Pauly said he needed a ride back to school. It was approximately a 25-mile trip to California, Pennsylvania, but I was able to borrow my parents' car to give him a lift. Naturally, Benny, Schiecko, and Johnny came along for the ride.

There were a number of college students milling about the sidewalks as we drove through the inner parts of town. We delivered Pauly safely to his dorm, and he asked us to stay for a short time. We reminisced about old times for a while, but this talk soon became boring.

"What are we going to do?" I asked. No one came up with any spectacular ideas, but then it dawned on me. *A warm and humid summer Sunday night in a small college town. What else should we do?*

"Why don't we get some water balloons and soak some of the people downtown?" I said exuberantly. My words were met with immediate looks of disapproval.

"No, no," Johnny said predictably. "No way."

Schiecko also hedged on the idea, thinking of his upcoming Petroleum Engineering field trip to the West Coast. He was never an outstanding athlete, but Schiecko excelled in the classroom at Penn State. He knew any possible foul-ups might jeopardize his much-anticipated trip.

"Come on," I agitated him more. "What kind of trouble can we get into? (The incident in Canonsburg must have slipped my mind at that moment). Besides, what are you going to tell your grandchildren someday?"

After further prodding, Schiecko was convinced, so everyone except Johnny loaded the car with water balloons, and we were back in business. It wasn't long before we hit the main street, and fortunately, the people were still out en masse.

Instantly the windows were down, and the balloon-bashing was underway. One after another, people were drenched. We hooted and hollered over our recent victory, and I surmised that we should circle the town once more to rid ourselves of the two extra balloons in the back seat. The consensus thought we should quit, but naturally, I convinced my friends to take one more trip around the block.

We reached a red light at the edge of town, and as we stopped, a policeman jumped into our path from out of nowhere and ordered everyone out of the car.

"Turn around, and put your hands on the car!" he ordered. Again, it sounded just like the movies.

"I can't believe this," I muttered to myself as the officer frisked each one of us. He directed me to pull my car off the street and park it. He then ordered us to march in front of him, where it seemed as though the whole town had bought tickets for an arrest parade.

"We usually turn punks like you over our knees," one person shouted. *"Throw the book at 'em,"* squealed another irate — and wet — pedestrian.

The march ended at the town jail, where the officer opened the door and pointed toward the front desk. Talk about familiar sites. The only difference between this place and the Canonsburg jail of a year ago was the order we received. Instead of stopping at the desk, the officer gave us a hearty instruction to keep moving. I guessed we were beyond the usual lecture or reprimand. Somehow, we had developed a reputation, and this police force was going to let us have it. The arresting officer made his way to the front of the line and ordered us to follow him.

The hallways echoed from the sound of the doors as they opened and closed before us — then behind us. Our long march finally ended around the corner of a dark hallway with very dim lighting. My stomach churned at the sight in front of us. The heavy steel bars; the singular exposed lightbulb. We were about to face the finality of our latest "just for fun" prank.

"In here?" Pauly Bird asked the stoic-looking officer.

"In here," was his simple reply.

"Are you sure?" The words came from Pauly's lips, but it was, no doubt, a question that lurked in the back of all our minds.

"I'm sure," the officer continued. "Now march!"

"S-L-A-A-M-M-M!!!" That awful sound echoed through the entire hallway as if to say: *"Welcome to you new home, boys. Look forward to a nice long stay."*

The room had all the modern conveniences one would expect from many of your finer jail cells. It had the concrete floor, the standard rectangular shaping, and, of course, what jail would be complete without the single, open toilet bowl standing in the corner?

I studied the others around me and perhaps finally realized that our antics were sophomoric to say the least and just not as much fun as they used to be. Not when you end up in a place that many consider just a few short steps from hell. Especially young people, like ourselves, who should take notice that nothing is worth going to jail over.

"That does it!" I cried out. "I'm gonna grow up and cut out all this nonsense." My tone slowly softened. "How are we going to explain this?"

I backed against the wall and sank slowly to the floor, not exactly sure if I could answer my own question.

The room was still for what seemed like a very long time before Benny finally broke the silence.

"You guys aren't going to believe this," he said as he tried to crack a smile. "I have an exam tomorrow for Officers Candidate School with the United States Navy. Anybody have any ideas whether I'll make it or not?"

Pauly Bird could only shake his head.

"I knew it," Schiecko said as he eyed the ceiling in disgust. "I just knew it."

After an hour or so had passed we resigned ourselves to the fact that we were going to spend a night in jail; who knew—maybe longer. Then we heard the clang of those awful sounding doors again. And footsteps coming down the hallway.

The first face we saw was Johnny's. "I told you so," he chimed with a smug grin on his face. Only our loyal friendship with Johnny kept us from reaching through those bars and strangling him.

Johnny entered the cell with the arresting officer and explained how he started searching the town for us when we didn't come back at a reasonable time. Along his path, he had spotted the many remnants of our expedition through California, Pennsylvania, and decided to ask some passersby who still lingered in the streets what had happened. They told him the story — including the parade through town, which Johnny seemed to relish — and he finally found the arresting officer, who led him back to the jail.

We were later released on bail — $25 per person — but no one had money, except for Schiecko's $50 he had saved for his upcoming field trip. Right now, there were more important matters, so Pauly Bird and I used Schiecko's money to bail ourselves out and then returned to the dorm to borrow the remaining $50 from Pauly's friends. Once we freed Schiecko and Benny, we were told by the arresting officer that we could appeal our case in two days if we wanted to plead not guilty.

I think a part of growing up was having fun in ways such as we did. Of course, it's no fun when your actions land you in jail, but part of the excitement — probably the greatest part — is in the danger.

On our way back to the dorm that night, we agreed that we would not file for a hearing. We had been through enough trouble in this town, not to mention an expensive water balloon battle.

Schiecko attended his field trip that year, and Benny passed his test for Officers Candidate School and went on to receive his commission. Pauly Bird finished his studies at California State with little fanfare, and

Johnny, well, good ol' Johnny graduated from Franklin & Marshall College.

As for me, I vowed to remember my words of despair in that dank and lonely jail cell. The ones to the effect of growing up and cutting out the nonsense. I think Art's boy has grown up quite a bit since then, but the nonsense? Well, I think there's still a lot of that left to spread around.

6

The Bug House

I WAS 12 YEARS OLD WHEN WE MOVED into the Brownson House Recreation Center. We lived in the one-and-a-half bedroom apartment upstairs, and though it was small, my mother and father did everything they possibly could to see that it was comfortable.

To me, the whole place was comfortable. The Bug House, which is what we called it because of all the "buggy" people who ventured through its doors, was an ideal place for me to grow up because it helped me to meet so many different people and take part in so many different activities. I learned sports there and developed whatever talents I had on its always competitive playgrounds.

The main building of the Brownson House was a large stone and brick structure with a clock embedded in the top and facing the main avenues of Tylerdale. The basement housed a game room with pool tables and ping-pong tables, and it had a stage covered with mats for boxing.

The first floor had offices, a rehabilitation clinic for crippled children and adults and a small gymnasium. The ceiling in the gym was supported by a pole that was right in the middle of the playing surface. I am probably most responsible for the protective mat that surrounds that pole because I just couldn't avoid running into it during the rough and tumble games we played. I ran into the pole on one occasion and knocked two of my front teeth into the roof of my mouth and the second time I received five stitches in the back of my head — again, because I wasn't watching where I was going.

The main building also housed kindergarten classrooms, a kitchen and a lounge. Up in the attic was a universal gym for exercising and weightlifting, and a room for the janitor.

Another part of the Brownson House was a larger gymnasium that was connected adjacently to the main building. It was dome-shaped and made mostly of stainless steel. This was where a lot of the intramural basketball games were played. Across the street was a large playground with an old bar in front of it. Right next door was a laundromat and parking lot that was, at one time, occupied by a dilapidated two-story house that was condemned. Three of the main factories in Tylerdale were in the surrounding area, and directly behind the Brownson House was Catfish Creek, which flowed softly underneath the railroad trestle.

My mom and dad wanted the Brownson House to be more than just a recreation center. They wanted it to be a home for kids to come to during the day; where their chances for getting into trouble would be lessened considerably.

There was rarely a time when a kid couldn't find *something* to do at the Brownson House. There were always pickup basketball games, football games; ping-pong contests, pool tournaments, and dart and card games. There were even dance classes and socials held usually once a week or once every two weeks.

There were plays that the kids rehearsed very hard for and performed for the adults, and there was also a boys club. And to think, this was all held right under the very roof where I lived. Kids came and went every day. They were the brothers and sisters I never had.

The Brownson House was more than just a structure. It was the people who made it, the people who walked its grounds and the people who kept it going.

To the kids, my father was a father; a grandfather; an uncle. Whatever they needed, he was there for them. He had a heart of gold when it came to sharing, but he also ruled with an iron fist. Just as he acted as coach or instructor, he was also forced to be the peacemaker when arguments or fights broke out. The altercations never lasted very long because Art just wouldn't tolerate that sort of thing. I have witnessed his short fuse by seeing kids literally thrown out the front doors of the recreation center by the seat of their pants.

I called my dad a "T-shirt executive" because he did everything at the Brownson House. His jobs varied from program director and accountant, to plumber, electrician, construction worker and janitor. He did it all.

There were also Syl and Popeye, who were the assistant directors of the Brownson House. They were part-time employees, but their love for the kids and their disciplinary abilities were always displayed with a full-time effort. They approached their work with enthusiasm, and I grew up learning and playing so many wonderful games with them.

Art, Syl and Popeye formed the nucleus of the Old-Timers football team. They were a bunch of older men who played touch football with my friends and me on Sunday afternoons in the late fall. Our games were very competitive, and once you were on that field, there was no backing out. Every Thanksgiving Day, we played the Turkey Bowl, which was kind of like our Super Bowl of touch football. Somehow, the old-timers usually found a way to win. The big play was when Syl and Popeye would run a wall for my dad and protect him with their bellies. With all this open time and space, he usually found someone wide-open in the end zone for a touchdown. It just seemed like that was the way it was supposed to be.

All through my high school and college playing career, I've experienced the opportunity of playing against some of the greatest athletes I have ever seen, but I wouldn't put any one of them against those old-timers on a sunny Sunday afternoon. They were certainly terrific athletes in their own right.

Besides blocking for my dad on the football field, Syl and Popeye were part of the tremendous volunteer support that faithfully rallied around many fund-raising situations. One time, my dad, Syl and Popeye led an effort to build a new gymnasium for the Brownson House. They headed up the fund-raising committee and organized other volunteers into work groups — everyone got into the act and did their share.

Sure enough, with the support of a very successful businessman named Tom Fitch, their mission was a success, and the new gymnasium was built.

It amazed me to see the number of people who were always there to lend a hand to my dad. It was also amazing to see how he found a place for each person and managed to get the most productivity out of them. There was one particular family in the community that had three mentally retarded brothers. The oldest, whom we called "Big Ern," was a special buddy of mine, and we always did things together. I used to take Ernie to the movies or we'd go swimming together, and I taught him how to play basketball. Art gave him a special uniform and appointed him the bat boy for the recreation center's baseball team.

My dad always felt it was important to make Ernie a part of the Bug House, and Ernie loved to put on a show when the center held dances.

Sometimes, the other kids thought it was funny to tease Ernie or his brothers, but I never let that stuff go too far.

Ernie wasn't a totally innocent individual, however. He had his fun and used to go around calling everyone a punk. Everyone, that is, except Big Art. I used to try and goad him into calling my dad a punk or a big Polack all the time, but he wouldn't budge. Ernie loved my dad and remained loyal to him all the way.

Although we were such close friends, Ernie sort of got away from me when I married my wife, Dottie. I don't know whether he felt betrayed by me — his friend — but things have never been quite the same. I see him sometimes when I visit the Tylerdale area, and he is still cordial with me, but somewhere along the way, his outgoing and friendly manner is no longer a part of his relationship with me.

Ernie's brothers, Joey and Gary, also spent many of their waking hours at the Brownson House. They were just like Ernie in that they could fill a room with warmth and love in a matter of seconds, and they loved to show off when they knew I was around to watch. Joey and Gary handled the down markers at the football games, and in the winter, they officiated some of the peewee basketball games. They gave all the signals that real officials used, but usually they were at the most inopportune times. All in all, a game officiated by those two usually ended in chaos. Art enjoyed every minute with these brothers, and they loved him dearly. Their laughter could be heard from one end of the gymnasium to the other, and neither of them had a mean bone in his body.

Frank Gaulteri, the one we called Chico, was Art's right-hand man. Although he had a disability, Chico and his brother, Russ, spent a lot of time at the Brownson House, and together they served as chaperones at many of the dances. If anyone got out of line, my dad could count on those two to handle the situation.

One evening, Chico had to deal with a young man who had become disrespectful. Usually, the matter is cleared up with a few words, but for some reason, the kid hit Chico square in the jaw. In a fight, Chico would have been no match for that particular kid, but in his own style as a fighter, he began to swing right back. Chico didn't connect, but fortunately someone was there to break it up. Nobody would ever consider telling Chico he was no match for the overzealous teenager, but we were glad Russ interfered, and no one got hurt.

Chico's fuse was always quick. My dad often used him as the timekeeper for various athletic events at the rec center, and the first person who questioned anything to do with the time would get an earful from Chico. He would then quit his position, but after a few words from Art and one of Evie's meatball sandwiches, Chico was back in business in just a couple of days. I used to distract him sometimes to the point where he didn't know whether the clock should be stopped or running. Once, I had him laughing so hard the buzzer went off to end the game while a player was getting set to pass the ball in bounds.

Chico was one of the biggest Notre Dame fans I have ever known, and as close as my dad and I were to him, we could never change his allegiance. I called him one Saturday afternoon from the bowels of Notre Dame Stadium just before Penn State was set to kickoff against the Fighting Irish. Another time, I had some friends bring Chico to State College to see us play Notre Dame in person. I don't think I ever saw him more excited, and that was usually the case when people brought up Notre Dame in his presence.

Another person my dad could always count on was his secretary, Shirley. She never understood the meaning of the word "can't," and her energy level was astonishing. Shirley also worked for the Crippled Children's Society in Washington, Pennsylvania, and she negotiated life's twists and turns herself from the seat of a wheelchair because of her inability to use her legs since her childhood.

Shirley did everything that other people found routine, such as living alone and driving a car. Her house was specially equipped with smaller dimensions so she could maneuver and function easier, and her car was also specially built so she could get in and out with ease and use the hand pedals to operate it. Nothing stopped Shirley from reaching her goals. She traveled when she felt like it, and she was very active in her church. She worked the extra job and also served as president of an organization called Open Doors, which was designed to assist handicapped individuals in their quest for as normal a life as possible. I always stop in admiration for Shirley, and I think of the tremendous inspiration she was to anyone who ever passed through the doors of the recreation center.

Even the janitors at the Brownson House made life interesting. Andy Corwin, a man who was born in Poland and spoke very broken English, was the first. Andy always told stories about his days in Poland, and he bragged about playing trumpet as a youth in a Polish band. We often wondered if his stories were merely fantasy, and I became even more suspicious when my dad handed him an old trumpet he had found in the basement one day and asked him to play. "Trumpet no good," Andy said in his Polish accent. "It need new spigot."

One evening, Andy was in the recreation center's lobby trying to call his brother. I said hello to him as I passed by, and two minutes later, as I was standing outside, Andy walked by me mumbling something about the telephone. "Where ya goin', Andy?" I asked as he headed across the street to Bernard's Bar. "Ah, I try to make phone call over there," he answered quite sure of himself. "Line busy over here, maybe no busy over there."

There was another young caretaker whom we called Jingles, and he was much like my wife, Dottie, in that he had a love for country and western music. I wasn't real crazy about it, but I did agree one summer to take my wife and Jingles to the country music jamboree in the hills of Wheeling, West Virginia. I didn't let it slip to many people that old Jer was going to a country music show, but when we got there, I turned to my right, and there was one of my old junior high school football coaches. He must have had the same feelings about country music as I did because we both just sort of ducked so as not to be seen by the other.

I used to spend many of my winter nights at the Brownson House when I was out on the recruiting trail for Penn State. One night, I was scheduled to see a high school basketball game so I could evaluate one of our prospects. I was dressed rather nice in a sport coat and tie, and as I made my way down the stairs and through the lobby, I ran into Jingles, who was dressed to kill in his new cowboy suit. The outfit featured a shirt and vest with several wild and decorative designs and a 10-gallon hat that Jingles seemed awfully proud to wear. He was a slightly rotund person, and this outfit did not help make his appearance any slimmer.

As I moved around the corner, Jingles asked me where I was off to. "A basketball game," I told him.

"Can I go along?" Jingles asked excitedly. I didn't know what to say because I didn't want to hurt his feelings. I thought it over for a minute and realized I didn't have the heart to say no.

"Come on," I said as I waved my arm at him, and we were off to Uniontown, Pennsylvania, which was about a 35-mile drive from Washington.

The parking lot was packed when we arrived at the school, and then it hit me that this was a game involving crosstown rivals. I finally found a parking space after maneuvering through several side streets, and together, Jingles and I hiked back to the gym's front doors. When we got to the gate, I could see through the doors that the game was a sell-out and my notion was confirmed when the ticket-taker gave me a sorrowful-looking shrug of his shoulders.

I explained to the gentleman that I was a Penn State football coach, and I was there for a very important scouting assignment. I told him I'd pay double admission or do whatever I could if he would just let us into the game. The man looked at me, then shifted his eyes at Jingles, then back at me again.

"You can come up with a better story than that, can't you, buddy?" the old ticket-taker said. I looked at him inquisitively as I had no idea what he was talking about. He then pointed at Jingles and said: "And I suppose *that's* Joe Paterno!"

From that point on, my pleas were drowned out by the man's laughter, and since I had no identification — no proof that I was a Penn State football coach — I was forced to simply walk away and miss the game that Jingles and I had driven about 45 minutes to see. As Jingles and I walked back to the car, even I had to laugh at what the old man said and how unbelievable my story must have been.

My father had a sign in his office that read: "Don't give up on a bad boy, because he might turn out to be a great young man." That sign was his way of life, and when someone mentioned the Brownson House, they were sure to mention Art Sandusky. He took on challenges from all types of kids. There were good ones, bad ones, juvenile delinquents and kids who might never have had a purpose in life but found it because they found a guy who cared about them and believed in them.

One particular challenge was a boy named Pat. He was very bright, but he often used his intelligence in devious ways. He seemed to be in constant trouble with the law, and my dad even supposed that Pat had stolen from the recreation center at one time or another. My dad, however, never gave up on him. Patrick spent some early time in reform school and my dad never lost contact with him. He visited him on a number of occasions at the detention facility and maintained his strong interest after Pat was released.

Patrick was a daredevil. He loved to climb around through the trees or make attempts at scaling some of the higher buildings in town. Art always felt that if Pat could channel some of that energy into something constructive, he could become a successful person. Eventually, Patrick became a steeplejack and started by painting flagpoles. One thing led to another, and just like that, Pat had his own business. He took the time to straighten out his life, and because he did, he became a productive citizen in the community.

Success like Patrick's was built around the love and determination of a father figure who cared about the kids in and around the Tylerdale community and did whatever he could to see that the kids had a chance. Unfortunately, however, there were tougher situations that even Patrick couldn't challenge.

There was once a black youth named Jimmie who seemed intent on causing problems around the area. He hung around the recreation center quite a bit, and Art felt that deep inside this young kid was a lost soul searching for love and attention. My dad tried everything he could think of, but nothing seemed to work. Until one day when he decided to use a little bit of role-reversal psychology.

Art called Jimmie into his office and told him that just for that one day the two were going to switch jobs. Art told Jimmie to pretend that he was the boss and that Art was the student named Jimmie. When their respective roles were established, Art went to work on his new boss and began to rattle off all the times he had misbehaved and had been disrespectful. He spoke of his experiences of hitting other kids and of writing on the walls.

"Now Jimmie," Art said to his pupil with a watchful eye. "If I had done all these bad things, would you suspend me?"

"Yes, sir, Mr. Art," Jimmie said. "I 'spend you."

My dad then proceeded to tell Jimmie that he simply had no choice but to suspend him for three days. Jimmie seemed to acknowledge Art's decision and gave a friendly wave as he walked out the front door.

The next day came, and my dad couldn't believe his eyes when he went out the door and spotted Jimmie turning the corner and heading for the recreation center.

"Jimmie!" Art shouted. "I thought I suspended you yesterday for three days."

"Oh no, Mr. Art," Jimmie said with a puzzled look on his face. "That was *you* that was 'spended yesterday for three days."

Art simply threw up his hands in disgust, knowing that Jimmie had somehow won again.

My dad often saw kids turn to trouble at very young ages, and he did everything he could to steer them in the right direction. He once watched a group of boys whom he considered to be *very* young walk out from under the railroad trestle. They looked about eight years old, and my dad had suspected they were smoking cigarettes under there. He called the boys over and asked them point blank if that's what they were doing, and one of them said in a very tiny voice: "Oh no, sir, that wasn't us. We

quit smoking." My dad studied the boy's face in amusement and wondered just exactly at what age the boys could have *started*.

Everything my father had ever done for the Brownson House was
accentuated by a testimonial dinner in his honor several years ago. It was
a night I'll never forget because it brought back all the memories that
were so special to me as I grew up in that house and all the people that
made growing up so special.

A man named Larry Romboski told how Art had worked with him
and started him on his way to a productive basketball career. So many
others like him said were it not for my dad, they might have been roam-
ing the streets looking for trouble and having little difficulty finding it.

I was asked to speak on that special evening, and though I wasn't
quite sure of what I was going to say, I knew I would find it nearly impossible to hold back the tears. As I stood at the podium and looked over the
audience, I saw everyone who was a part of my life: Shirley, Big Ern, Joey,
Gary, Chico Gaulteri, Syl, Popeye, Jingles and so many others who grew
up with me. It wasn't a guest list filled with marquee celebrity names, but
it was the group of people that were special to my dad and those whom he
wanted by his side on this special evening.

I began my speech with a joke, as I had intended, because I knew
this was the only way I could get through the speech without everyone
noticing my tears. Things became easier when I reached the punch line
because, once again, I had my support system cheering me on in the audience. There were shrieks of laughter from Joey and Gary, and soon, everyone joined in.

"You tell 'em, Jer. You tell 'em!" Joey and Gary were yelling. They
were my number-one fans when it came to being funny, and I always said
if I could take them to all my speaking engagements, I'd be a guaranteed
smash hit. Those two seem to bring laughter and happiness with them
wherever they go.

I never was able to take them with me on the speaking tour, but I
take their memories. And I take the memories of all the other people from
the Brownson House who have touched my life over the years. Even though
I currently live in State College, and no matter where life's roads might
take me, the Bug House will always be my home, and its people will be
the fondest memories of the greatest days of my life.

7

Growing Up in Sports

ATHLETICS WAS A VITAL PART OF LIFE NOT ONLY FOR ME but for practically everyone who grew up in Washington, Pennsylvania. Sports played an important role in many people's lives because for some, it was a chance to stay active and keep a body in shape, while others knew it might be their only ticket out of what would soon become a depressed area.

I learned to love athletics because I saw how much fun my dad had as a player in several baseball leagues and as a coach for many of the various sports teams in the community. As I said, he coached a Pony League World Championship team in 1955 and was successful because of his strong desire to get the best effort possible out of each individual. I'll never forget the look on my dad's face when they pulled it out after facing the tremendous odds that were stacked against them.

That championship also gave me a tremendous feeling of accomplishment about athletics, and it taught me that success comes through hard work, effort, discipline and, sometimes, maybe even a little bit more.

My hard work began at an early age when I signed up for midget-league football. I played whatever position I had to at the time and felt fortunate to just be learning the game around the many fine teachers —

including my dad — the town had to offer. I also played basketball and baseball right up through high school, but something told me football would be my ticket, and I'm glad I paid attention.

I was also fortunate to constantly be surrounded by other fine athletes. It seemed like no matter what team I played on, we were always in the hunt for a championship. We were junior high champs in football and basketball, and, of course, there was the Pony League World Championship in baseball.

As I said, football was my secret love, and fall was definitely the time of year I couldn't wait for. I was kind of a late bloomer and didn't start to seriously mature physically until my sophomore year of high school. I became a single-wing blocking back, and the most fun I had was being able to play both varsity and junior varsity during much of my high school career. I was the single-wing fullback in the JV games on Monday, and I played defense during the varsity games on Friday. The dual roles kept me busy, but I don't think any high school player would pass up the opportunity.

I'll always remember the first play of a JV game we played against Canon-MacMillan. I was responsible for taking the snap as the single-wing back, and I was to spin around, fake a handoff to the tailback and then head up the middle. I spun, as I was supposed to do, and just completed the fake when *"B-A-N-G!!"*, I was smacked hard by one of their defensive linemen.

I headed back to our huddle with my nose bleeding, and as I looked around the huddle, one of our offensive linemen, who was a good friend of mine but maybe not at that moment, said: "Uh, I guess I missed my man."

"Uh, yeah," I said right back to him. "I guess you did!"

I got pounded pretty much throughout the rest of the game because we were playing against most of their varsity players, and they seemed more than willing to take it out on us on almost every play. My day was complete when I received a kickoff on the last play of the game and once again took a jarring tackle. I remember wishing the ball wouldn't come my way this time, but it did, and it seemed the perfect ending to an otherwise miserable day.

As I grew older, football became more and more an instrumental part of my life. I never took it seriously until my junior year in high school, probably because that was when I finally began to mature enough physically to stand up to the constant pounding that so often accompanied the game.

There were always exciting events going on while I was on the football field. My dad used to handle the down markers for the Washington High School football games, and once, when there was a controversial call in a very tough game against Uniontown, my dad threw down the sticks in protest of the official's call and was promptly thrown out of the game.

All the communities were very competitive in those days, much like they are today, and teams loved to hand out punishment to each other, whether it was warranted or not. The first lesson you had to learn back then was to look out for the guys on the other side of the field because they were going to come after you with everything they had — on every play.

Unfortunately, I didn't always remember this rule, and when I kicked off to open a game against Connellsville my senior year, I took a miserable shot as I headed down the field.

I did everything perfect on the special teams. My head was down as I followed through on the kick and sent it booming into the night sky. I failed, however, to notice the bruising hulk of a lineman that Connellsville had set up on the opposite side, and he sent me flying with a crushing forearm block.

The truth is you're *supposed* to keep your head down when you kick the ball, much like a golfer or baseball player following through on a swing. But after that, the head should come up so you can see where you're headed, and that was where I failed. The Connellsville player who got me had at least a 20-yard head start, and his timing was perfect. I somehow managed to avoid that guy for nearly the rest of the game. Until the last play, that is.

We found ourselves ahead comfortably after scoring an insurance touchdown with just a few seconds left in the game, and I felt ashamed of myself for having avoided the guy who clocked me in the beginning. I had one more kickoff coming, and I felt I just had to take one last shot at redemption. My plan worked to perfection as I figured right and nailed that guy from Connellsville with a vicious hit before he could dish it out to me. As far as I was concerned, we were even.

My senior year saw many interesting experiences in football, and we, as a team, experienced many highlights and, fortunately, very few lowlights. We played one game in the mud and rain, which was not the ideal situation for a single-wing offense like the one we ran. The game was against Canon-MacMillan, a team that we had a mutual disrespect with, and when the sliding and sloshing took us to halftime, we were in a very tight game.

Our coach, Dave Johnston, was none too pleased with the way we were playing, and he let us know in his loudest of voices at halftime. As he berated us up and down the locker room, we could hear a chorus of words from a group of young boys who stood huddled around our locker room window above.

"Hey, you guys," they chanted over and over. "What are ya doin' down there? Get out here and play!!!" They repeated this song-like chorus for two or three more minutes before someone escorted them away from the window. As the coach grew hotter and hotter with every thought of the little kids' bantering, we did everything we could to hide the laughter that we all felt inside that locker room. That particular game ended with a huge fight, and it was so bad that I remember seeing a Canon-MacMillan player biting the finger of one of his own teammates.

We lost only one game that senior year. It was against Uniontown, a school which had great football and basketball tradition back then. That particular game was memorable for me because I had gone through a flu shot earlier in the week, but when game day came around, I was, most assuredly, struck with a case of the flu.

I played that evening despite a high temperature, and whether I suffered from weakness or not, I wasn't sure, but I missed an extra point, and even though I blocked a punt later in the game, I didn't have enough energy to pick up the ball and run it in for a touchdown. Our offense had the ball, and we were driving in for the winning score, but a bad snap resulted in a lost fumble and a lost game.

Our next game was against Mount Lebanon — another school steeped with football tradition — and this was a game our coach particularly wanted to win because he was from the Mount Lebanon area. We didn't have school the day of the game, but we all got together at the locker room that afternoon just so we could be together as a team.

First, we went for a long walk — as a team — just to get away, and when we got back, our coach told us that he had gotten hold of a scouting report that Mount Lebanon had made of us. He ran down the list of every player on our team and reported Mount Lebanon's strategy against us as well as their feelings about each player. Of course, the report was phony, and our coach was using it to psyche us up, but we didn't know it at the time.

Some of the findings in this bogus scouting report said: "This guy is too slow; this one's lazy; this one won't do this; this one won't do that." He made every report negative just so we would get ourselves fired up about sky-high.

That's just about the way every player became, but the feelings were on the inside. Outside, we were listening intently, waiting to hear what those nasty Mount Lebanon coaches had to say about us. The room was filled with an eerie silence, until finally, a kid on our team who was in special education classes spoke up.

"Coach?" the young man asked as he raised his hand. He was a little slow academically, but he worked hard, and he loved his football. "What did that report say about me?"

"Well," our sly coach answered. "It doesn't say anything about you. Evidently, they don't even feel you deserve to be on the team."

That was what finally set things off. "I'll show them!" the boy answered with a fiery look in his eyes. "We'll show them who's on this football team!"

From that point on, our entire team was pumped up and excited to take on the powerful team from Mount Lebanon. They were very talented that season, but we were a team that wasn't about to be denied that evening. We were never more motivated, and even though Mount Lebanon had defeated Uniontown earlier in the season, 28-0, we took care of Mount Lebanon, 28-0, and went on to win our conference championship.

We were considered one of the great football teams in the area that season. We had a number of outstanding players, including six who went on to play major college football (two each to Penn State and Nebraska, one to Ohio State and one to Wyoming). We also had two players who made it in the National Football League (one to the Washington Redskins; the other to the Atlanta Falcons). Our class featured many gifted athletes — not just in football — and although I didn't consider myself to be one of them, I felt very fortunate to be one of the Washington High players to make it in major college football.

Football was everything to me, but I still tried my best at other sports and did whatever I could to make myself a better athlete. When you find one sport to be your strongest, it never hurts to participate in others because it keeps you active on almost a year-round basis, and that keeps you in shape for the sport you want to succeed at.

I went out for the basketball team at Washington High, mainly because most of the players were also from the football team. The best way I can sum up my basketball career is to highlight the time I was responsible for the other team completing a *five-point play in a span of one second.*

It happened in a tournament in Aliquippa, Pennsylvania A kid was driving in for a layup, and I fouled him. He made the basket and the subsequent foul shot, and when I tried to pass the ball in, I was looking for a fast break opportunity, but my pass was picked out of midair and laid in for an easy hoop — just like that. I think Bill Russell would have been proud of that kid.

I was open-minded, and I was also not afraid to speak my mind, which our coach usually didn't appreciate. We were playing against a team that played strictly a zone defense one time, and I was out on the wing, moving the ball around the perimeter the best I could. We couldn't get the ball inside because this team matched up so well with our offense, and the more we passed it around, the more easy steals that team turned into layups for them.

Our coach called a time-out to try and figure out a way to crack their zone, and I decided to give him my philosophy.

"Coach," I asked him. "Do you want me to break in behind my man when he overplays me because I know I can get by him?"

"Jer," the coach replied calmly. "What I want you to do is sit down."

I answered him in a tone that was just as calm but unrelenting. "Well, I really didn't have that in mind, but I guess I'll have to do it."

On another occasion, I came to the sideline during a timeout and said rather excitedly: "Coach, I'm open if you get the ball to me on this side (pointing to the right baseline). I think I can get a good shot off there."

That same coach looked at me and said: "Well, that's really great, Jer." He then turned back to the huddle and continued. "Tommy, you move over to the right side (my side) and Jer, you move over there (the opposite side), since that shot is open."

That should give you an idea of the type of basketball player I was and the confidence my coach had in me.

I also did my best to succeed in baseball, but I wasn't the most coordinated athlete on the field. I played the infield a lot, and once, I called for a pop fly that looked like it was headed to short center field. I turned my back to the infield and sprinted toward center, but when I turned to look for the ball, I saw it drop to the ground right behind second base.

The coaches then thought they'd get a look at me in center field, but that didn't seem like a smart idea when they saw me rush in for a line drive and forget to put my glove up. The next thing I knew, *B-A-N-G!!!*, the ball popped me right in the nose.

My favorite baseball experience happened when I played in a summer league following my senior year of high school and before my big move to Penn State University. The league had a mixture of older and younger players, and we played in various locations throughout the different communities.

We were playing at West Liberty State College one Saturday afternoon, and since it was summer, the college was pretty much closed up tight. During the game, I discovered I had a bad case of diarrhea, and there wasn't a bathroom to be found. I was hanging on for dear life from my shortstop position during the last inning, and I couldn't wait for that last out.

The other team had a runner on second base and two outs when the batter hit a line drive to left field for a single. As the guy from second tried to score, our left fielder made a perfect throw to the plate, and I jumped excitedly (for obvious reasons) when I heard the umpire's "OUT!" call. No sooner did the word leave his lips, and I was headed to the patch of woods nearby.

What I didn't realize was that our catcher had dropped the ball on the tag, and the runner was ruled safe. The teams were ready to play again, but our coach quickly noticed that he had no shortstop out there. Soon, everyone else began to notice my absence, and everyone was looking around for me and calling my name. I was in the woods hearing: "Jerry, Jerry, where are you?" It took me a little while, but soon I came strolling out of the woods with an extremely embarrassed look on my face.

8

Recruiting (1)

DURING THE MIDDLE OF MY SENIOR YEAR IN HIGH SCHOOL, recruiting became a major part of my life. I experienced the soft talk and sometimes luring techniques that were utilized by the many coaches who came to our school in hopes of landing some of our strongest senior talent. Later on, as a coach at Penn State, I became one of those recruiters, and I soon discovered what it was like to be on the other side of the fence.

As a teenager, it was a fun and enlightening experience to be sought after by some of the most outstanding football schools in the country. I wasn't kidding myself. I knew these great coaches weren't looking, first and foremost, at me. Washington High School had some of the finest football talent in the state, and it was very rare for one school to send *six* players to major college football programs in one season.

When the recruiting all started, we were in the middle of our basketball season. Most of the football players whom the recruiters were after were on the basketball team, and it was not uncommon for the recruiters to attend a basketball game or two because it would give them a better knowledge of a certain individual's overall athletic ability. Our basketball coach was a strict disciplinarian, and he wasn't too keen on the idea of us going through these outside distractions. In other words, having college football coaches constantly lurking through our school halls looking for that special prize. I never thought of them as actually "lurking," but I do admit the recruiting was a distraction to our business on the court.

The first distraction came when an assistant coach from the University of Tennessee sent plane tickets for me and a couple of my teammates for the purpose of one our legal visits to the Tennessee campus. We had told him we probably couldn't come right away because of basketball, but he sent the tickets anyway. We asked our coach about it, and needless to say, he showed his first signs of unhappiness with our whole situation.

Another time, I had received about three recruiting calls the afternoon of a very important basketball game. The football coaches all said they'd be in attendance at the game that night, and I started to wonder how I should look to them as a basketball player. I went into the game deciding the best thing to do was be aggressive. I ended up having four fouls before the end of the first quarter — the fourth one because I shoved the guy with the ball out of bounds because of just plain frustration — and the coach showed his disgust in me by benching me for the rest of the game.

I was very naive when I made my first official football visit. I expected every large university campus to be a resort or playground, with lakes and palm trees capturing your eye at every turn. I guess I expected every college campus to be like one giant recreation center. When I first laid my eyes on Penn State University, it wasn't at all like I expected.

The realization of hard work and discipline hit me as soon as I spotted those ivy-covered walls on many of the older dormitories and classroom buildings that fronted the western side of the campus. In this central part of Pennsylvania, there was peace and humility like I had never witnessed before. There was a one-way street going into this little town known as State College and a one-way street going out. In between was a place I never dreamed would match the same affection I had grown for my home back in Tylerdale.

I guess I knew from that first visit that Penn State was the place for me. The thing I wasn't sure about was whether Penn State really wanted me. Later on, I came to the realization that they probably didn't want me very badly, but they sort of threw me in because they wanted two other guys from my class. Well, they only got one — Bob Riggle — who later went on to play for the Atlanta Falcons in the NFL.

My next visit was to the University of Tennessee. It was the first time I had ever been on an airplane, and as excited as I was for the trip, I was fully aware that I was traveling on a Friday the 13th. The plane arrived safely, however, and my host for the weekend took me to a party that Saturday night. I don't drink now nor did I drink at the time, but it was easy to see that this guy had had too much after just a short time.

That experience had a definite effect on my feelings for Tennessee because it seemed like I was the only sober person remaining at the party after a couple of hours, and my host's girlfriend was pleading with me to drive his car home from the party because he was drunk and going through red lights at intersections. The weekend was not enjoyable at all because I was young, and I couldn't picture myself attending a university where experiences such as this would constantly make me nervous.

Next up on my recruiting trail was West Virginia University. The coaches there were extremely down to earth, and I really enjoyed their company. The highlight of the weekend was staying up all Saturday night with some of the players and listening to the Wheeling Jamboree. As I said, I was never too fond of country music, but on this particular evening, in this backwoods setting, it seemed to be okay.

My final visit came in the spring. We were flown to the University of Kentucky by an alumnus in his own personal one-engine plane. The day was very windy, and I had just eaten spaghetti for lunch. When we got on the plane, our pilot sort of laughed and said: "There's a pail back there just in case anybody decides to get sick."

We were in the air for about an hour and the ride was feeling more like a roller coaster. We never made it above the clouds, and it felt like we were constantly going up and down. Needless to say, I threw up not just once or twice but *three* times. The third time was after the pilot said he couldn't gain clearance to land, and we'd have to stay in the air a while longer.

The Kentucky coaching staff was new, and I found their style to be very aggressive. We were invited to watch one of their spring practice sessions, and I noticed how they used live players with chest protectors instead of tackling dummies during certain drills. They had the defensive player hit an offensive player, then pursue and make the tackle on this stationary human dummy. On the last play of this particular drill, all 11 players hit the stationary dummy.

I presumed these "dummies" were just players that the coaching staff didn't want to keep around. Kentucky lost about 40 players that spring, and I don't think it was a coincidence that their aggressive-style drills had something to do with that.

The Kentucky coaches continued to send me clippings and literature about the university, and they thought I was seriously considering going there. But when I witnessed the kind of practices they ran, I knew that was an experience I didn't want to be a part of.

Three of us went on that visit to Kentucky from Washington High, and during the course of our stay, we were housed in the athletic dorm. We goofed around and had pillow fights, and though I started out on the top bunk, I eventually spilled down to the bottom. Bob Stock, one of the recruits from our group who eventually went to Ohio State, was just about to swing a vicious pillow at me when one of the Kentucky coaches opened the door. The coach really let us have it as his tongue-lashing had us frozen in the same positions for a long time afterward.

I made all my visits and truly tried to give each school an equal chance. But in the end, I would never argue with my decision to attend Penn State. I still wasn't too sure how much they wanted me, but my high school basketball coach had me believing that Penn State would definitely be the right place for me. As it turned out, choosing Penn State was one of the best decisions I had ever made in my life.

9

A Nittany Lion

I BECAME A COLLEGE FRESHMAN IN THE FALL OF 1962. I'll always remember my first ride to State College with my parents. They had never been there before, and I enjoyed telling them how beautiful and scenic the drive was. There were a couple of different back roads that one could take to Penn State, like Route 45, which wound along the valleys with the streams and mountains always in your sight.

Those mountains weren't as beautiful, though, when the day finally came for me to leave my hometown and my family. It wasn't a very happy time, and after the first few days at Penn State, struggling through the ordeals of freshman orientation, I became very homesick. I lost some of my papers I was responsible for, and the beautiful place I had bragged about had suddenly become just school. It was difficult to accept, but I had to keep telling myself I was here to stay, and I wasn't just visiting anymore.

Being a freshman at Penn State was easier at that time than it is today. We reported in the middle of September, and if you could make it to football practice you went. Getting settled in for school was the most important thing for freshman players. It was obviously helpful to you as an individual if you got things settled quickly and took part in as much practice as possible, but you weren't penalized if it didn't work out that way.

We helped out here and there, but there was never any organized practice for the freshmen. We had a freshman team, and we stayed together as a freshman group, with study hall in the evening. Really, it was kind of a neat experience, sort of like misery loves company. It was a way of bringing everyone closer together during the tough times.

The practices weren't very difficult, even when we did start practicing more regularly. The fun times were when we got to run against the varsity. I'll always remember the first time I ever lined up against the varsity in a practice session. I got down into my stance on the line, and there across from me was Dave Robinson, who was an All-American player in college and later became an All-Pro with the Green Bay Packers. I took one look at him and thought to myself: "What *did I get myself into?*"

I wrote a letter to my parents early in that first year. I thought of how easy it is to take someone for granted and think so much of them when they weren't nearby. I had sort of cruised along in my life up until then, with no real determination to do anything special. Going away made me really see what all my parents had done for me, and I had suddenly found that these were the moments I should put the most thoughts toward what I wanted to do with my life. The letter was just my way of letting those people know how much it meant to me to have them as parents.

I also reminded them of what meaningful lives they had led and of how much they had done for so many people. It was at this time that I decided I would like to give to others in much the same manner that my parents had done over the years. I wanted to show them what a great example they had been to me, and hopefully, they would realize their influence had fallen greatly on me.

My first commitment to doing something special for my parents, to make them proud, was to do well academically. I had never been a strong student in high school, but this I felt I owed to them. I wanted to be a success in football, even though I realized that was probably not the most important thing in their lives. I wanted to do the best I could to make everyone back home proud.

I became a very committed and studious person. I reminded myself of the pressure and probably tried to stuff too much into not enough hours in the day. I went to classes in the morning, worked out and ran in the afternoon and stayed up many late hours studying. It was not uncommon to see me stay up until midnight and then rise for another day at 5 a.m. It was really the first time in my life I had become so committed to both academics and athletics.

As a freshman, the football program at Penn State was not very intense. I'll always remember a trip we made to play Army — a five-hour bus trip. When we got there, we ate with all the freshmen cadets, and it wasn't difficult to notice the sharp discipline they had to endure. I immediately realized this was much of the same discipline I had imposed upon myself in the early part of my freshman year. Seeing the discipline, however, did give us a perspective on the freedom of choice we had at Penn State.

We slept right in the barracks, and on the morning of the game, our coach woke us up to get ready. After we had washed up and brushed our teeth, the coach told us he had wakened us too early, and we had another hour or so if we wanted to get some more sleep. We went back to our bunks, and needless to say, I started wrestling around with some of our other players. The coach didn't like it, I was in trouble and, of course, I didn't get to start the game. We won, however, and our big treat on the way home was a stop at a gas station for a candy bar and an apple.

Winter was always a tough time for me for some reason, and I became more homesick than ever during my first winter at Penn State. It was very hard—maybe because I spent less time with football, although I did work out very hard and spent a lot of time getting ready for spring practice.

I played intramural basketball to keep busy—something I really enjoyed. My dorm team was very good, and we ended up winning the championship. Throughout my career, we got just as excited for those games as we did for the football games.

As winter wore on that first year, I became very anxious for spring football practice. It would signify the big start to my varsity career. The thing I remember most when it finally came was looking around the locker room that first day and sizing up my major competition. He was a very talented young man about 6' 3", 225 pounds. An outstanding athlete. Right then, I knew how tough it was going to be.

But for all of this player's size and stature, fortune seemed to turn my way. It turned out this guy really didn't find great enjoyment in the game of football, and he turned out to be not much of a player. Because of these circumstances, I suddenly had an opportunity to play a lot of football the next year.

Dick Anderson, who was a great player at Penn State and has worked with us for many years on the coaching staff, was a player on that team. He was a redshirt senior, and going into the season, he was the heir apparent to the starting end position. I was to be his backup because we played both ways, offensively and defensively, in those days. Dick got hurt, and I ended up starting the first game at the University of Oregon.

Oregon had some great players of their own at that time: Mel Renfro (running back); Bob Berry (quarterback); Dave Wilcox (linebacker). Those guys were outstanding, and they proved their worth by going on to successful careers in the NFL. I looked at those guys and thought of their tremendous success, and then I realized this was my *first* game.

We had a meeting the day of the game, and Joe Paterno was an offensive coach. He was going over some plays and said: "Jerry, what would you do if they did this?" As he said this, I could see he was pointing at the blackboard to emphasize his question. I was very nervous, and I couldn't get myself to say anything. I opened my mouth, but nothing came out. Joe said: "What's the matter? Are you a little bit nervous?"

I just kind of stuttered my answer. "W-w-well, I g-guess." I remembered telling one of the other players a few minutes later that I wasn't sure if I was really going to enjoy this experience.

The anxiety sometimes does make it difficult to enjoy your first big-time football experience, but I soon learned to overcome that. Once you got involved in the middle of a football game, the anxiety would fall right behind you. Emotion would usually take over and carry you the rest of the way. But I could never hide the fear of failure. It was always in the back of my mind. The fear that I would never live up to the expectations of those who were back home; those who meant so much to me.

There were some real characters on our football team. One guy's name was Bernie, and he could throw a fit at the drop of a hat. The whole locker room would start shouting: "We want a fit! We want a fit!" Sure enough, Bernie would throw a fit.

Glenn Ressler was an All-American lineman who went on to an All-Pro career with the Baltimore Colts. He was very big and strong. An outstanding football player. For some strange reason, Bernie was probably the only person who could tease Glenn and get away with it. Glenn grew up on a farm, and Bernie would say in kind of a slow, singing tone: "Hey, Okie, you got a letter; M-O-O-O, it would say." Glenn would just stare at Bernie as this continued on.

Bernie was a little bit different, but he was a highlight for everyone's amusement in the locker room. He used to catch a fly every once in a while, tie a string of thread to its wings and then watch it try to fly away. One might think that with all of his oddities, Bernie might have seemed out of place on the football team. But sometimes teams need a character like him. While Bernie really didn't like to practice, he became totally concentrated and very intense when it came time for the games. He was a really tough football player who, in reality, was always secure in his knowledge for the game.

He weighed only 195 pounds, but I remember a time when he ran head-on into a 235-pound running back. The ball dropped one way, the back dropped the other, and the back never returned to that game.

We had another player at that time who never moved very far up the depth chart but gave every effort he had. He was usually a member of the foreign team in practice, which meant his job was to run the other team's plays during game preparations. One day, he taped handles to his back and wrote the word "SPALDING" on his shirt to simulate a practice dummy. He then went on to the practice field like that and turned a tense and serious practice session into a few minutes of welcome and relaxing laughter.

I make it sound like the locker-room scene is nothing but shenanigans and comedy, but that is really quite far from the truth. When it is time to get serious, the locker room turns into a place for meetings, film sessions and then more meetings. College football is played for 60 minutes on the field every Saturday afternoon, but the week leading up to the game involves hours upon hours of preparation.

As a player, these meetings can often lead to pain and discomfort. Sometimes, you just sit in the meeting room and look at the clock. Your mind can lead to disbelief that you're going to have to be on that field again in a short while and struggle through another practice. That is where the camaraderie comes in. The word "team" should really begin to mean something when these thoughts enter your mind because this is the time when you should look around and see that you're all in it together. You're all working for that one common goal.

The locker room is not always fun and games. But the comic relief I speak of is really quite good for everyone. And believe me, there are times when, plain and simple, it is a necessity.

I have quite a few Penn State football experiences to remember. As usual, you tend to remember the players more than anything else. One player who will always stick out in my mind from that first year was Gary

Klingensmith. He was a young man who was almost totally deaf, but we used to say that Klinger would only hear what he wanted to hear. If a coach yelled at him, he'd stand there stiff, pretending he couldn't hear. But if a coach said, "Good job," his head was the first to turn in acknowledgment.

The game at Oregon was the first for both Gary and myself. He was a running back, and since he was almost totally deaf, he would go on the snap of the ball instead of listening for the snap count. On the first play, Gary took off early and ended up five yards deep into the defensive secondary before the ball was snapped. He was the first running back I ever saw who was both offsides and in motion at the same time.

There had been some attention in the media about Gary's disability and how he had worked hard to overcome it. When a number of reporters asked him after the game if it was just excitement or emotion that made him jump on that first play, he replied: "Well, there had been so much talk about this deaf kid on the Penn State football team, I just wanted to make sure everyone knew which one he was."

There is something about me that turns even the most mundane activity into a real adventure, and it was really no different in football. On the opening kickoff against UCLA in my sophomore year, which was our first home game, I was running downfield on coverage, not really paying much attention to the way they ran their kick-off return setup. I was on the end — the contain person — and it was my job to not let their runner get to the outside. I had my head down and I remember the guy who blocked me knocked me clear out of bounds. The same guy then jumped on top of me, and I started yelling and kicking, trying to get up. While this was going on, our head coach at the time, Rip Engle, was yelling at me: "Sandusky! Sandusky! Get up and get back in there!"

By this time, I had become furious, and I wanted revenge. I was playing opposite their tight end, and I remember wanting to hit him with everything I had. But when I charged him to let him have it, he hooked me, and the play went around my end for a 20-yard gain. The guy I was up against in that game was named *Sports Illustrated*'s lineman of the week, and he sent me a thank-you note for everything I had done for him. Needless to say, the day started out bad and only got worse.

Remember, in those days, we played both offense and defense, and while I played mostly on the defensive side, I did get to play a little bit of offense. On the first pass that was ever designed to be thrown in my direction, our quarterback, Pete Liske, looked at me in the huddle and said: "Now make sure you run a good pattern." And that I surely did. I concentrated really hard on that pattern. I hustled; I made the right cut. I did everything right except look for the ball. I suddenly realized what was missing, but as I started to turn, the ball hit me in the back of the helmet.

In another game, this one against Syracuse, our coaches called for a fake punt. I had dislocated a couple of my fingers earlier in the game but was able to get them taped up and keep on playing. We were told of the fake in the huddle, and I was to be the primary receiver. I looked at the punter as if to say: "Are you kidding me?"

We went into punt formation, and I found myself alone in the flat. I was almost out of bounds by the time the punter threw me the ball, but I turned back to the inside and caught it. The play was designed to get a first down, of course, and as I ran, all I could see was that down marker. About 20 or 30 yards of open field stood ahead of me. I was running as fast as I could (which wasn't really that fast). Perhaps I could have scored, but my mind was so set on getting that first down that I got past the yard marker and promptly stepped out of bounds. That was all my mind could focus on at the time.

Another spectacular highlight of my playing career came against the University of Pittsburgh. I was supposed to run a down-out-and-down pattern, which I did to near perfection. I moved down the field and then into the flat. Suddenly, I broke free down the sideline, and I found myself again running with everything I had. My problem came when I ran right into the down marker. I was okay, but the marker was bent completely out of shape.

Some of my fondest memories as a player came in games against Ohio State. We played at their field when I was a sophomore, and they had future pros like Matt Snell and Paul Warfield on their team. We beat a great team that year, 10-7, and the next year we were facing them when they were undefeated and ranked number two in the country. I was on defense that day, and the guy I lined up against was a former teammate at Washington High. We beat them 27-0 and didn't allow a first down until the end of the third quarter.

It was a real thrill for us as players to win a game like that and it was one of those victories the student body enjoyed celebrating all over town. The students staged one of the biggest rallies ever at Penn State as they rocked buses and pushed a Volkswagen all the way up the campus mall and into the president's pond. All in all, it was an unforgettable experience full of extreme chaos.

My junior year started out disappointing, but we ended the season playing well. We had the shutout over Ohio State, and we won the Eastern championship. We had an opportunity to play in a bowl game, but we turned it down because it just didn't seem to be the right thing to do at the time.

I then endured a senior year that started out with high expectations that were never really lived up to as the season wore on. It seemed like one thing after another happened to throw us off course. It started off with losses to the number-one ranked team in the country (Michigan State) and number-two (UCLA). In fact, UCLA beat Michigan State in the Rose Bowl that year.

I didn't enjoy ending my Penn State career that way. It was a tough year that ended even more disappointingly for me because I was flagged for a conspicuous penalty on national television. The last game was against Maryland, and it was at the same time one of our astronauts was going up in space. At that time the space age was really coming to the front, and all of America became fascinated by the thought of space travel.

Unfortunately for me television, also had the split screen. On one side of the TV, people could witness the launch of another rocket, and on the other, they could witness me in all my glory. My biggest moment in the spotlight, and I ended up roughing the kicker. I usually don't mind working in front of an audience, but as I look back on that scene, I sure do hope the viewers had their eyes set on that rocket.

I went home quite often during the summer in my college days; back to the Brownson House where I could help out with things at the recreation center. Between working at the local Coca-Cola plant and the hours spent working with kids at the playground, I was rarely at a loss for things to do. It was also fun just to sit back on those summer evenings with family or neighbors and tell stories to each other like we always did.

One of the greatest things I learned at Penn State was maturity. I grew up a lot there and learned to make a commitment both academically and athletically. And the best part was I had a good time doing it.

I knew from the beginning that I wanted to be a teacher and a coach. Dick Anderson was on the Penn State coaching staff as a graduate assistant. It was only a couple of years since I had played behind him when I was a sophomore, and he was a senior. He had gone on to grad school, and he too wanted to get into coaching. My first teaching experience was in a class Dick taught called "Physical Conditioning." The class was designed to help condition young people who did not pass a basic physical fitness test at the university, mostly because they were not very athletically inclined.

I observed the class for a number of days before Dick finally told me I could take a stab at the teaching duties. I decided I would combine some basketball teaching skills and conditioning exercises at the same time.

First of all, I had the students form two parallel lines, and I showed them the simple art of passing the basketball back and forth. We eventually combined the passing with running up and down the court to get them in touch with conditioning, peripheral vision, judgement and hand-eye co-ordination.

One little thing about this drill that I neglected to tell the students, however, was that when they get to the other end of the court, they should wait until the whole class got there. The first group got to the end of the court and took a shot at the basket. I noticed the ball went off to the side, and I told the next group of students to run their drill. I watched them start on their way, and I turned back to the line to make sure the next group was ready. It was then that I realized I should have mentioned to the students to wait there until everyone had come through.

But by then, it was too late. I looked back to the middle of the gymnasium floor, and sure enough, the first group of students were on their way back proudly running the new drill they had learned. I couldn't have planned a better collision if I had tried. One of the students fell down and kept screaming over and over: "My head! My head! I think I broke my head!"

I'll always remember looking down at that student and saying: "You're head's not broken. I know a broken head when I see one, and believe me, your head is not broken." I think at that point, I wanted to crawl in a hole. I remember looking at Dick Anderson and seeing him shaking his head. "So, you still want to be a teacher, do you?" he said to me. At that point, I wasn't quite as sure as I was a few days earlier.

10

Dottie Gross

IT WAS THE SUMMER BEFORE MY SENIOR YEAR OF COLLEGE when I met the girl I would eventually marry. My family spent a lot of time with a couple named Todd and Kate Brown in Washington, Pennsylvania, and it was at a picnic the Browns were hosting that I met Dottie.

She lived in Washington as a young girl, but her parents moved to Chicago before I ever had the chance to meet her in our early days. She came back to visit friends and relatives every once in a while, and she was staying with the Browns during this particular summer. My friend, John, came to the picnic with me, and Dottie was there with a couple of her friends. They were singing songs — a lot of Tennessee songs because that was where Dottie and her family were originally from. I don't know whether the love bug had hit me right away, but I definitely enjoyed the good times we had together that day.

I got to know her better a short time later when John and I did an errand for the recreation center. Todd had an old couch that he was giving to the center, and John and I were enlisted to do some pickup and delivery work. I was fortunate enough to again run into Dottie, so after all the work was done we spent the rest of the day talking and generally having a good time.

I'll always remember Todd being upstairs in the house, kind of coaching me — rather loudly at times. It was his way of reminding me that it was getting pretty late, and I had better get going. We knew Todd had to get up early in the morning, but I managed to hang around, and we kept on having a good time. It was a good thing Todd was a friend of my family, because he might have thrown me out otherwise.

I was always very shy and backward; never one to be aggressive socially. Even though I spent time talking with Dottie a couple of times, I couldn't quite bring myself to ask her out on a real date. It was a good thing my mother wasn't as shy and backward as me. It was thanks to her, after all, that I ended up getting together with Dottie on a regular basis. She asked her to come to a softball game I was playing in, and I ended up taking her home. Maybe I just needed that one little push because one thing led to another, and before long, we had become closer.

We got to know each other very well, and Dottie ended up spending a lot of time with me that summer. Once, we loaded a bunch of kids into the back of the rec center pickup truck to go to a Pittsburgh Pirates baseball game. I'll never forget that experience, because it nearly cost us our lives.

It was a two-lane highway we were traveling on, and things were rolling along rather smoothly. All of a sudden, a car came barreling around a bend seemingly out of control and sort of bounced over the median strip. In a flash, it somehow went by the truck without hitting us, but I still shudder to this day when I think of all those kids in that truck and the tragedy we avoided.

I worked with kids on the playground in those days, and Dottie would often find her way there to keep me company. She enjoyed playing with the kids as much as I did, and we both still remember a little boy probably no more than four or five years old at the time whom we called Pee Wee.

Pee Wee didn't come from a very good home, but I know how much he loved that playground. I had to close things up usually around nine every night, and I don't think I can count the number of times when, after I had closed the last gate and driven away, I would look in my rearview mirror and see little Pee Wee climbing the fence in order to get back into the playground. I often wonder about a lot of those little kids—what they're up to today. I especially think of Pee Wee and find myself still amazed how unafraid of those dark summer evenings he was.

In the fall of my senior football season, we had just lost a heartbreaker at the University of California. It was a tough and disappointing loss because we were ahead the whole game and ended up losing it in the last seconds.

This weekend was of great importance to me, not only for the trip to California, but for the trip home as well. Our plane was to make a stop in Chicago on the return, and since Dottie was back home now with her parents, we decided to plan my first meeting with them during the team's stopover.

They came to the airport to greet us, and right away, I knew they were going to be nice people. They made me feel comfortable right away — even after the disappointment of our loss — and I was very impressed with them and their attitude toward me. It was almost as if I was ready to breathe a sigh of relief because I had finally got the chance to know this couple I had heard so much about in the summer.

September 1966 will always be a special time to remember in the Sandusky household. It was the time when the girl I had met two summers before had officially become my wife. Our big honeymoon was a short trip to Presque Isle in Erie, Pennsylvania. We drove there in a rainstorm and stayed at a Howard Johnson motel. We had to keep the trip short because I was due to start graduate school at Penn State in just a few days. We spent a couple days at Presque Isle and a couple more at the recreation center before we headed back to State College. It wasn't the best of starts for Dottie and I as we had to leave a lot of our belongings in the car during our short stay at the rec center. As luck would have it, someone broke into our car that first night and stole a number of things— mainly most of our clothes.

When we discovered what had happened, the S & S Detective Agency went into action. Translated, that was simply my dad and me. He obviously had a good rapport with the people around town, and he knew his methods would help us solve the case. We began talking to many of the kids around town, and eventually a couple of them sent us on the right path to the culprit.

We found some of our lost items simply discarded along the railroad tracks, and unbelievably, the person responsible for the theft was an AWOL soldier. My dad and I went to his trailer, hoping to get the rest of our things, and for some reason, I found it fortunate that he wasn't at home. The man's mother was there, however, and she made sure we got all of our things back.

I wasn't afraid of how the soldier would treat my dad and me, but I think the reason I was glad he wasn't there was simply because we didn't need any unnecessary confrontations over a few pieces of clothes. Why the man would steal a woman's clothes, too, I'll never know, but it truly was a strange situation and a not-so-pleasant start to our marriage.

Right after I started my graduate work at Penn State, Dottie and I had to return to Washington for the wedding of my good friend, Benny Biceps. I was aware that he had asked me to be in the wedding, but what I didn't know until the day before the game was the fact that I was the best man.

One of the guys who was supposed to be in the wedding got sick the day before and couldn't participate, so he was replaced by Benny's future brother-in-law. This man was much larger than the rest of us, and we had to do some scrambling to find a tuxedo to fit him. I ended up giving him my pants, and I wore the pants of the sick man. We both had a tight fit, but at least we were suited up for the wedding.

I worried about my pants tearing during the ceremony, and it seemed like everything, even the reception, was turning into utter chaos. As the bridal party was seated at the head table, Benny's brother-in-law elbowed me lightly and said: "You better get some champagne for the toast." I was so naive I didn't know what champagne looked like, so Benny had to get it himself.

"You have to untwist the top and pop the cork," Benny told me as I stood there with a dumb look on my face. I didn't know what I was doing, and my inexperience showed as I tried to twist and turn the bottle, then the cork. Finally, it popped and flew into the air. I felt relief, which soon turned to embarrassment when I saw the cork hit the top of the wedding cake. A portion of the cake flew into the air like a mound of dirt from a mortar shell, while the fake bride and groom fell helplessly to the floor from their perch on top of the cake. In my toast, I spoke my true feelings at the time: "Well," I said. "I haven't gotten Benny and his bride off to a very good start, but I sure hope things get better."

Dottie and I would surely never forget our first Christmas together. We spent part of it with my parents in Washington, Pennsylvania, and then we traveled by train to Chicago to visit Dottie's parents. It was a long train ride, and I couldn't get much rest because they kept turning the heat way up, then way back down. There was no consistency in the air temperature, and that kept me awake most of the time.

We arrived in Chicago to a freezing rain, which Dottie's father had driven all the way to the station in just to meet us. He was very excited to see us, and as we were driving home, his excitement, unfortunately, had kept his attention from knowing how fast he was going on the highway. He was talking to us as he drove on the inside lane of a six-lane highway. He noticed a car moving slightly toward his lane and touched his brakes to avoid any contact. As we learned, however, the slightest touch of brakes on an ice-laden highway usually spells trouble.

Suddenly, we started sliding, and the car sort of skated to the right across all three lanes that remained of the highway. With no more room, we slid off the road but fortunately into an exit lane. If we would have hit the guardrail, we would have bounced right back into traffic, and there was no telling how many out-of-control cars would have jostled us around like a pinball machine.

As it was, we were still in grave danger because, although we didn't head back into traffic, we were thrown into an embankment and sent in the direction of a concrete bridge. It was one of those times—one of those experiences—where I can honestly say I saw my life flash before my eyes.

Fortunately, the contour of the land helped us to avoid the bridge by sending us down a fairly steep hill. Given a choice of slamming into a concrete bridge or sliding down a snowy hill, I would feel more fortunate with the hill. The car swerved one way, then the other, and as I watched this all transpire, I had resolved myself to the fact that it was all over. I saw the bridge, then the hill, and everything seemed to be moving in slow motion.

We skidded to the bottom of the hill, and the front end of the car sort of jumped on top of the guardrail. At last, we came to a stop, and Dottie began to scream: "FIRE! FIRE!"

We were all shaking, and I was so full of adrenaline I looked at her and said as calmly as possible: "Oh, why don't you be quiet." She looked at me with surprise, but we both understood why we said what we did, and there were no hard feelings between us. We were all okay and that was the main thing. In fact, the worst that happened was my father-in-law's glasses had fallen down over his nose from the jarring knock the car took from the guardrail. Overall, we had experienced an extremely close call. We were all aware of that as we said a prayer of thanks for our survival. I thought of the accident Dottie and I had almost been in on our way to the baseball game during one of our first dates together in Pittsburgh. We had been through two experiences now where we could very easily have lost each other. Two was enough as far as I was concerned. The experience in Chicago was too close of a call, and as we sat there in the car, we knew we very fortunate once again—this time with our very lives.

Married life was a bit of a struggle in the beginning, but not in the sense that we struggled with each other. We were tested, but we survived on love. Our struggles came simply from the rigors of living off campus at Penn State, trying to keep a small apartment running with some sense of organization and keeping up with my graduate studies.

We took a third-floor attic apartment, Dottie and I, and the fire escape was a rope tied to a radiator. The apartment was heated by coal, and it was my responsibility to help fire up the furnace in the evenings during the cold weather season. The apartment was furnished, but the couch could swallow a person whole if you weren't careful.

Even though we were newlyweds, I felt I still had exceptional mechanical abilities. On one occasion, Dottie asked me if I would be able to change a lightbulb in the bathroom. I looked closely at her to make sure her question wasn't presented in a sarcastic manner, and then I answered proudly that it would be no problem.

I stood on the toilet seat to get a better reach at the disabled light bulb and began to put my mechanical prowess to work. "This will be easy," I said through muffled breath. But it wasn't. Like so many odd jobs I had tried in the past, things began to go wrong. First, it was the toilet seat. My feet were steady, but the seat was not. It slipped from under me and sent me flying. Instinctively, I reached for the closest thing one can find when in the midst of a free fall.

With my luck, the closest object happened to be the medicine cabinet. It was within reach, but it didn't do much good as the combination of my strength and desperation to hang on pulled the medicine cabinet from its supports and sent it crashing—along with me—to the floor.

There I was, sprawled out on the bathroom floor, with a broken toilet seat lying to one side and a partially destroyed medicine cabinet—with most of its contents—spread around the other side. And through it all, a dark, unchanged lightbulb stared down at me from the ceiling. I could swear it was alive and that it took pleasure in my struggles.

Dottie came running at the sound of crashing metal and porcelain, and for a moment, it looked like she had a smile as wide as the lightbulb. She helped me to my feet and brushed me off. That was when I looked into her eyes and said: "Dottie, maybe you ought to change that bulb." She nodded her head in agreement, and within five minutes, she did exactly that.

I hadn't totally given up on my mechanical abilities, and after a day or two of recovery from my fall, I decided to take on the task of fixing the medicine cabinet. I spent hours and hours working on plans and putting them into action. Finally, I was ready to replace the cabinet. I placed it in the area on the wall where it had originally stood and proceed to pound it back into place. I was just about finished when Dottie came strolling up the stairs. We stepped back to take a *good* look at the medicine cabinet. We turned our heads to one side, then the other, and leave it to Dottie to suggest that next time I should use a level when I put something like that on the wall.

It seemed Dottie was always the one to bail me out when things didn't go right in my fix-it experiences. We had an element burn out in the hot water heater one time, and she asked me to take a look at it. I joked that maybe she should get a water man to fix it, but when I got home that night, I decided to tackle it myself.

As I worked on it, I immediately had the feeling that something was wrong. The water was supposed to flush out quickly, but it was just sort of bubbling and gurgling. I opened the hot water heater to find the element that was burned out, and sure enough, the water gushed out, seemingly flooding the house in a matter of minutes. I screamed for Dottie and in her haste to get to me, she cut her foot on something in the basement. She was holding her foot, and all I could say was: "Forget your foot and help me stop this water from flooding us out." I was a pretty compassionate guy, as you can tell.

We finally got everything cleaned up, and I somehow got the heater fixed. I thought it was amazing that I didn't electrocute myself. I proceeded to fill the tank with water, and of course, I became impatient. So, I turned the hot water heater on before the water level had reached the top element. This resulted in me burning out the top element in the heater, which was just about where I had started. I finally gave up and instructed Dottie to find an expert to fix that blasted water heater because I was surely no expert.

It was quite obvious I wasn't mechanically inclined, but Dottie always seemed to find the wherewithal to stand beside me. She saved me when I was babysitting our first son, E.J., after he nearly flooded our garage.

I decided to wash the car in the driveway, and I figured he could help me by turning the water on and off from inside the garage. My hose had no nozzle to control the flow on my end, so I told E.J. to listen for me to yell: "Turn it on!" and "Turn it off." We had good teamwork going for the first 15 or 20 minutes, but at one point, when I yelled for him to turn it on, the hose gave no response. I yelled it again and decided I better check it out. When I got inside the garage, there was E.J. holding the nozzle on the other end of the hose in his hand while the water rushed out of the faucet at his feet.

I tried to put the nozzle back on, but it wouldn't go. To top it off, I couldn't turn off the faucet in the garage either, and a very important long- distance phone call came at just the right time. Fortunately, Dottie arrived just in time to bail E.J. and I out before we were forced to swim our way out.

When I met Dottie, it was the summer before my senior year at Penn State. Football camp came much too soon that season, and on the first day, I was still in pretty good shape—meaning the practices hadn't tired me out yet. I found myself missing my new-found love, so as I sat around the dorm area with some friends on the team, I decided to write Dottie a letter to show her how much I missed her.

"Dear Dottie," it began. *"As I sit here staring at Mount Nittany, I see no towering, majestic mountain. Instead, I only see your face. Amidst all this violence and brutality we call football, I feel no pain or hatred. I feel only love for you. J.T. White, my position coach, says I should 'HIT!,' but I cannot hit. He barks 'RUN!,' but I cannot run. He screams 'HATE!,' but such is not my fate. You, you, you are my destiny! Amidst all this violence and brutality, I can only feel love for you..."*

The letter went on and on like that as my friends helped me piece together the words. After I signed my love to the letter, I decided to add a little supplement: "*P.S.,*" I continued. "*You can buy tickets for all the Penn State home football games through the ticket office for five dollars a ticket.*" I thought Dottie would get a kick out of my letter, but actually, she thought I took a hard hit to my head in practice or something.

Dottie was born in Tennessee, and so many of her relatives lived there. One of the first years I was back coaching at Penn State, we were scheduled to play at Tennessee in the last game of the season. We had a very good football team with Franco Harris and Lydell Mitchell in the same backfield. We were undefeated at the time, but we went into Knoxville and got our butts kicked. The Volunteers ran back two punts for touchdowns, and they intercepted a lateral and ran it back for another TD. The final score was something like 31-19. We lost, but it was a terrific atmosphere to play in. I was also proud that we were playing in Dottie's hometown territory, but I wish we could have given them a better display of football.

We were invited to the Cotton Bowl that season to play the University of Texas. Bowl games often have functions for both teams to attend in order to draw crowds, bring a bit of camaraderie to both teams and to basically keep the teams together as much as possible. Less chances for players to find trouble individually that way also. We were invited to a country and western cookout in Texas. They had a country-western band and a barbecue. When the leader of the band asked if anyone had any requests, Dottie spoke up immediately that she wanted to hear "Tennessee Waltz."

Keeping in mind our recent thrashing of a few weeks before, several of the players and coaches heard the song playing and started looking around, wondering who would ask for such a song. Maybe it was a prank from one of the Texas coaches, someone stated. Coach Paterno slowly turned around and said: "Who in the world requested this song?" Then I started looking around, acting as if I didn't know. "How could anybody be so dumb to ask for this song?" I then looked at Dottie and said: "I can't believe you did that to me." She just smiled, but maybe it was a good motivational tool for the team because we came back strong from our season-ending loss and beat the Longhorns, 31-6.

Come to think of it, we haven't been invited back to the Cotton Bowl since, and I might be the one responsible for that. On the night before the game, one of my responsibilities was to go around and make sure the players were in their rooms for the night. No one was allowed to enter or leave the floor. I had just finished checking everyone in and was headed down the hallway when I heard the elevator bell ring. I stopped in my tracks and peered cautiously around the corner as I heard the doors slide open. I couldn't believe my eyes as a young lady came strolling out of the elevator and proceeded to walk down the hall.

"Excuse me, miss," I said with a nervous, yet forceful voice. "Where are you going?" I tried my best to keep my composure as she disregarded my question and brushed right past me down the hallway. I couldn't believe she had the audacity to completely ignore me. Even a simple "Get lost!" would have been something.

I asked her again, and she took off running down the hall. She caught me a bit flat-footed, but I felt the old speed and agility of my youth would still be enough to catch her. I was dead wrong. She ducked around a corner, but I still felt I could catch her. When I found that same corner, she was nowhere in sight. I heard a room door close and figured she had slipped into one of them, but I had no idea which one. Instead of knocking on all the doors, I decided to get one of our rooming lists and see if I could figure things out from there.

Figuring it would be a difficult task and wondering if I'd ever see this mysterious girl again, I stood in the hallway poring over my room list. I was about to give up my seemingly fruitless search when who but that very same girl came strolling by me as if nothing had happened before. I decided to calmly speak to her again.

"Excuse me, miss," I said in the most polite manner I could muster. "Who did you go down there to see?" Again, she refused to acknowledge me, so I calmly repeated myself. Just when I figured there was no hope for an answer, she stopped in her tracks and turned to face me.

"I beg your pardon, sir," she said, "But the word is 'whom,' and *whom* I went to see is none of your business."

To this day, I don't know the correct way to say it, but I kept my cool while I thought about what she said. "Don't tell me that, miss," I said with an equally straight face. "The word is 'who,' and it certainly *is* my business what you're doing on this floor."

With that, I checked the rooming list again and determined who was in each room. When I checked the area this young lady had come from, the list read: "Cotton Bowl Executives." As it turned out, she was married to one of those very same executives. My first thought was to crawl into a hole, but I tried to keep my dignity. "Ma'am, I beg your pardon," I said with a thousand apologies. "But it *is* whom, and it is *definitely* none of my business."

Trips like this were part of the many vacations Dottie and I have taken together. I will always remember them. Sometimes I would get myself in trouble, like the time we took a family vacation to Wisconsin. My parents were there and so were Dottie's, but my dad and I spent most of the time by ourselves fishing. That didn't go over well with most of the family. They were kind of upset, but for the most part, we all enjoyed many great times and vacations together, and everyone took part in everyone else's interests through the years.

Dottie really helped me get through graduate school at Penn State. She had a job at the university, and I taught in the physical education department on top of my graduate assistant's job with the football team. I really enjoyed the teaching and the competition. I played in graduate school basketball leagues, and I traveled with some of the Penn State football players for a "football" basketball team we had.

Even though school was tough, and I wasn't the most mechanically inclined person, Dottie and I enjoyed that year in our small attic apartment, and we also enjoyed my service as a graduate assistant football coach. Part of the job of being a grad assistant at that time was to work closely with the freshman team. Freshmen didn't play with the varsity then, so we had to be their coaches and help them through a very critical time in their lives. It's a phase where they were on their own for the very first time, yet they still needed someone to be there for them and gradually help them break their ties from home. So we, as grad assistants, were kind of like fathers and coaches. We spent time with them in study hall, making sure they knew how important that was to their academic success. We checked them in and tried to help them make it through their initial struggles—which were often plenty.

The head coach of the freshman football team at that time, Earl Bruce, was a great person, and he fit the mold of the father figure very well for this group of players. We played two games as a team together that year—one against West Virginia and the other against Pittsburgh. Before we played West Virginia, Coach Bruce delivered his pre-game speech with a lot of emotion.

"West Virginia will probably be the toughest team you'll play all year," he said with fire in his eyes. "Unless Pitt is tougher."

I think about those beginnings of my coaching career quite often, and I realize they were times that were very instrumental in where I stand today. Some young coaches would look at an assignment with the freshman team at that time as a step down, but I liked helping young men at that age. I looked at them, and I remembered the letter I wrote home to my parents when I was a freshman, and I recalled how that time in *my* life was so critical. They were some very special moments, indeed, and I had a wonderful woman like Dottie to share every one of them with me.

11

No Kids

FROM GRADUATE SCHOOL, I went to my first full-time coaching position at Juniata College in Huntington, Pennsylvania Juniata was a very small liberal arts college—enrollment around 1,100 students at the time. It was different from Penn State, obviously, because of the size of the schools. It wasn't as intense as the practice regimens I had learned at Penn State either, but one element of sports that was definitely present with Juniata football was pride. Everyone affiliated with the football team wanted to win on the field, and everyone worked hard to accomplish that goal.

Competitive instincts also took over even when we weren't thinking about football. As individuals, both coaches and players were always trying to be a little more competitive than the next guy. The preparations we had before practice weren't as difficult as they were at Penn State, so I used to challenge the other coaches —and even some players—to kicking contests or whatever competitive activity we could think of. I played basketball in the winter, and I especially loved being able to get to know what seemed like every student on campus because of their involvement in sports or my other job as a physical education teacher. In that capacity, I had the great fortune of meeting a lot of good students and definitely outstanding people.

College football at a small school can be a real treat at times. When you've been a part of one of the largest and most successful programs in the country, you learn to realize how good those opportunities are, but you also realize you can take some of that experience and incorporate it into the small college atmosphere.

We played our first game that season against Westminster College, and I learned a very important lesson right away. We had a saying: "You win with performance; you lose with potential." We lost to Westminster that day because we played quite a few players who had potential but lacked the performance qualities it took to get the job done. The kids made several mistakes, and we, as coaches, probably made the biggest mistake by not paying attention to the words of our own team's saying.

Through the rest of that season, we played guys who were perhaps smaller, but they played the game the way coaches like to see it played. They went all out, and even though they were smaller, they were quicker and more aggressive than the players we started out with against Westminster. And wouldn't you know it, we ended up winning the rest of our games that season.

In major college football, you get used to traveling by plane to almost all the away games, but at a small school like Juniata, buses were the common mode of transportation. We even had a regular driver every week who was truly a great man who loved to do what he could for Juniata College. He became very good friends with our trainer, and wherever we played, those two would scour the town we were playing in looking for a restaurant that served steamed clams—once, of course, the players and coaches were delivered to the stadium we were playing in.

At Juniata, I also helped coach the basketball team at that time. Russ Trimmer was the head coach, and he seemed to always press the right buttons. He was a great coach who practiced the man-to-man defense to exhaustion. He was a fiery individual, and defense was his specialty. He always loved to win, but if there was one team he took a little extra satisfaction in beating, it was Susquehanna University. The problem was, he also got a little carried away if we didn't do well against Susquehanna.

His biggest frustration came from the fact that he worked so hard on team defense and this team looked like a pickup team when we played them. They played a 2-3 defense and looked like they never really worked on it. In one particular game, we were losing to them at home, and finally, Russ couldn't hold it in any longer. He let out his inner frustration to such a point where he could be heard throughout the gym, which earned him a technical foul from the referee. To make things worse, when he realized what the call was—and that it went against him— he instinctively threw a towel at the official.

Naturally, the officials threw him out of the game, which left only myself to take over. There was a minute and 26 seconds left in the game, and I wasn't very familiar with the system, because I had just come from football. I looked at everybody in the huddle and didn't say much to start. The players stared at me, I looked back at them, and this continued for what seemed like forever. They were looking for words of wisdom, and all I had to offer was a dumbfounded look on my face. Finally, I said with fire in my eyes and thunder in my voice: "All right! Let's go get 'em!"

The players went out and did their best, but my sage advice wasn't enough to help us pull out the game.

I coached the junior varsity basketball team, and that was a challenge I thrived on and enjoyed, even if we didn't have the greatest athletes. On the Division III level, freshmen were eligible for varsity action, unlike the higher levels at that time, so we lost a few of the better athletic undergrads because of that. But I enjoyed the involvement with a lot of the great young people, and they always gave tremendous effort in whatever I asked of them.

The players worked and practiced hard, just as I had expected they would, but even to my surprise, we started the season undefeated before we hit final exams and the semester break. Soon after the break, we were scheduled to play St. Francis—a Division I school. They were tough to begin with because of their own success and the higher level of competition they faced throughout the season. What made dealing with St. Francis even tougher was the fact their freshmen had to play JVs because they were ineligible for varsity ball due to their Division I status.

To top it off, our team had run into some academic problems. We were undermanned, but I was still hopeful we could beat St. Francis or at least give them a run for their money. I even went there to do some scouting before our big game right after the semester break. St. Francis has always been known for large basketball crowds in a very small gym, and the night we played, there was no exception. It was early, and the varsity game was still a couple of hours away, but the gym was full, regardless. It was our chance to shine if we could somehow pull off the upset. I even picked up a couple of our football players for the game to make sure I had enough people in case we ran into foul trouble.

Despite all my efforts, we were depleted. My roster was down to six players, and St. Francis simply wore us down. We lost something like 90-50 or some absurd score like that. The large gathering showed no sign of mercy either as several of the students and fans became downright obnoxious. They ridiculed and laughed at my players, but I was able to remain calm and put up with most of it. Remember, I said *most* of the crowd.

There was one guy who became particularly obnoxious with his constant chatter. A coach should never react to negative comments from the fans, but this guy had gotten on my last nerve. He wasn't far up in the bleachers behind our bench, and he kept up his chatter to the point where I finally turned around and said: "Aw, why don't you just shut up!"

It appeared the whole gymnasium had fallen silent for just that moment because everyone realized who said what, and that was all they needed. The fans started booing me directly and throwing jelly beans at our bench. I knew I had probably made a huge mistake, and I decided to sit on that bench the rest of the game and keep my mouth shut, no matter what the fans had to say. I was hoping it was the best decision I would make that night.

As we walked off the court, I told our players: "You know, they still have to come to our place. Somehow, some way, I don't even know how, but we're going to find a way to beat that team."

My guys were fired up, and when the time came for St. Francis to play at Juniata, my players had remembered my promise. It seemed like even more of an insult when we found out that St. Francis had even left their coach at home. Instead, they brought the equipment manager and a trainer. That was how much they thought of us. I told this to our players, and they wanted so badly to go out and prove that team wrong.

Our players listened intently to my plan, which was simply to freeze the ball for the first half. The shot clock wasn't brought into college basketball for several years after that, so I think I can safely say my ball-possession tactics were not the reason for the rule change. I wanted my players to control the ball and not take any unnecessary shots. I instructed them to only shoot if they had a clear lane to the basket, which would not be often against St. Francis. I told them we wanted to keep the score within two or three points by halftime, then we would change the whole tempo by pressing them early in the second half. We would try to get a lead and then hold on for dear life.

The plan was actually working the way I had hoped until there was about a minute-and-a-half left before halftime. Somehow, St. Francis broke loose with a 10- or 12-point spurt and held a 13-point lead at halftime. In the locker room, I was extremely frustrated, and I reminded the players how they disrespected us by not bringing their coach to the game.

We pressed them early in the second half, got as close as five or six points, but that was it. I was disappointed in the loss, but I enjoyed the game because our kids showed they will always give their best effort—win or lose.

Dottie went with me to Gettysburg College one time on a scouting assignment, and when we came out of the gymnasium, we noticed freezing rain in the air. We took our time and made it safely to the top of a mountainous road we had to climb. When we reached the top, however, there were several cars parked off to the side of the road, their drivers seemingly not sure if they wanted to brave the downside of the mountain in these conditions. My own car started sliding a little bit when I got there, but fortunately, I was able to pull along side the other cars parked out of danger.

I got out of my car to check out the conditions, and my feet slipped right out from under me. I hit my head on the concrete and I'm quite certain I had a concussion. It was like a dream. There was a nurse up there on that mountain, and she patched my head for me. We were talking to a guy and trying to decide what we should do. Finally, we began talking in bolder tones.

"If you follow me down the other side of the mountain," the man said boldly, "I think I can go through a reservation down there and get you on your way." I looked at Dottie and it seemed like neither of us knew what we should do. But we wanted to get going because the idea of spending the night on top of an icy roadside mountain in the car didn't seem very appealing.

As we made our way slowly down the steep hill, Dottie finally spoke up. "I don't know if I like this, Jerry," she said as the cold rain ticked at our windshield. "There were some people who have been killed by strangers in that area. What if this man is setting us up for something like that?"

"Oh, stop thinking of such crazy things," I told her. I didn't want to think about such a thing at a time like this, but she did manage to put the thought right there in the center of my mind. What made it even more scary was the guy stopped his car at that very moment, got out and began walking toward our car. I wasn't really sure if I should open my window, but I did.

He was ominous looking as he approached our car. I almost expected him to pull a gun or knife, or something out from behind his back. "I just want you to know I'm the preacher at the local church in this area, and if you keep going on this road for about two miles and turn to the right, you'll be on your way."

I shook hands with the preacher and thanked him for his troubles. As we drove off, I looked at Dottie and said: "Yeah, aren't you a great judge of people?"

Dottie and I had many goals in our lives, and one of them was clearly to start our own family. We both had always loved kids, and we felt like we were ready to start our own family while we were at Juniata. Things weren't going exactly as we had planned, and finally, we were given the news that we would not be able to have our own children. We were told it would just not be possible.

It was a devastating blow, to be sure, but one of the first things that crossed my mind was something that Bob Phillips, a good friend to me and a great coach at Penn State, once told me. "It's not what happens to you in life that's important," Coach Bob said. "It's how you react to it."

More recently, I think of Dave Dravecky, the major-league baseball player who lost his pitching arm to cancer. He battled through all of the radiation and chemotherapy treatments after he was diagnosed with the cancer and even got a brief chance to pitch again. He won his first time back on the mound, but in his second start, his left arm snapped right there on the mound, and his career was over. He lost so much muscle from various surgeries and treatments that his arm couldn't handle the stress of pitching anymore. Dravecky was eventually forced to have his arm amputated because the cancer had returned, but you never heard a negative word from him, and you never saw him feel sorry for himself.

His words stick with me every time I feel that so many things are against me: "It's not 'Why me, God?'" Dravecky said in recalling his feelings. "It's: 'What is your *plan* for me, God?'" This experience happened to Dave Dravecky long after doctors informed Dottie and myself that we couldn't have children, but they were words we used back then to get us through the initial sadness of what we discovered.

Dottie and I didn't want to dwell on the unfortunate. Instead, we accepted what we were told as quickly as possible and didn't hesitate to take the next steps necessary in our healing process. If we couldn't have children of our own, we reasoned the next logical step would be to adopt. So, we began the necessary steps to start our family in a very different way. At just about the same time, I was offered an interview at Boston University.

It was an interesting interview, one I thought I handled pretty well, but I didn't get the job right away. I didn't know their reasons for not hiring me at the time, but later, much closer to summer, someone from the Boston University athletic department called me and asked if I would like to coach in a different capacity. I had basically worked with the defense ever since I started coaching, but Boston University wanted me to take the opening as their offensive line coach. It seemed like a step up—a step in the right direction—so I accepted.

It was a whole different experience. One minute, I was coaching at the Penn State summer camps, and the next minute, Dottie and I were saying: "Boston, here we come." It was 1968 and we didn't know what to expect as we headed toward one of the biggest cities I had ever lived in. We didn't know what we were doing; we had no place to live. I love to look at trees and it seemed like Boston had none to look at. But I was ready for the job nevertheless. If nothing else, I figured living in a city this large was certainly going to be an interesting experience.

In the beginning, I had to live in a dorm because I got busy with football right away, and it was hard to find a regular apartment on top of my coaching duties and everything else. Dottie couldn't stay there in the dorms with me, so she went back to her home in Chicago until I had time to settle in somewhere.

On the day we were supposed to check in, I didn't have my room key, but I went to the dorm thinking I could get it there. When I was a grad assistant at Penn State, we hardly ever worried about locking our doors, so I figured it might be the same here. I should have known better being in the city, but it was one of those times when my naive nature would catch up to me and cost me a hard lesson as well.

When I arrived at the dorm, I found my room and was pleasantly surprised to find the door already open. I figured this wouldn't be a problem as I would just move my stuff in and get the key later. I went to work and left the room just the way I found it, but when I returned, I found that my clock radio and some of my clothes had been stolen. I wondered right then what I had gotten myself into. Life was much faster there in the big city, and the people weren't very friendly. I knew as each day passed, I had walked into a totally different atmosphere than what I was accustomed to.

On one occasion, I was driving down Commonwealth Avenue in a snowstorm, and I had to decide whether to turn into the entrance of Boston University. There was a lot of snow everywhere, and that area hadn't been plowed at all. But, of course, I didn't know this until I decided to attempt the turn. I got stuck in a heavy snow drift, and the car wouldn't move. I was grinding the wheels as I tried to lurch the car back and forth. As I did this, a number of people stood around on the sidewalks and simply stared at my frustration. I thought of all the small towns I had been associated with up to then and how a group of people like this would have dropped anything they were doing in a second to rescue a stranger in trouble and not give it a second thought. It was only after I asked for help that anyone on this Boston street bothered to step up.

I knew this was going to be a learning experience, and I was going to have to ask for as much toughness out of myself as I would ask of the players I would be coaching. I had a job to do, but as I drove around that city, I saw so many helpless and hopeless people. There were so many down-and-out souls who experienced so much hurt while displaying obvious needs. That was something I never thought I would get used to during my stay in Boston.

I tried to forget those experiences by immersing myself into my duties with the football team. Boston University had a very liberal atmosphere in previous seasons. Sometimes, that can be okay if you're good enough to back it up, but this team wasn't and it showed in their records of the past few years. There was very little discipline, and we as assistant coaches convinced the new head coach that this lack of discipline most likely had lots to do with the past failures.

We went to New Hampshire for our preseason camp and began to instill the discipline from the very beginning, right down to setting a rule that the players were not permitted to wear long sideburns, which had become the fashion of the time. If any of the players even came to breakfast with those long sideburns, we didn't allow them in. I'm sure that sideburns weren't the answer to all of Boston's football troubles over the previous few years, but we made a lot of progress by sticking to little rules and dress codes like that and it actually helped us grow together as a team.

I was assigned to coach the offensive line at Boston University, and unfortunately, I didn't do as well as I had hoped in our first game. It was my first time at that position and we were beaten by Colgate, 28-0. We had a lot of problems, but we stayed with the discipline we had instilled from the beginning.

We had to dismiss a player who was elected as a captain by the previous coaching staff. He thought he was tough because he was a bouncer in a couple of bars, but I didn't think he had the toughness we needed on our team. I didn't think he would be the kind of player we would want on the goal line when the game was on the line. Instead, we played a lot of younger guys and grew as a team. They were players who responded to us, and together, we got better and better as the season went on.

At one point, there was some dissension when some players quit the team, and we had to dismiss some other players. Boston University never got much attention in the press, but when the problems developed, the media was right there to report it. The press could be brutal in a city like Boston, even at that time, and they spent a lot of time talking to the players in question. Those players gave their versions of what happened, and it led to some unfair statements toward our head coach, who had to make the difficult decisions. He elected not to return phone calls to the media, and on the Saturday that we were supposed to play Temple, the sports headlines in the Boston newspapers glared at everyone who read it: "DISSENSION AT BOSTON UNIVERSITY." It was my first experience with the coldness of a big city publication, and I thought it was very unfair, not only to the head coach, but to the entire Boston University football team.

I'm sure we all weren't totally right as football coaches, but the players that were interviewed for these stories said a lot of unfair things about the coach and the university, and they never got a chance for rebuttal. The players gave a very disturbing view of things, but believe it or not, the negative articles actually seemed to unite us even more as a football team. The experience made those who hung around and believed in the program work even harder. We probably played beyond our potential on that particular Saturday, but we upset a very good Temple football team. That was the start of a great year for us. Everyone came together, and it turned into one of the better seasons Boston University had experienced in quite some time.

After the first month of living in a dorm, I was able to find a place for Dottie and I to live. Foge Fazio, who was also on the Boston coaching staff at the time and went on to become head coach at the University of Pittsburgh, had found a duplex in Boston, so Dottie and I simply rented the vacancy above.

Boston is a city that is well known for its seafood, so when Dottie wanted to cook steamed clams one day, I was very hungry for the idea. They smelled great as they cooked to perfection on the stove, and it was then that I heard the scream from downstairs. It was Foge's wife, Norma. Knowing that Foge was away at the time, I rushed down the stairs to check on her, and I discovered she had fallen and twisted her ankle. It looked like a sprain, and since I wasn't very sure about things like that, I called for Dottie to come down right away with some ice.

We had a dog at the time—a little mutt named Mitzie. She was an excitable dog to begin with, and she followed Dottie everywhere. In the haste and confusion of these sudden events, Mitzie jumped at our apartment door and somehow managed to close it behind Dottie. Suddenly, we were locked out of our own apartment with clams steaming on the stove and the landlord at least an hour away. By the time we got back into our apartment, the clams had exploded, splattering the stove and walls with bits of clam. For a meal that I had anticipated greatly, it turned into the worst seafood dinner I had ever experienced.

Foge Fazio was a good friend to me at Boston University, and as time went on, we had become even closer. He was a Pitt alumnus, and, of course, I was from Penn State. We often talked about the great rivalry between our two alma maters, and one day, Foge came upstairs and told Dottie and I he had been asked to return to Pitt to join their staff as an assistant coach. It wasn't maybe two weeks later when I received a call from Joe Paterno, who had recently taken over at Penn State. He asked me if I would like to come back to Penn State and coach on his staff. It was an opportunity I couldn't believe came to me so quickly, and I couldn't wait to get back to the life I had known as a student in the small town of State College. After I accepted Coach Paterno's offer, I hurried downstairs and told Foge in a friendly rivals sort of way: "If you're going back to Pitt," I bellowed: "I'm going back to Penn State."

It seems like we have been battling ever since.

12

Family

OUR FAMILY HAS ALWAYS BEEN A BIT OLD-FASHIONED. We tried to eat meals together. Usually, breakfast and dinner were the best bets, with lunch being together as much as possible. Those were fun times because we tried to make a point to share the day's events. It was an opportunity to laugh together and share interesting stories.

Dottie was the leader. She prepared just about all the meals and made all the kids' lunches for school. Most of our "together" time was spent at home. The kids spent a lot of time with Dottie and I growing up. We were definitely a family that enjoyed one another.

We were often entertained by Jon and Jeff battling each other in the living room, and I'd play basketball with the boys or get a neighborhood football game going in the yard. We enjoyed trips to the lake, picnics and having football players over to the house where we could all play games. Having friends and neighbors and Second Mile kids over, it seemed like our house was always a place for fun. We enjoyed the simple things in life, and that's what made our experiences so neat and special.

It seems like there have always been dogs in our lives. There was Mitzi when Dottie and I were first married. Then there was Fifi, who was given to us by my mother-in-law. After that came Stosh and finally, there was Justice. They were a constant source of entertainment, also, as they did their tricks, played with the kids and generally misbehaved the way lots of dogs do.

One time, there were some Second Mile kids at our house, and Dottie was concerned that they might be misbehaving in the basement. She asked me to check on the source of the noise down there, so I decided to do it just to ease her mind, if nothing else. I descended the stairs, and as I turned the corner, there came one of the dogs flying over the sofa. I barely had time to turn my head when next came one of the kids hurtling over the same sofa, much like the dog. I rolled my eyes, threw my hands in the air and went back upstairs.

"Everything's fine," I said to Dottie. "Just another typical, normal evening in the Sandusky household." And that really was a common way of life for us. Kids sometimes turning the place upside down, and I was often the biggest kid in attendance.

Our own children: Ray, E.J., Kara, Jeff, Jon and Matt are all adopted, and they have all formed a special place in our hearts through so many different ways. Matt is the youngest, and we got to know him through The Second Mile. We became very close to Matt and watched him develop from a shy boy who kept to himself most of the time to a young man who finally allowed himself to see that he could enjoy the same wonderful things so many other children enjoyed in their lives.

Matt was around seven or eight years old when he first became involved in The Second Mile. He would visit our house occasionally, but he was never one to get very attached to anyone. He would stand off in the corner somewhere and watch as I would be wrestling with the other kids. He became an instant challenge for me. I didn't want to see him go through life by himself at such a young age. I didn't want to lose him to whatever other fates might have awaited him, so I kept trying and trying to pull him in.

Gradually, Matt did become more attached. He spent more time with us and got to know our family very well. He especially became close to Dottie and Kara, but he was still very shy and quiet. He lived with his biological mother, brother and sister. His mom was a person who tried very hard, but she kind of went from one crisis to another and never really gained control of all the circumstances she was faced with. As a result, Matt seemed to be neglected in many ways. He was put down a lot and told that he really wasn't any good.

I would take him home sometimes, and there wouldn't be anyone there. He resented me and he wouldn't talk when I took him there. At one point, he cried out to Dottie and Kara. He wanted out, he told them. His mom was getting abused by a boyfriend, and it was a very difficult situation.

When Matt was entering eighth grade, he was a record-setter when it came to disciplinary referrals, and he just wasn't doing very well at all. I convinced his mother to start a program where he could study and work out and spend time with us, and in turn, he would be rewarded with money that would go into a fund for his college education. He would have to sign a contract to do his share, and he would also receive some money in hand.

I traveled the 20-mile distance between State College and Howard many, many times. Matt adhered to the program we started for him, and all of a sudden, his grades improved at school, and he began to participate in football. He was also able to go to a bowl game with us. It was the Citrus Bowl in Orlando, Florida. Things seemed to be going in a positive direction for Matt, but following that bowl trip, another decline started.

Matt started missing his responsibilities he had with me, and I had to try and track him down. His mother became very jealous of what was happening. I think because he had been doing so well, she didn't know how to react. I remember driving Matt home one time and talking to him about what was happening in his life, the good things as well as the bad. I told him he had a big challenge ahead of him, and he was the only one who would be able to get through it. I told him he had to stop lying to people and stop accusing others for the problems that he had to deal with. I told him he had to have the strength and courage to fight out of the lifestyle that was making him so despondent.

Things remained difficult for a while, but Matt hung in there. Finally, everything kind of climaxed when his mother and her boyfriend decided to end the program he was going through with us at home. All of this occurred at a baseball game, and Matt acted out in frustration, anger, so many emotions were coming out. I wasn't really able to see him, but I had to test him. He cried out to me and said, once again, that he wanted out. But I needed to know whether he had the strength and the courage to stand up for what he wanted. I also needed to know whether I was going to be able to pull all of this off. I talked to him in front of his mom's boyfriend, and Matt passed that test with flying colors as he stood strong and seemed to want to fight to get out of that situation.

Time went on and I couldn't see him very much, and things began to falter. I went through all kinds of channels, such as children and youth organizations to probation systems, trying to devise a way for Matt to be relieved of those difficult circumstances he was embedded in. Then, as

Matt drifted away even further, we lost touch, and things really went downhill.

I'll always remember seeing Matt at a Second Mile camp. I hugged him and cried because he had become such a part of my life, and it appeared as though I wouldn't get to see him very much anymore. The school year started, and Matt was now a sophomore in high school. He didn't do well in football. He wasn't prepared at all, and it was apparent he had lost his motivation and incentive. He didn't do well in school, and he came close to quitting school altogether. And then, whether it should be considered fortunate or not, Matt got into trouble with the law.

The incident happened right before we went to Los Angeles to play Oregon in the Rose Bowl after our first Big Ten championship in 1994. While I was in California, I was able to make several phone calls back home, and I decided to explore the possibility of having Matt come and live with us. Tim Janocko, who was the head football coach at Clearfield High School, went to the detention center to visit Matt and see if he would be willing to live with us. Tim saw him, and we learned on either Christmas Eve or Christmas Day that Matt did want to take that step. I talked to him by phone while he was in the detention center, and I thought everything would be fine if he was placed with us in foster care. But it didn't happen that way. The challenge we had with Matt, and the one he faced himself, was still very great.

We thought we knew Matt and that he knew us, but he really didn't understand the rules and guidelines that were expected of him. He violated so many rules, and there was so much frustration. He wasn't responding to us or his new surroundings at all, so we sought help through counseling.

That, too, became confusing because none of us really understood what the people were saying, and there were many differences of opinion. Matt, especially, became very confused, and eventually, everything hit bottom. Our relationship floundered, and one problem surfaced after another. It got to the point where the authorities were going to take him away from us, but fortunately, two people stepped in and, in our eyes, saved that young man's life.

One was Dr. Fox, a psychiatrist assigned to Matt's case. He wrote an assessment showing his opinion that Matt should be placed back with us because that was what Matt wanted. The other person was the judge who made the tough call—the one that said he would indeed be placed in our custody, despite very strong opposition from people who believed that Matt should be sent away.

We had new hope, but things still continued on a downward trend until the whole situation looked very bleak. It appeared, once again, that we wouldn't get very far and that everything was coming to an end. Subconsciously, I started to withdraw from Matt because I just couldn't deal with the hurt anymore. I felt we had done everything we could for Matt, and the end of our relationship was approaching. I told him there was nothing left and that we had played our last card. I told him if he did something wrong again, he would be out of our control, and there would be nothing more I could do for him.

Matt sensed my withdrawal, and one day, when I was working in my den, he came in with a piece of paper in his hand. "Here, you may want to read this," he said with a sad look on his face. "You gave it to me a long time ago. I read it, and now may be a good time for you to do the same thing."

I took the paper from his hand and read the title of the article: *Keep Climbing*. The gist of the article was a statement about never quitting; never giving up. When I finished the article, I looked up to find his eyes had never left mine. I was humbled once again by a young man who had been through so much adversity in his life, but here he was teaching me how to keep on fighting even when the odds are stacked tremendously against you. "I ought to punch you in the nose," I said as I smiled and hugged him. "You drive me nuts!"

"I love you," was his simple reply. But you have to know Matt to know how much those three words meant.

From that point on, it seemed Matt had changed. He grew a desire to succeed after so many experiences of me pushing and pulling and shoving to get him to do this or that. He was now doing it on his own, and it was a great thing to see. He got tutored for his college boards and began to do very well in school. He turned his life into a positive direction. He was accepted for college at Penn State and became an equipment manager with us on the football team.

Matt has traveled a long, long road since those days when he wanted to quit school. He is an official adopted member of our family, and he was with us through the death of my father as well as both of Dottie's parents. All of this helped draw him closer to us, a family that has always cared so much about him.

Regardless of what happens down the road, we witnessed a young man who had the strength and courage to stand up and say: "I want to be something special." He had the strength and the courage to stay loyal to us even when we weren't sure what would happen. He could have hurt us.

He could have driven us out of his life, but he didn't. And that will always mean the world to us.

At this time, Matt is still a student at Penn State, and we all, at times, still experience some highs and lows. There will always be battles, just like we have experienced on the football field, but we're still in the game. We will continue and fight onward together. Hopefully, we will have a positive conclusion, but just witnessing Matt carry himself this far has certainly been a national championship experience for us.

We took trips with the kids a lot, and some of them would be to state parks and swimming areas. I always loved to fool around in the water, often to Dottie's embarrassment because it usually took a lifeguard or park ranger to tell me to straighten up or get out. Once, I was throwing a volleyball around in the water and the lifeguard's whistle blew. "No volleyballs in the water," he said as I turned to the sound of the whistle. Next, we were tossing around a lighter beach ball until we heard the whistle again. "No beach balls in the water."

The young lifeguard sounded a bit more perturbed, so I did what he asked and threw the beach ball out of the water. After a while, the pool was fairly empty except for the kids and me, so in an impromptu sort of way, I began to pick up one child after another and toss them a few feet into a safe spot of the pool. The kids were laughing, splashing, and having a great time—almost as much fun as I was—until we heard that dreaded whistle again.

"No throwing children in the water," he said in that same drill sergeant tone of his. I was starting to get annoyed now, because the kids were just having fun, and we weren't jumping around in anyone's path. I thought of letting him know how I felt, but Dottie politely told me that probably wouldn't be a good idea. After thinking about it, I realized the lifeguard was just doing his job.

Bowl trips have always been fun and exciting for our family, and were usually met with great anticipation by everyone involved with Penn State football. Our family often piled into one room, five and six kids at a time, along with two adults. This was certainly one way for us to experience the togetherness that we cherished so much.

At the Fiesta Bowl one year, Dottie and I were sleeping in one room and the kids in the room next to ours. I was awakened at 3 a.m. by Kara yelling at Jeff. It seemed he had rolled over and kicked her and then he wouldn't roll back. I listened for a while, hoping they would settle it on their own, but when it started getting louder, I knocked on the wall and said, "Jeff, move it!"

There was quiet at first, and then I heard what sounded like legs kicking rapidly under covers, like a loud swishing sound. I soon discovered it was our oldest son, Ray, and he was indeed running in place in his sleep. The sound was amusing enough, but when he began talking in his sleep, we couldn't hold in the laughter.

"There, was that enough for you?" Ray asked rather loudly. We broke out laughing in both rooms, and even though it was three in the morning, we ended up having a nice family conversation.

I often think of Jon's first experience in a big city. We were in New Orleans for the national championship game against Georgia in 1982, and he was so impressed by all the tall buildings, the pigeons and the experiences of just being in a big city. The one thing I probably wish he didn't have to experience then was a car driving by us and an elderly lady hanging halfway out the window. Chances are, either Jon or myself was wearing some kind of Penn State clothing because this woman started wailing at us: "How 'bout dem Dawgs! How 'bout dem Dawgs!....Woof, woof, woof, woof...!" Jon would learn there are fans of all shapes, sizes and personalities out there, and they are not always cheering for the blue and white of Penn State.

Bowl trips were always a time for us to spend together as a family away from home. It was a vacation for everyone but me, but they understood why we were there and what made the trip possible. And when my coaching day would finally come to an end, I made sure that family came first. There was always the swimming pool and the jacuzzi for the kids to enjoy, and Dottie did her part by taking them to the zoo or whatever attraction was in that area.

Even without bowl trips, we often traveled together. There was a time when the kids all wanted to go to Disney World in Orlando. I didn't know if I'd be able to swing that much time to do it, but some good fortune came about when I had to take a spring football trip to the University of Florida. I had contacted a former teammate of mine, Mike McBath, because I knew he had a condominium in Orlando. It was owned by his future wife at the time, and they graciously allowed our family to use it.

So, Dottie packed the kids and two dogs into our Citation Hatch-back and drove south. They stopped in Tennessee and stayed with her parents for a short time and then drove on to Orlando. In the meantime, I bummed a ride from Gainesville to Orlando, and I met my family there. We had a great time, and the kids wore themselves out every day in the park.

Toward the end of the trip, we had planned to spend the day at Epcot Center, but Jon, who was the youngest at the time and probably the most worn out because we had been up a long time and had done a lot of walking, had decided he definitely did not want to go there. He was adamant in his stance, and I can still remember the tears in his eyes when he said: "I thought this trip was for me."

"Jon," I said as I looked him in the eye. "This trip *is* for you. And it's for Ray, E.J., Kara and Jeff. It's for all of us." After that, he understood, and he was fine. We ended up enjoying a nice time at Epcot Center.

On the way home from Florida, we were squeezed into the hatch-back with a rack on top for our luggage. We drove back to Pennsylvania, stopping in Tennessee to pick up the two dogs. It was a great car to travel in. We put Jon on one side and Jeff on the other so they couldn't get at each other. We managed to make it back without much incident, and as we traveled along, the kids started calling themselves "The Sardinskys" because everyone was packed so tightly in there. That was an example of our togetherness, and we made it a fun and memorable trip.

There were other times when we would travel together in the car, and the kids worked together in assembly-line fashion addressing and stamping envelopes for fliers regarding a book I had written about developing linebackers. We often worked on different things while we were traveling, and we played games that families often play in the car to keep the harmony as smooth as possible. Dottie also liked to sing songs, and she got the kids to sing along with her. They were songs she had learned from church camps when she was younger.

E.J. and I always competed hard against each other in basketball. When he was younger, I would always beat him, and he was the one who came back each time more determined than ever that this would be the game he would finally beat me. When he was a senior in high school, I got ahead of him in one of our contests, and I made the mistake of relaxing a little bit. E.J. seemed to notice this lapse in my judgment, and he pounced on it. He suddenly found his game, and before I could do anything about it, he had won.

When we got home, E.J. walked into the house and said: "Hey, Mom, would you like to meet Mr. Humility?" That upset me, and I told him right away we were playing again tomorrow. Now it seemed like our roles were reversed. I had become the one who had to try extra hard to beat E.J. The next day, I couldn't hit a shot to save my life, and I lost again. This, of course, thrilled Dottie because she had always rooted against me in games and contests with the kids.

When we came home from the playground after E.J.'s second win over me, he walked into the house and said, "Mom, you better be kind to this guy. He may be going through a midlife crisis." That just about destroyed me.

There was just something about the competitive nature between E.J. and me. No matter what the contest was, we made it fierce. We even had an argument in a State College fast food restaurant about basketball and whether we would be playing another game. The whole family was there, and most looked embarrassed to be seen with us. My dad thought he would have to step in. Dottie kept telling me to grow up and quit acting like a child and my mother said she couldn't believe it was all happening. But that was life in our family. Never a dull moment.

One evening, some good friends of ours, Jim and Becky Martin, were expected at our house for dinner. Jim was a national championship wrestler at Penn State and Becky was his bride-to-be at the time. They were also special friends of our family as well as friends to The Second Mile. Before they arrived, E.J. and I were watching a boxing match on TV. We started some friendly sparring of our own, and sure enough, it soon became heated. Finally, I told him we better quit, but he took one final jab at me, which, of course, didn't sit too well.

I went after E.J. with full force, and by accident, I knocked him through the bathroom door, and the door broke completely off its hinges. Fortunately, the doorbell rang at just about that moment, so we knew with the arrival of our company that we were safe for at least a few hours from the wrath of Mom. When Jim and Becky left, however, she still let us know in no uncertain terms how angry she was.

The next evening, I was downstairs doing some work, and E.J. came down to talk to me before he went to bed. We talked for a while, and as he turned and started up the stairs, he tripped, hit the bannister and tumbled back down, making a loud thumping noise as he went. When his mother heard this, she started screaming: "You guys will never grow up! You never listen!" E.J. was unhurt, and as he sat on the floor laughing, I walked to the bottom of the stairs with my hands raised in the air. "I had nothing to do with it," I said before Dottie came after me. "I had nothing to do with it."

We had one particularly notable family summer vacation at a camp in South Fork, Ohio, with my parents, Dottie's parents and the Browns, some very good friends of ours who actually helped bring Dottie and I together. My family was in one cabin, and the parents and the Browns shared the other one. Dottie got a little upset with me through part of the vacation because I spent so much time fishing, golfing and swimming with my dad. On the last night we were there, we celebrated my parents' anniversary, along with Ray and E.J.'s birthdays. One was on July 25, the other on the 27th, and my parents' anniversary was on the 25th.

We had a cake and spent a great evening together, just having fun with family and friends. In the middle of the night, with everyone seemingly fast asleep, one person lay awake listening to the sounds of a summer night in the woods.

"Jerry," Dottie whispered as she nudged me in my sleep. "Jerry, listen to that. She does that often, so I didn't really pay much attention. She did it again, so I decided maybe I better listen to what was bothering her. I sat quiet for a few seconds, until finally, I heard some noises myself. It sounded like someone was trying to break into the cabin.

Jeff was sleeping in a room adjacent to the kitchen, while Ray and E.J. were in a room next to ours. I decided the best thing I should do is go and investigate, so I made my way to the kitchen and awakened Jeff. "Turn very slowly and tell me what you see," I instructed him once he was awake enough to understand me. Jeff turned so he could get a better look at the kitchen and told me the figure in the darkness looked like a man with a big tail.

I was even more confused now, but I decided to get Jeff out of there, and we went to Ray and E.J.'s room. I didn't want any of us to get sprayed in case it was a skunk, but I also didn't want a bunch of animals rummaging through our kitchen. I finally decided enough was enough, and I had to carefully find out what this creature was. I worked my way closer and closer, and I finally realized our friendly intruders were a couple of raccoons that had pried open the screen in the window, and they were rifling through the aluminum foil that covered the birthday/anniversary cake we had enjoyed a few hours earlier.

One of the raccoons ran into E.J.'s room and jumped across his bed. I had never seen E.J. move as fast as he did right then. After a few minutes, Ray and E.J. got the raccoons positioned onto a couple of tennis rackets, and they were able to get them outside. It turned out to be an amusing experience.

Family will always be important to me. I watched our children grow into fine young adults and go off in their own different directions. Ray is

married and living in Tennessee now; E.J. is the head football coach at
Albright College in Reading, Pennsylvania, and is married with two kids
of his own; Kara is married, and she and her husband are expecting their
first child; Jeff is married and stationed at Camp Lejune, North Carolina,
where he serves in the Marine Corps.; Jon just completed his senior year
of football at Penn State, and I was glad to have my retirement coincide
with his last year. Jon is going to help out with the team this season as an
undergraduate coach, and it appears he, too, has a future interest in coaching. And Matt is still attending Penn State, where we hope his life will
continue to go in a positive direction.

I am proud to think I had some bit of influence on the lives of my
children. Dottie has always been there to look after them when I was
away, and usually from the minute I was back in town, I became another
big kid for her to supervise as well. As I said before, there was never a dull
moment in the Sandusky household, and I don't think any of us would
have wanted things any other way.

13

The Old Guard

I WAS FORTUNATE ENOUGH TO WORK WITH MANY GREAT COACHES at Penn State, both as a player and as a coach. The unique aspect of Penn State football is the stability of the coaching staff. There have been only five head coaches in the modern history of Penn State football. The assistant coaches that were here when I was a player were mostly the same ones that I ended up coaching with over time. I can't think of one other university in the country that has had more coaches retire in the same community. That stability was one of the biggest reasons I chose to attend Penn State, and it was an even bigger reason why I wanted to return as a coach.

In his first season as head coach, Joe Paterno asked me if I would like to be a graduate assistant. I knew I wanted coaching to be part of my future, so I accepted his offer without much discussion. I worked a lot with the freshman team, and sometimes we had to run plays with the varsity. Usually, we communicated through flash cards we held up to run the other team's offense and defense. I say "usually" because sometimes we were told to come in and run, say, Navy's defense, and we wouldn't have a clue as to what we were doing. But somehow we would manage to find a way to get the job done.

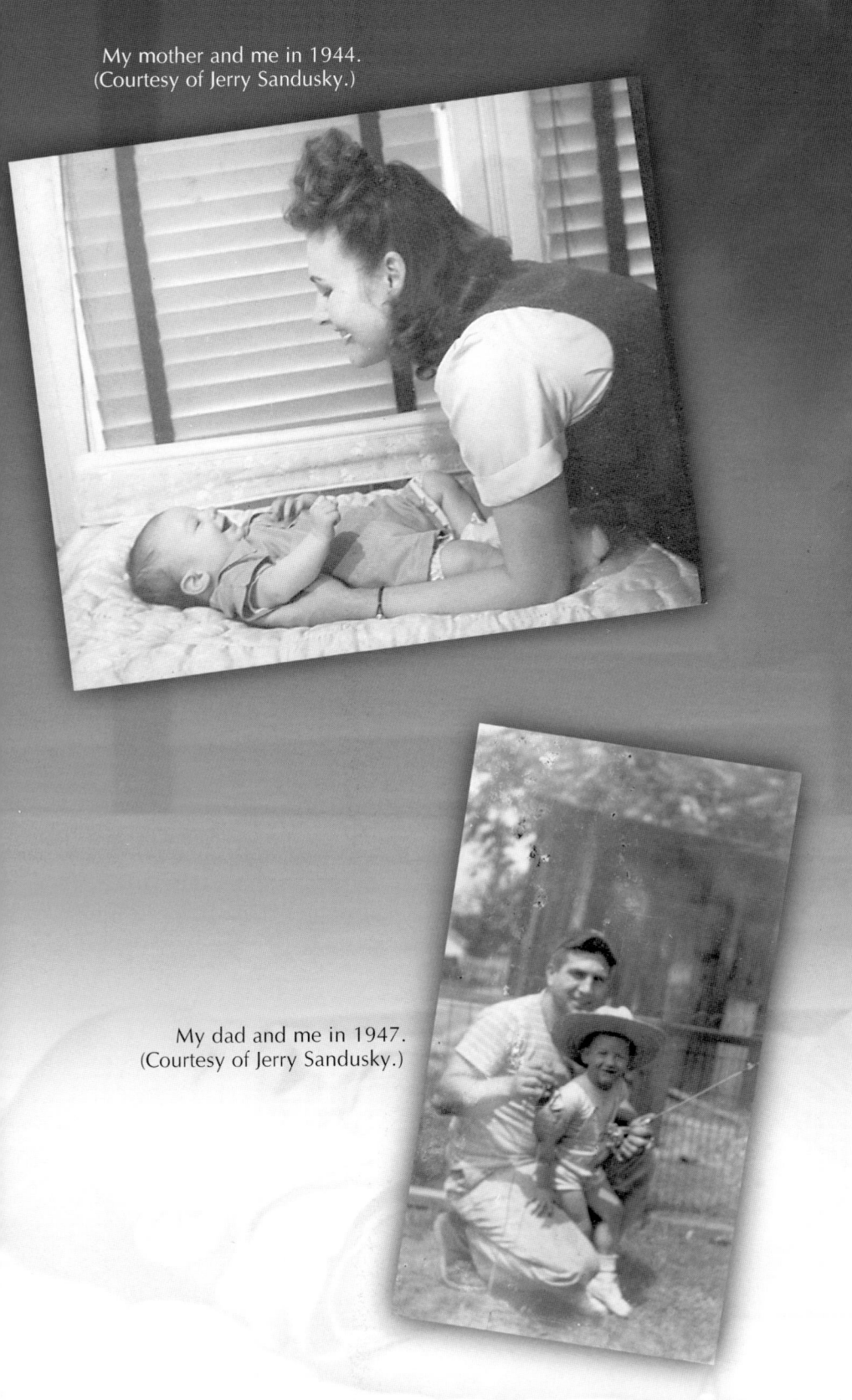

My mother and me in 1944.
(Courtesy of Jerry Sandusky.)

My dad and me in 1947.
(Courtesy of Jerry Sandusky.)

Me as a youth football player posing with my grandfather, whom I called "Judge." (Courtesy of Jerry Sandusky.)

I was a mascot for my father's basketball team in 1950. (Courtesy of Jerry Sandusky.)

I was part of the Clark School Midget Football championship in 1956. (Courtesy of Jerry Sandusky.)

My high school basketball team in 1962. I'm in the back row, third from the right. (Courtesy of Jerry Sandusky.)

I received a trophy after playing crosstown rival Trinity High School in 1961. (Courtesy of Jerry Sandusky.)

Sophomore year for me at Penn State. (Courtesy of Jerry Sandusky.)

Dottie and me with our parents at the rehearsal dinner the night before our wedding. (Courtesy of Jerry Sandusky.)

Me with Dottie's father amming it up as we prepare for our own outdoor "rock concert." (Courtesy of Jerry Sandusky.)

Jack Ham (33) in 1969. Ham went on to a great NFL career with the Pittsburgh Steelers. Jack received the last scholarship Penn State had to offer in his senior year of high school. (Courtesy of Jerry Sandusky.)

These players were part of the 1978 team that went 11-1, losing only to Alabama in the Sugar Bowl. Unfortunately, that loss cost Penn State the national championship. (Courtesy of Jerry Sandusky.)

Penn State's defense held All-America running back Herschel Walker (34) of Georgia to 111 yards rushing in the 1982 Sugar Bowl. The 27-23 victory gave Penn State its first national championship in school history. Walker won the Heisman Trophy that season. (Courtesy of Jerry Sandusky.)

Gregg Buttle poses with E.J. (left) and Tim Kulka. (Courtesy of Jerry Sandusky.)

My oldest son, Ray, referees a wrestling match between brothers Jeff and Jon. (Courtesy of Jerry Sandusky.)

Jon Sandusky (in costume) with family friends (left to right) Becky, Robin (cousin), and Jim at an elementary school play. (Courtesy of Jerry Sandusky.)

I am joined by national wrestling champion Jim Martin (left) and Bobby White after a high school benefit involving pudding wrestling. (Courtesy of Jerry Sandusky.)

The Sandusky family poses with our favorite lion. (Courtesy of Jerry Sandusky.)

Kids from my Second Mile Foundation join me at my home following a Penn State home game. (Courtesy of Jerry Sandusky.)

Chad, a special friend and former Second Mile participant who is a senior at Robert Morris College.(Courtesy of Jerry Sandusky.)

A Second Mile postgame football game with Jason, Zach, Mike, and Brendan. (Courtesy of Jerry Sandusky.)

Postgame gathering with friends Frank Mosier and Dom Toscani (left to right) and three young people I got to know through The Second Mile: (left to right) Brett, Frankie, and Jason. (Courtesy of Jerry Sandusky.)

Shirley Reynard, longtime receptionist at the Brownson House Recreation Center. (Courtesy of Jerry Sandusky.)

E.J. and I play basketball while Jon watches. (Courtesy of Jerry Sandusky.)

Family picture with a couple of kids from The Second Mile. Many of these kids grew to be a part of our family. (Courtesy of Jerry Sandusky.)

Justice and Staush, our family dogs. (Courtesy of Jerry Sandusky.)

I carry the Fiesta Bowl trophy in celebration in 1987.
Behind me is Jim Caldwell, now the head coach at Wake Forest.
(Courtesy of Jerry Sandusky.)

Penn State linebacker LaVar Arrington (11) laughs as I try to fire
up fellow linebackers Mac Morrison (31) and Brandon Short (43) during Media
Day on August 6, 1999. (Photograph by Craig Houtz.)

I try to motivate my players from the sideline during a game against Arizona in 1999. (Photograph by Michelle Klein.)

Courtney Brown gives me a hug after the Lions stopped Purdue on the last drive of the October 23, 1999, game. (Photograph by Pat Little.)

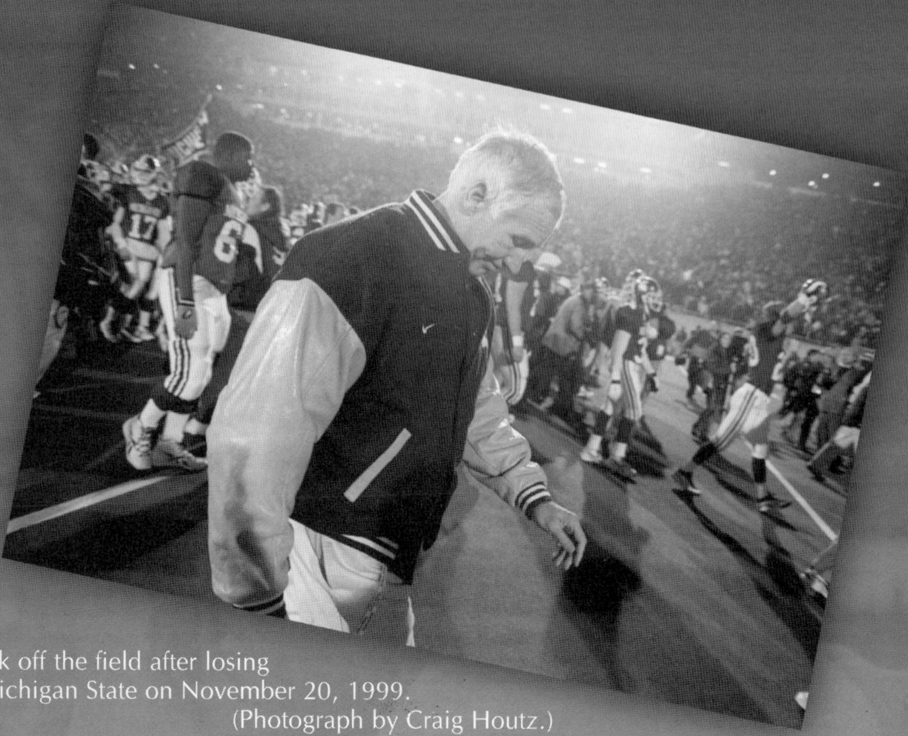

I walk off the field after losing
to Michigan State on November 20, 1999.
(Photograph by Craig Houtz.)

My son Jon hugs me after both of us were introduced before the
Michigan game in 1999. (Photograph by Pat Little.)

We had some good freshman players in that group. Players like Steve Smear, Jim Kates, and Dennis Onkotz, just to name a few. This group, along with several other players, went on to produce two undefeated seasons at Penn State.

It has always been my nature to goof around with the players and personnel at Penn State. It didn't matter whether I was a grad assistant or defensive coordinator, I liked to have fun. Sometimes—no, usually—this got me into trouble. I was known as the "Breakdown Coach" because one of my assignments as a graduate assistant was to watch the players covering punts. We wanted them to hustle down the field and get into a good hitting position, ready to make the tackle. We called it "breaking down," therefore, the nickname began.

One day, there was a scrimmage planned, so I wasn't needed on the field at that moment. Unbeknownst to me, however, Coach Paterno had changed his mind about the scrimmage, and he wanted me and my punt coverage team on the field. As usual, I was joking around with some of the players on the sidelines, and I wasn't paying attention when he called for me. In the distance I heard his voice grow louder, but I still was unaware that his cries were aimed at me.

"Uh, Jerry," one of the players interrupted me. "You better get out there. Coach Paterno's yelling for you."

Just then, the screaming became doubly intense from the middle of the field, but instead of hanging my head and shaking in my shoes, which is probably what I should have done, I ran onto the field waving my arms and shouting: "The breakdown coach is on his way! The breakdown coach is on his way!" Luckily, Coach Paterno didn't see or hear me doing that, but I was not about to get off the hook that easily. It turned out my antics were caught on the practice film, and I was called into his office the next day. I knew he would be furious because Penn State practices are organized right down to the last minute, and Coach Paterno doesn't believe in wasting one of those minutes.

I visited his office the next morning, and it was much like I had expected. "Jerry," he said, starting out calmly. "I would like to be able to recommend you for future coaching jobs, but I don't want to recommend a guy who's going to act like a complete goofball." He went on to bawl me out, and he told me he didn't like what he saw on the film. I felt bad at the time, but I still take a good-natured attitude with the players, and I subsequently have heard about it once in a while over the last 30 years or so.

Through the years, the assistant coaches are the ones I remember the most. J.T. White was the defensive ends coach and my coach when I was a player. Frank Patrick coached the defensive secondary; Jim O'Hora coached the defensive line, and he was the man I replaced as defensive coordinator. We called him Steady O because he never got too high or too low. Dan Radakovich was the linebacker coach before I took that position; and Bob Phillips was our quarterbacks and wide receivers coach, not to mention a great friend.

I had known some of these coaches when I was a player, but I got to know them in a coach-to-coach relationship a lot better when I went to a summer football camp with them in Northwestern Pennsylvania. It started out as a wide receiver camp, but it eventually grew into a camp for all positions. It was a camp where no pads were worn, and strictly fundamentals were taught. It was actually quite primitive at this camp. We were in the middle of the woods with no hot water and one shower that we couldn't even use. We had to wash in the river. It was, by no means, considered luxurious living.

It was my first experience at a camp like this as a coach, so I was very concerned about getting these young peoples' respect. I was in charge of one of the cabins, and the kids decided to carry on an age-old tradition they had heard about of ringing the bell at three in the morning. Ordinarily, it was a bell that we used as a wake-up call, but they had other ideas for it. I heard them rustling around, but I waited a while to see what they might be up to. It wasn't long after that I heard the bell and checked the time. I stormed out of the cabin and chased the culprits down. I found each one of them in their various hiding places. As I took them out into the street, I reminded them of the time and how awfully early it was to be ringing that bell, not to mention how wrong it was. To emphasize my point, I decided to have them run several sprints under the lone street light. That only proved to be a bigger mistake because I spent the rest of the night trying to get them settled back to sleep.

J.T. White was in charge of the camp, which was a responsibility he loved. He was a competitor, and he ran the camp in a military-like fashion. He conducted inspections of the cabins; the kids' tonsils; everything. The cleanest cabin was always guaranteed to win an award of some kind.

The kids would send postcards home to their families, and J.T. would often take a peek at a few of them, just to get an indication of how the kids were enjoying the camp. I observed him do this several times over the years, and there was finally one occasion where I couldn't resist giving old J.T. a rough time. He was having a particularly difficult time with one young camper who seemed to give him grief every chance he could, whether it was intentional or not. I noticed how the kid was getting to him, so I got a postcard and wrote the following, keeping in mind that J.T. would especially find it in his best interests to read what this kid had to tell his parents:

"Dear Mom and Dad,

This camp stinks. I can't stand anything around here, especially the coaches. There is one coach named J.T. who goes around and tries to destroy peoples' brains. The J.T. must stand for Jumbo Talker because that's all he's full of. Somebody must have destroyed his brain some time. I can't wait to get out of here."

I ended with "Love from your son..." and I put the pesky kid's name on it. The next day, I watched as J.T. scanned the outgoing mail. Sure enough, he came across my bogus postcard, and I could see the irritation growing inside him. You could always tell when J.T. was getting mad because his nose would begin to wrinkle. That day at practice was torturous for that innocent and unsuspecting kid because J.T. put him through the ringer. I thought about telling him it was me that wrote the postcard and not the kid, but I decided not to because, actually, I didn't seem to mind. When it came right down to it, the kid got on my nerves, too.

Even though I was an only child, I've always said the kids in my neighborhood who came to the Brownson House were my brothers and sisters. I had fun with them, and I feel it was through these football camps later in my life that I really learned how much I loved working with kids. I learned by watching Bob Phillips at a camp we went to in Buffalo, New York. It was run by a man named Jim Kellogg Clark, who was friends with Coach Bob.

Coach Bob is an extremely conscientious person who had always taken a great interest in young people. He got to know every one of the kids at the camp by their first names, and he wrote letters to them, and it was quite evident he enjoyed a great association with them. At this particular camp, I was in charge of a room with about 40 kids in it, and I found it to be just as much fun working with the kids as Coach Bob did. Sometimes, I even sang in the morning, which was my form of a wake-up call to get the kids out of bed. Imagine how much they loved hearing my voice in song so early in the morning with practice looming on the horizon.

Eventually, we established our own camp at Penn State, although the first one was not very well-prepared or organized. It started on a Sunday night, and after a light practice, I was out running when one of the coaches yelled out to me: "Jerry, we have a meeting." I thought he was joking, so I kept running. The next thing I knew, Coach Paterno was out there yelling at me again. That was the way the week started.

Coach Paterno wanted me to take charge, so I held a meeting with some of the other coaches to try to come up with activities and plans for the campers. Some recreation ideas were bounced around, but they weren't very popular ideas. Not many of the coaches gave suggestions, but when the ideas bombed, they were awfully quick to criticize.

It got rather frustrating by the end of the week, and I heard some of the coaches still trampling on some of my ideas for recreation activities that we had planned for the kids. Finally, I couldn't hold it in any longer and decided to let them know how I felt. "Oh, that's right," I said harshly. "No one speaks up in meetings, but you all sure don't have any trouble talking behind my back."

Coach Paterno could see that I was rather upset, so he played the father figure and calmly took me aside. "What's wrong with you, Jerry?" he asked.

I told him I didn't like the way everybody was talking behind my back and second-guessing me. He remained calm and said: "Now you know how it feels, right?"

"Yeah, you're right," I answered. I understood his point, but I was still upset for some reason. "I admit that I talk behind your back, but I also say what I feel to your face." That has pretty much been the rapport between Joe and I through our many years together and it has always seemed to work just fine.

Joe Sarra, who was an assistant coach at Lafayette College at the time and would later become an assistant at Penn State, has always lived for coaching football, and he would constantly stay awake until three or four in the morning. I've always told him he sleeps with just one eye closed because the other one is still open looking at films. We were roommates at one of the football camps (we would later become roommates for Penn State road trips for many years to come), and we had some young people who were causing a lot of problems. They took us to the edge, but I tried to stay with them through the week and talk to them in hopes that they would change.

It didn't work out, however, because when the last day came, some of the kids squashed oranges on the cabin doors and left their rooms in a total mess. Joe Sarra and I caught up to those specific kids at the bus station, and we told them what we thought of their stupid tricks. We said we hoped they felt good about themselves for what they had done, and they should never think about coming back.

We were highly disappointed with those kids as people because they had disrespected positive efforts that we set out to achieve with every camper who comes through our doors. But kids like that are a rare occurrence when I think of all the great young people who have visited our camps. One young man in particular was a boy I got close to by the name of Shane. He came to our house on several occasions to visit and stay. I climbed Mount Nittany with Shane, rode bicycles and did just anything I could so we could spend time together. Shane was a prime example of many of the kids who became just like a part of my family.

As a part of my family, I have also been able to take some of these kids to bowl games with us. For kids who might never have been out of their own community in their lives, let alone out of the state, the experience that a bowl trip provides is hopefully something they would never forget and provide a positive force to carry with them in their own future endeavors.

Probably the neatest thing about coaching at the camps is the way young people come to improve their skills, knowing they won't all be great, great football players. I really enjoy being with them because, basically, we're all there for one reason—to get better. It's a sincere relationship that develops between us, and as I travel around, I try to remember as many of the kids as possible. I've had the great fortune of seeing many of them at various locations throughout mostly Pennsylvania but several other places as well.

I had mentioned Shane as one of the campers who has touched my life in the past. Shane came to our camp as a small blond-haired, blue-eyed kid from Seattle. I was always worried about him being homesick, but he did okay. Shane was a really good high school football player. He could move laterally extremely well, and he was an intense competitor. The only thing he had trouble with at camp was his 40-yard run, but we worked with him on that, and he did improve. As I said, he was small, but he always battled despite his size. That was one of the biggest things that always impressed me about Shane. He is currently working as a part-time football coach for my son, E.J., who is the head coach at Albright College.

There was another young man named Troy, who was always laid back and slow moving. I'll always remember Troy, because I worried about him when he would head down to the practice field. He constantly looked tired, but he would make it through. We were recruiting a player from Troy's hometown, so I asked to recruit that player so I could visit with Troy while I was there. I ended up staying with Troy and his family at their home, and I got to know all of them very well. His family proved to be special and warm people who took me into their home and made me feel very comfortable. I will definitely cherish those moments.

Another kid who stands out in my mind over the years is Alex, whose family often brought him to Penn State football games. Alex went on to play college football at Holy Cross. Then there was Steve, who attended one of our camps and went to Hillsdale College in Michigan, where he turned out to be a good football player. Most of the kids I met and interacted with over the years were wonderful family people. I was glad to get to know all of them and become a part of their lives.

I've also talked about some of the coaches I've worked with over the years, but they deserve more than just a casual mention. First, there was J.T. White, who coached the defensive ends and linemen.

He was my coach when I was a player, and he was still coaching when I took over as defensive coordinator in 1976. It was odd because I became responsible for overseeing him, but in reality, no one could do that. He was the old drill sergeant with great coaching abilities. He was "6-foot-3-and-3/4 and still shrinking," as he used to say. He also used to describe himself as "198 pounds of dynamite."

J.T. was gruff on the field, always barking and yelling at anybody in his path. He called everybody knuckleheads or hammerheads. But underneath that hard shell he was a very warm and caring person. If you were one of the people J.T. cared about, there wasn't anything he wouldn't do for you. He was an extremely sensitive person.

Another sincere coach who belonged to the old guard was Frank Patrick. Frank was an All-American football player at the University of Pittsburgh and just a great athlete in his day. He coached the defensive secondary and the punters at Penn State. He and J.T. White always played racquetball together, and that usually led to some animated, and sometimes heated, discussions. They did a lot of things together, including a class they taught, and they loved to scout. Whether it was future opponents or high school prospects, Frank and J.T. were always watching films together, which was soon to be followed by an argument. Frank Patrick knew a lot about the coaching profession, and he made certain that a lot of that knowledge rubbed off on the rest of us.

Some coaches are nonconformists, and that's what I always thought of Dan Radakovich, who coached the linebackers during his stay at Penn State. Dan believed very strongly in what he did, and he was often able to convince a person toward his line of thinking. Rad, or "Bad Rad," as we liked to call him, was a very intelligent person. He was always most productive at night because he stayed up all night watching films and working on the Xs and Os. Because of that habit, however, he usually found it very difficult to wake up in the morning and be in the office by 8 a.m. But his attention to detail is what stood out most about him, and it helped him to continue his successful career in several other places. Rad was a great technician and a great strategist. He was also an outstanding fundamental football player during his career.

Jim O'Hora was considered the father of the staff. He was a steady and solid person as well as a fun-loving Irishman. When you got to know Jim off the field, you realized what a fantastic person he was. He seemed to epitomize the father image one could look for when his or her own father wasn't around. I learned many things from Jim O'Hora, but one of the main things was that there wasn't much sense in allowing yourself to get too low when things go bad, or too excited when things go well because those same things would undoubtedly turn in the opposite direction.

Bob Phillips, whom I have mentioned earlier, was the final member of the old guard. He coached the wide receivers and quarterbacks, and he, like the rest of the coaches I've worked with over the years, cared so much for people he came in contact with. His whole life revolved around football, but more importantly, it also evolved around the young kids he coached. Bob had a phenomenal high school coaching record in Western Pennsylvania—I don't think he lost more than 10 games in his whole career. It wasn't necessarily because of his great strategy and planning, but more so because he cared about his players. He motivated them and molded them into being great team players. You could see that in the hours he spent with kids at the football camps, going over things with them, while showing a genuine interest in them as people.

Between the kids who have come into my life through camps and various other avenues, and the coaches whom I've worked with over the last 32 years, my life has been touched in so many unique ways. The old guard molded my thoughts in coaching and, besides my dad, were probably the most influential people I have ever come across.

As for the kids, my home has become an extended family. We've adopted many brothers and sisters who turned out to be great people. They are people whom I've grown to love through association; by simply spending time together and learning from each other. They gave me moments to cherish and experiences I will never forget.

14

Back to Penn State

IN A LOT OF WAYS, IT FELT LIKE I HAD COME FULL CIRCLE. I came to Penn State as a freshman in 1962. My intention was to get an education and also to learn more about the game I had cherished playing in high school. I had four moderately successful years, and I graduated from the university in June 1966. I knew in my heart I wanted to get into coaching, and I was fortunate enough to do my graduate assistant work at Penn State.

From there, I took the assistant's job at Juniata College in 1967. In '68, I was hired to coach the offensive line at Boston University, which gave me my first taste of Division I football as a full-time coach. Finally, the circle became complete when I was asked by Coach Paterno to return to Penn State to coach the offensive tackles. I knew I had made it back to the place I would always love—the open country of central Pennsylvania, with its rolling fields and beautiful mountains. State College was a perfect fit for Dottie and me because of the friendships we had made earlier on, and the peace and quiet it would no doubt provide us.

We were fortunate when we returned to Penn State because we were able to rent a house that some friends of ours had been renting the previous year. But we didn't want to rent for very long. We were intent on buying our own house, hoping we had indeed finally found our niche back in State College. We rode around the area whenever we had a free moment, looking at houses and wondering what we could afford. I was never much of a negotiator, so I didn't expect to do very well in the wheeling and dealing that often accompanies house buying. It was late summer, and as we took one of our drives around the town, we came across a nice looking house with a FOR SALE sign in the yard. We talked with the owners, whom we had learned would be leaving the area and needed to sell. As we talked, I thought about our need to buy and their need to sell, so I figured I had nothing to lose by making them an offer.

I waited until Dottie and I got back to our rented home before I told her what I thought and she gave me that "Why not?" look in agreement. So I called the owners of the house and made them my "educated" offer—which they abruptly turned down. I was disappointed, but as I said, I wasn't much of a negotiator, so I didn't view the rejection as a major setback. I pondered for the next couple of days whether to raise my offer, hoping the house wouldn't be sold in the meantime. As I did this, the owners called us back out of nowhere and said they had decided to accept our offer. I was never sure of their reason, but I wasn't about to look a gift horse in the mouth. I was able to find a person in the banking and loan business, and before we knew it, we had everything taken care of for the purchase of our first house.

It's true that I coached the linebackers for most of my Penn State career, but when I returned for that first season, I was actually in charge of the offensive tackles. I didn't have a lot to do in that role as far as difficult assignments, so I would sometimes go down the hall from our coaches offices in Rec Hall and play racquetball while the other coaches were busy working on their daily routines for practice. As usual, Coach Paterno often got upset with me, and he came charging down the hall, looking in on the different racquetball courts so he could scream at me. That first year, we played in the Orange Bowl, and I think I got moved to the defense simply because I upset Coach Paterno enough with my constant questions about why we did certain things on offense, which was always where he spent a large part of his practice time.

Jack Ham was the first linebacker I ever had the opportunity to coach. Jack, of course, went on to a legendary NFL career with the Pittsburgh Steelers and is now in the Pro Football Hall of Fame. Joe Paterno gave me some simple advice on how to coach Jack Ham: "Jerry," he said, "you just leave him alone." That's exactly what I did, too. I never said a word to him, and that's what I've done with every linebacker since. Oh, I talked to them. I just said as little as possible. Basically, I just told them about Jack Ham and said: "Do it the way Jack did it and you'll be fine."

I had to do a lot of scouting early in my coaching career at Penn State. Just like almost everything else, it seemed like every experience in scouting turned into some sort of adventure. I first learned scouting through J.T. White, who was paired up with me in the beginning to make sure I did things right. My first scouting experience was a game between Kansas State and Baylor. We were scouting Kansas State, and J.T. taught me that we had to diagram each play and formation as they happened.

The game was moving by so quickly, I was obviously having trouble keeping up. I was getting frustrated because as I would look down to draw the diagram, the Kansas State offense was running the next play. I missed the first three plays, and J.T. just sat there and laughed at me. I wanted to impress him and Coach Paterno by asking as little as possible, but it seemed I was only getting myself in deeper. Finally, J.T. asked me if I was ready to stop messing around and learn the right way to do it. He showed me the way that night and eventually clued me in on the ins and outs of scouting until I was finally ready for my first solo assignment—a Saturday night game between Kansas State and Arizona in Tucson.

I knew I would be up all night charting plays on the flight back to Pittsburgh, so I had the foresight to mark down the area where I parked my car at the Pittsburgh Airport. I did so for the simple reason that my tendency was to forget such things when my mind was occupied so heavily, as it would be on this occasion. As I had figured, I was up all night working on the Kansas State scouting report. I was tired when I got into the airport that Sunday morning, and I was glad I had marked the area where my car would be. I went to the designated area on my papers, but there was no sign of the car. I searched the whole area. There weren't that many cars parked there, probably because it was a Sunday morning, I had figured, so it shouldn't have been so difficult.

But it was. I searched and searched and searched, but I couldn't find it anywhere. I brought the airport police into the picture and reported the car as stolen. They were writing their reports, and when the officer who was taking down the information asked me about the year, make and model of the car in question, it hit me like a falling rock. I had spent most of that morning looking for *my* car, when in reality, I should have been looking instead for the car that was issued to me by the university. So from that point on when I went on a recruiting trip or a scouting assignment, I had to remember not only to mark the *area* where I had parked my car but also *which* car I had driven.

Another scouting assignment that almost went awry was one I had arranged to switch with J.T. With the change, I was headed to a game being played on a Saturday night at North Carolina State. My plan started out well as I got up very early that Saturday morning and drove to Washington, D.C., from which I could catch a flight to Raleigh. I had planned to get into a hotel there early, rest up before the game and then stay overnight until I could catch an early flight out that Sunday.

My day became rushed fairly early because I got caught in a steady rain and fog on the drive to Washington. I just made the flight, thanks to a small delay, and when I got to my downtown Raleigh hotel, I didn't have as much time to relax as I had hoped for. Some people at the hotel told me the stadium was only about a mile away, so I figured I could get some exercise by walking to the game. I walked a mile, but there was no stadium in sight. I walked another one—still there was nothing. I walked a little further, when I finally saw a sign of life. I saw some students walking by, so I asked them if I was close to the stadium. They looked at each other, then at me, and one of them said: "Not really. You're about five miles away." With that, he pointed in the opposite direction.

I couldn't understand how I got lost from what seemed like simple directions, but somehow I did it. I did the only thing I could do at that point—I ran. I didn't even know how close they were to kickoff. I just started picking my feet up and laying them down, one at a time, hurrying and hoping I could make it there in time. Luck seemed to change for me a little bit because a city bus just happened to come by at the right time. I caught up to it at the next stop and found relief when the driver told me he was headed toward the football stadium.

The game was just starting when I got to my seat. I was glad I wouldn't miss any plays, but I did miss the kicking charts, which is what we diagram before the game in warm-ups. The game itself had little more excitement in terms of my usual misadventures, but when I got back to the Washington airport the next morning, I found that in my haste to get to my flight the day before, I had left the headlights on in my car. I found someone who had jumper cables to help me get it started, and after many thanks for their kindness, I was on my way home.

Along the way, I passed through the town of Huntingdon, Pennsylvania, which was where I had my first full-time coaching experience at Juniata College. One would think I should know my way around the place, having worked there only a short time ago, but there I was driving the wrong way on a one-way street. When I realized my mistake, I was hoping I could maybe straighten myself out without much notice, but much as the rest of this trip had gone, luck was not on my side. There was only one policeman patrolling the town at that time, and I happened to get him. To sum it up, I learned in a very short time that scouting assignments are not always as boring as they would seem to be. At least not when the assignment fell on my shoulders.

Besides scouting, I was also responsible for looking at films, getting medical reports from the trainers and anything else Coach Paterno could yell at me about after I turned everything over to him. Great organizational skills were never one of my strong suits, as could easily be noticed by the loose pieces of film and paper scattered all over the floor of my office.

I was also responsible in those early days for film exchanges with our opponents. It was a common practice and courtesy to allow the upcoming opponent to view films of our previous opponent, and they would do the same for us. There was one particular week where we were scheduled to play Army, and I had our films wrapped and ready for the exchange. We made the necessary plane connections for our films to get to them and, for what I thought would be, Army's films reaching us. The tough part, however, was that Army's films weren't delivered. To make things worse, I had to show up at our Sunday night coaches meeting and tell my boss we didn't have their film. Needless to say, he wasn't too happy.

"Get those Army coaches on the phone!" Coach Paterno said in a demanding tone. I did what he asked, and when their film coach came on the line, Coach Paterno took the receiver out of my hand. He didn't take long to say what he wanted to say, but he basically let the guy have it for not coming through with the delivery. I felt bad because he messed up, but I'm sure I messed up too. But mistakes happen, and we all have to live with them.

An interesting footnote to our film fiasco is that Army's coach who was responsible for the film exchange was Bill Parcells, who later went on to coach the New York Giants to two Super Bowl championships. He also coached the New England Patriots to the Super Bowl during the 1996 season and the New York Jets to the AFC championship game in 1998. Any time I run into Bill, we usually share a laugh about that film experience way back when.

Of all the things that ever came with coaching, I would have to say that the players I worked with were probably the greatest part of the job. I coached so many outstanding athletes at Penn State, but more importantly, they were also outstanding young men. The ones I remember are the ones who took our lessons on the field to heart and turned them into some of the many great moments of glory in Penn State football history. There have been many, far too many for me to include all of them here, but I would like to mention a few who had some kind of influence either in my life or in my coaching style.

Greg Buttle was an outstanding linebacker at Penn State from 1973 to 1975. He was a guy who came in as a freshman and exuded confidence from the very beginning. I became very close with Greg, although it certainly didn't start out that way. I said he had confidence, and that's always something I like to see in players. But I didn't like the way he displayed that confidence in the very beginning.

Greg was from the beaches of South Jersey, and he came into his very first camp wearing sunglasses and sort of strutting around the place as though he owned it. I knew right away this kid would never lack confidence. I took him right away to be an instant challenge, and I said to myself: "I'm gonna humble this guy. If it's in my power, he's gonna crawl out of this place." Well, after four years and an outstanding career, Greg Buttle strutted out of Penn State in the same manner as he strutted in.

Normally, I never tried to embarrass freshmen, but because of his somewhat cocky nature coming into camp, I decided Greg was going to be an exception. I was explaining the different responsibilities he would have to know for the position he would be playing on defense. I pointed out that judgment would be the best option to use in these defenses based on the speed and running tendencies of the opposing quarterback. After I went over the responsibilities Greg would have to know, I decided to quiz him on the things he should have learned.

"Greg," I said. "You're playing against the fastest quarterback in America. He sprints out. What do you do?"

"I go into my curl-pass zone," he said rather confidently. And he was right.

"All right," I continued. "Now, the quarterback gets outside of the defensive end. To contain, what do you do?" Greg's next assignment, in this case, was to come up quickly and make the play, but he answered with his own confident spin to the situation.

"I'm gonna hang back, wait until he crosses the line of scrimmage, and *POW!!!*, I'm gonna nail him." That was Greg's reply. On paper, he was totally wrong on the assignment, but Greg Buttle felt perfectly confident that he would carry out the play in the manner he had described.

"Wait a minute," I interrupted him. "You must not have understood me. I said you were playing against the fastest quarterback in the country." Greg looked me right in the eyes and said without blinking: "Yes, but he's playing against the fastest *linebacker* in the country."

We never told him how slow he really was, but he proved to be an outstanding football player at Penn State nonetheless.

There was one season in the mid-1970s when we had two defensive players—Greg Buttle and Tom Donchez. It was our last game of the season against the University of Pittsburgh, which was, by far at that time, our greatest rival. Pitt was a very good football team that featured a number of outstanding players, including Tony Dorsett, who would go on to win the Heisman Trophy his senior year.

The coaches always leave the players in the locker room before the game to collect their final thoughts, and before this game, Greg was bent over tying his shoes. Mike Hartenstine was always a quiet kid at Penn State, barely ever saying a word during his entire four years. But the players were especially fired up for this game, and Mike seemed to be harboring some pent-up emotions inside him as he readied himself for a tough afternoon of football. It wasn't Mike's words that triggered an unusual pregame incident, however. Instead, it was his actions. He was sitting down, mentally preparing himself, when all of a sudden, he stood up and kicked a helmet with all the ferocious emotion he had inside him. I'm sure his intention was to try to get the rest of the players excited for the game, but as the helmet left his foot, it started a chain reaction that could have had an effect on our entire game.

The helmet bounced off a wall, proceeded to hit Greg's foot as he was bent over tying his shoe and ricocheted straight into his forehead. He was out cold before he hit the floor, bleeding from his forehead, without any coach's knowledge. The players didn't know what to do, but one of them ran out to the field and got Eddie Sulkowski, who was one of our trainers. Eddie came in and patched Greg's head temporarily with a butterfly bandage, put his helmet on his head and instructed him not to take it off under any circumstances.

Greg staggered out of the locker room rather wobbly as the team took the field, but we really didn't notice at the time. We were on defense for the first series of the game and it was his responsibility to call the defensive plays—based on our calls from the press box and the sideline. I was upstairs, and we noticed right away from up there that Greg wasn't running the plays we had called. Jim Rosecrans, our other inside linebacker and a good friend of Greg's, made the first three tackles. I told Jim O'Hora that Greg wasn't calling the right plays, but instead of taking him out, we pulled Rosecrans, so we could find out what was wrong and get him to tell Greg to start calling the right plays.

Rosey looked up at us when he was on the sideline phone and said: "I can't believe you took me out of the game to tell him he's calling the wrong defenses. I'm playing the game of my life!" I stood over Greg at halftime as he laid on one of the trainer's tables, yelling at him about which pass zone he was supposed to be covering, while one of the doctors was putting 15 stitches in his forehead.

As I said, Mike Hartenstine was a quiet guy for the most part. He always got upset at practice during his senior year for one reason or another. I think it was just because he wanted to do his best all the time, and if he didn't perform the way he thought he was capable of, he would get upset. But Mike was never the type of player you had to hound all the time. He knew his assignments and responsibilities, and he carried them out well. Sometimes, J.T. White got on him during practices, and that seemed to be the only time Mike would speak up.

On one occasion, J.T. spoke up to him in a rather harsh tone and Mike turned and told him to "GET LOST!" He then simply walked off the practice field and into the locker room. We were scheduled to play Pitt that weekend, and I wasn't too happy with him for taking it upon himself to leave the field. I approached him in the locker room and told him I didn't think it was right for him to be talking back to a coach like that, number one, and also he had no valid cause or reason to walk out of practice like that.

"Who do you think you are to do something like that?" I asked him. He seemed to get a little more upset as we talked in the locker room, but eventually, he came back to the fold and showed his true leadership qualities. That period of rebellion was one of the few experiences where we ever had any such problems with Mike Hartenstine. He was always a first-class player and person.

Another player I grew very close to was Kurt Allerman. He was an intense player who gave everything he had, and he was one of the toughest linebackers I ever coached. Kurt wasn't a great athlete, but he made up for it with his intensity and effort. He was a young person I cared deeply about because he was always dedicated to his studies and the way he played football. I'll always remember an onside kick he went after in a 12-7 loss to North Carolina State one season. He got flipped in the air and landed right on his head. As he lay on the ground, I remembered how much I felt the hurt because I cared so much for him. I was very fearful that Kurt was hurt seriously. Actually, he did suffer a neck injury that forced him to miss the last couple of games that season, but he recovered quite well and went on to play pro football for the St. Louis Cardinals and Detroit Lions.

We had another linebacker during the Greg Buttle and Mike Hartenstine era named Buddy Tesner. He ran a 5.2 40-yard dash, which wasn't very fast, and we would learn to accept that Buddy wasn't an outstanding athlete by any standards. What set him apart from the marginal athletes of his day and allowed him to take his place at Penn State was his ability to stay ahead of everyone else mentally on the field. He was always sharp and alert, and that's what put him on the field instead of in the stands.

I can remember one game, however, where Buddy made a rare mistake that led to a big play by our opponent. He knew when he came off the field I was going to get him on that sideline phone from upstairs and give him what for. Being the thinker that he was, Buddy took a deep breath, picked up the phone and started letting *me* have it. "Who has the flat on that defense, Jerry?" he yelled. "I'm sick and tired of these mistakes out there."

I was caught off guard by his words, but I should have known he would come up with some method to keep me from yelling at him. "I give up, Buddy," I stammered into the other end of the phone. "You win." Buddy Tesner never went to the pros, but he made me just as proud by becoming an accomplished orthopedic surgeon.

Gary Gray was a unique individual simply because he was a player who had a great interest in hypnosis. He took it to the extent that he often tried to hypnotize players before the games, but I believe it was still their natural ability that helped them perform to such high levels. His interest in hypnosis not withstanding, Gary was a pretty outstanding football player. He led the team in just about every statistical category: tackles, assists, blocked punts, interceptions, and fumble recoveries.

He could do it all even though he was another one of those players with not much ability but a tremendous amount of heart. Gary was about 5'11", 205 pounds. He didn't run very fast, but he was extremely confident and intelligent. He had a great knack for knowing where the ball was going at all times, and that carried him a long way during his career at Penn State.

In a roundabout way, Gary Gray might have actually had something to do with me being named defensive coordinator. We were playing a game against Temple, and at that time, Temple had some pretty decent football teams that always seemed to give us tough games. On this day, we weren't playing very well. I was up in the press box watching Temple do things on the field that simply bothered the heck out of me. I was upset with everything and mad at Coach Paterno.

He is a great defensive strategist, but like everyone, we all have our days when things don't go right, and this was looking like one of those days for him. I was mumbling about the way he was handling the defense, wishing he would turn the game back over to the assistants. Gary was working as a grad assistant for us that season, and he was on the sideline headphones connected to me in the press box. At the end of the third quarter, Coach Paterno turned to Gary and said: "Ask Jerry what defense he wants to call."

I was still upset, and I told Gary in a stern voice: "You tell him. I don't care what defense he calls. He's messed this thing up through the first three quarters. He might as well carry us through the rest of the game." I knew Gary wouldn't actually say that to him, so I listened as he told Coach Paterno that I was calling for a defense that he had actually picked from the top of his head. They called the defense Gary had actually ordered, and it worked, but thanks to him, I looked like the genius, and it wasn't long after that I was named defensive coordinator.

So, it was thanks to these great players and many more who made us coaches look better than we actually were throughout the years. Some went on to professional football, while others went to professions in engineering and orthopedics, just to name a few. As football players, I will never forget the miracles I saw them perform on the field. As individuals, I'll never forget them as some of the finest young men I have ever known.

15

Recruiting (II)

I HAD SEEN THE RECRUITING WARS AS A SENIOR IN HIGH SCHOOL, watching several of my Washington High School senior teammates and I get courted by one school or another. I made my choice in my heart after my first official visit to Penn State, but I still went through with the other visits on my schedule, I suppose out of curiosity, just to see what else was out there in the all-too-competitive world of college football. I learned a lot about the lengths that coaches would go to in order to land their prize recruit, which certainly wasn't me, but others whom I had met during my journeys.

I learned a lot during those recruiting visits, and I was probably one of the few recruits who observed how the coaches handled the recruiting process as much as how the prospects handled them. I felt like I could see it in their eyes whether they were truly interested in the recruits they brought in. The coaches eyes lit up around the ones they were truly after, while they seemed to go through the motions around the players who were marginal or had little chance at all.

At that young age, I had no idea I would have a future of my own in coaching nor did I know I would even have the desire to do so. But when I did return to Penn State, when I realized I would be on the other side of the spectrum, it hit me that recruiting would soon become a whole different ball game. From now on, I would be the one who had to convince the young athlete of all the virtues Penn State had to offer, instead of being the one who needed convincing.

The one thing I learned from the very beginning about recruiting from a coach's perspective is how difficult it was. It's an inexact science, to say the least. As each high school prospect comes in for a visit, you're never really sure of what you're getting. We try to make the right decisions, but the plain fact is many of our decisions are wrong. Some of the greatest football players we've ever had at Penn State were people who we didn't think would have what it takes to be successful on the Division I level.

Earlier, I spoke of Jack Ham and the Hall of Fame career he carved for himself in professional football. In the recruiting process, Jack was offered the last scholarship we had during his senior year of high school. Furthermore, probably the only reason he got the scholarship at all was because his good friend, Steve Smear, was really pushing hard for him. If that one scholarship wasn't left over, Jack Ham probably would not have attended Penn State.

Shane Conlan was a great linebacker at Penn State during the mid-1980s, who played most of his pro football career with the Buffalo Bills. He had just one major college scholarship offer, and that was at Penn State.

Another former player who had a unique recruiting experience was Scott Radecic, a former All-American linebacker who played at Penn State from 1978-82. As I recruited Scott during his senior year of high school, his choices were narrowed down to either Penn State or Brown. I was aware of his dilemma, so I thought I would give him something to think about. "Name me one person who ever amounted to anything after going to Brown University," I said, kind of tongue-in-cheek to him, knowing that Brown was the college that Coach Paterno had attended and played football for. Scott thought about it for a second and decided I must have had a point because he made up his mind to choose Penn State right there and then.

Mark Markovich was another young man we weren't quite sure about. He was a nice kid, and Earl Bruce, one of our coaches, had Mark and his family, up to the campus for a visit. They were a nice family and his mother was a sweet, gentle woman. But as we sat in our meetings after recruiting week was over with, Earl said: "I hope that Markovich kid doesn't want to come here. I just don't think we should be recruiting him."

By a sheer matter of coincidence, the phone rang in our offices right about then, and lo and behold, it was Mark Markovich calling to tell

Coach Bruce he had decided to come to Penn State. "Oh, that's really great, Mark," Earl said. It looked like he rolled his eyes a little, but it was hard to tell. "We're going to look forward to having you here."

Mark turned out to be another great player at Penn State, and he was a captain for one of our undefeated teams in the 1970s. From his Penn State career, Mark went on to become quite a successful business-man in his professional life.

Another kid we debated on was Mickey Shuler. He was kind of in between on our list of high school players because he played wide receiver, but we didn't think he was fast enough to play the position on the college level. If anything, we thought—maybe—he could play tight end in col-lege, but as I said, most of the coaching staff wasn't real high on him. Coach Tor Toretti liked Mickey, however, and at his request, Dick Ander-son and I went to one of his high school basketball games to watch him for his athleticism.

Dick and I went to Mickey's basketball game, and we determined early on, just from watching warm-ups, that he wasn't fast enough to play wide receiver. Early in the game, Mickey bumped his elbow going for a rebound and he looked like he was in real agony. We didn't think he was hurt that bad, so now Dick and I had also drawn a conclusion that the kid wasn't tough enough to play college football on the Division I level.

We were a bit disgusted, wondering why we were even there in the first place. "We shouldn't be recruiting this guy," we kept muttering to each other. In those days, recruiting rules were different. Coaches were permitted to talk to players and parents at the site of high school athletic events, whereas now they are only permitted to observe, with no contact permitted to the recruit or his family. Dick and I knew we might be facing a dilemma if we were to run into Mickey or his parents after the game because we wondered what we should say, knowing we weren't really in-terested in recruiting him.

We agreed to compromise. We would talk to his parents, to say hello and be nice, but we wouldn't make a point to talk to Mickey him-self. We were cordial without saying too much to his parents after the game, and we managed to sneak away without talking to Mickey. Later that week, we got a call at the coaches office from Mickey Shuler. "I've decided to come to Penn State," he said to whomever he spoke with. "I made that decision because you guys never badgered me or bothered me at the basketball game the other night." As I said, Coach Tor Toretti had a belief in the kid, so we pursued him, and he kept his word and commit-ted to Penn State.

Mickey is a prime example of a kid who sometimes makes a monkey out of a coach, because although he didn't possess the athletic ability we are constantly searching for in a high school recruit, he did have the work ethic that is often overlooked. He worked and worked to make himself stronger and better as each and every season went by. He turned into an outstanding tight end at Penn State and went on to a prolific NFL career with the New York Jets.

There were also times when players a coach recruited impressed enough to be offered a scholarship, but they turned out to be not so impressive on the field. One of those types of players was a young man named Chuck Correal. We really didn't pursue him at first, but I ran into him at his school while on a recruiting trip. As I talked to Chuck, I became more impressed with the way he handled himself, and I kept thinking that maybe we were making a mistake by not recruiting him.

His coaches spoke highly of him as a person and as a leader, whether it was sports or anything else in life. I went back to Penn State and spoke to Coach Paterno about him and he said: "Well, have him come up and see us." Coach Paterno liked Chuck, too, when he met him, so we gave him the one scholarship we had leftover.

He started out as a linebacker and simply looked terrible in his first pass coverage drills. Those thoughts of doubt crept into my head again, as they did with several borderline recruits we took chances on. But Chuck had that special work ethic too. The kind that overcomes almost any lack of talent an athlete might have. He worked and worked very hard after a position change, and soon, Chuck Correal became an outstanding offensive lineman for us. He was a two-year starter and anchored the offensive line that carried us through an 11-0 regular season in 1978 before we lost to Alabama in the Sugar Bowl. Chuck even played a little pro football, and he was another prime example of a player who taught me that first impressions are not always as they seem.

I remember a time when one of our recruits could easily have been unimpressed with me as a coach and representative of Penn State. Derek Bochna came to Penn State in the early 1990s from a small town in Pennsylvania called Mapletown. He broke a Western Pennsylvania career rushing record in high school, but we wanted him more for his play on defense. I had scheduled to meet him at his house at around seven one night, but I called him and told him I was a little behind schedule, and I probably wouldn't be there until close to eight.

I double-checked the directions with him and started on my way, but sure enough, I got lost. I found Derek's school; his church; his friends, but I couldn't find his house. It was a small town, but very way out. It probably should have been easy to find, but this was me, and I somehow find ways to make everything difficult. I never made it to Derek's house until 9 that night, but he and his family were very gracious toward me.

My first recruiting experience as a coach was not a very good one. We were really high on Randy Gradishar, who would eventually have an All-Pro career with the Denver Broncos. His college choices were narrowed down to Penn State, Purdue and Ohio State. I went to his high school one day to visit with Randy and his coach, but I had to wait because I had arrived a bit early. I had about a 25- or 30-minute wait, so I spent the time talking with a young high school girl who was serving as a student receptionist in the school office.

She knew I was there to speak with Randy, probably because she had seen many other coaches come and go with the same hopes and intentions. I was friendly with her, and she insisted over and over during our conversation that Randy would be going to Ohio State. "No way," I told her defiantly. "Penn State is the right place for him." Our good-natured teasing went back and forth until I got the chance to talk with Randy and his coach. He seemed eager to make a visit to Penn State, so I made all the arrangements, even though visits were tough for him because his weekends were filled with high school basketball as well.

It was decided a Sunday afternoon would be the best time for Randy to visit the Penn State campus, so I arranged to meet him—accompanied by his high school basketball coach and girlfriend—at the Nittany Lion Inn, which is a quaint little hotel/inn on the Penn State campus where we used to meet and entertain a lot of recruits and their families. I watched as their car pulled into the driveway of the inn, and as I approached the car to greet them, who should I see first but the very same girl from the high school office who insisted that Randy had Ohio State on his mind all along.

He later married that girl, and I lost both of them to Ohio State. In fact, I was in charge of three recruits that year. Two of them went to Ohio State and one to Pitt. So, that sums up why I didn't feel like I was cut out for recruiting after my first year as a coach.

My success ratio would get a little better as the years went by, and there was one young man I was recruiting named Ron Crosby whom I really wanted to land at Penn State. He had a tremendous personality, and his family was extremely genuine. Ron had narrowed his choices to Penn State and Ohio State, and I had to give him a call to see if he had made up his mind. My family and I were on a trip, so I decided to call Ron before we went all the way home. If he knew he was choosing Penn State, we would stop at his home on the way, but if his final choice was Ohio State, we would just continue on to our own home.

I called the Crosby home, and Ron's dad, who was a former coal miner, answered the phone. The Crosbys were my kind of people, and I admired the courage Ron's father always showed. He was down to one lung, and he had been through some major medical problems, but he wouldn't hear of feeling sorry for himself, nor would he like anyone else to feel sorry for him. When he knew it was me on the other end of the phone, his tone became sorrowful, as though he had to deliver me some bad news. "Coach," he said. "I'm sorry to have to tell you this, but Woody Hayes came by earlier today and picked Ron up in a big car full of green. I'm not sure, but I think he's going to Ohio State."

He couldn't stifle his laughter, however, and I knew right then that Ron had decided to attend Penn State. I was very happy with that decision, not only because I thought highly of Ron's athletic ability, but simply because of the kind of people his family were. I knew he would represent Penn State in the most positive of ways, and he never let us down in any way. Ron played one of his best games ever in front of his father in a game against the University of Pittsburgh. He had the same smile and same toughness as his dad, not to mention the same competitive nature. That has always been one of my favorite elements in a football player.

Ron started out as a linebacker at Penn State, but he accepted a move to defensive end that we suggested, and from then on I don't think he would have played anywhere else. In that game against Pitt, Ron was all over the field, as were guys like John Quinn and Ron Coder. They weren't household names, but they did their jobs. We won the game, 7-6, and the key play came because of a young man named Tommy O'Dell, who watched film of Pitt's special teams unit with Gregg Ducatte, who was a former player working with us as an assistant coach. Gregg spotted an opportunity from Tommy O'Dell's side of the field in the kicking game, and Tommy broke through to block an extra point.

The game sticks out in my mind because it was the last regular season game for guys like Greg Buttle and Jim Rosecrans, who had served us so well during their careers. Carson Long was Pitt's usually reliable kicker that season, and I know the blocked kick really shook him up because he missed, I believe, two other field-goal opportunities. I'll never forget seeing Rosey and Greg wrestling around on the Three Rivers Stadium field when the game finally ended. I can still feel their joy and elation because it was a great victory for Penn State over our toughest rival in those days.

There were plenty of times when I became attached with a recruit and his family, but I wasn't as fortunate in having them make Penn State their final choice. One such case was a young man from Phillipsburg, New Jersey, named Ned Bolcar, who had us on his list but ultimately decided to attend Notre Dame. It was difficult to see Ned choose anywhere else but Penn State, because he always carried himself with very high grace and esteem. His recruitment was being documented by *USA Today,* and in the midst of such national coverage, Ned handled the whole process with great poise. I especially admired that quality in him.

I always enjoyed the recruiting process—meeting people and trying to present a great university to them. I have been told, at times, that I didn't have enough B.S., but I always tried to take that as a compliment, because recruiting is very difficult, and you really get tempted once in a while to say things that aren't true. It's also difficult because you do get attached to the players, and you want to be a part of them. Hopefully, they'll be smart enough and strong enough to see through so much of what goes on and base their decisions on sincerity.

As I dealt with each young man individually, and in most cases his family too, I held out hope that they would look at Penn State as the kind of place where they could grow and develop as people. If they could do that, they would no doubt live their college careers in much the same fashion as I did.

16

Experiences, Teams, Players

As a player, I remember the tough practices, the first practice in my first spring and what fear that brought. I remember my first game and the hot August practices in preseason that came before that first game. Preseason gave us two long and full practices to look forward to each and every day for two and three weeks straight. I was always so tired and sore. I ached and sometimes cried before those practices, wondering practically every minute if this was all worth it. But what got me through it were the other people—the other players who were going through the same things as I was. We backed each other all the way and knew we'd have the opportunity to grow and improve as people and players.

I'll always remember the many tough games we had, which seemed like every week, and our wins against some great Ohio State teams. And, of course, I will always treasure a touchdown catch I had against Pitt.

More than anything else as a player, though, I will remember my junior year when we lost four of our first five games but came together at just the right time to win all the rest—including an upset win at Ohio State. Despite the early adversity, we managed to win the Eastern Championship.

We rode a wave of momentum through the second half of that season, which made us feel good about what we could accomplish the next season, when I would be a senior. We had high hopes and even higher expectations, but we suffered some heartbreaking losses for reasons that we just couldn't understand. We never reached our potential that season, but I chalked it up as a simple part of life. I learned not to celebrate too much on the highs and not to dwell too much on the lows in my life. I didn't know it then, but as I ended my long career, as both a player and as a coach after the 1999 season, I can think back to many other seasons where we went through similar highs and lows.

As a student, I tried hard to excel all the time in the classroom. I can recall staying in on Saturday nights with tears in my eyes as I studied my lessons with hopes of reaching a higher plateau. They were often hard times, and there were many times when I wondered if I really enjoyed what I was doing. To top it all off, I suffered from the homesickness factor when I missed my family, and the rest of the people from back home who were so near and dear to me.

Whenever I was down, however, I always had football to pick me up. I knew early on that going home would be the worst decision I could ever make, no matter how much I missed the place. To think of all I would have missed if I would have followed my first instinct long ago and gone back home. I shudder at the thought today.

If I would have left Penn State, I would have missed all the great football teams we've had over the years. I look at those teams today and wonder what made them so different from others. I truly believe it was the intangible qualities; special situations that matched special people who were able to rise to the occasion when times were at their toughest. The character and intelligence of the Penn State teams from the past shone through with the teams of 1968 and '69. Those teams had great defensive players like Jack Ham, Mike Reid and Dennis Onkotz. Chuck Burkhart never lost a football game at quarterback in high school or college. He accomplished a great deal in his career without a tremendous amount of athletic ability. We always had a great supporting cast with players like Franco Harris, Lydell Mitchell, Charlie Pittman and Ted Kwalick. They were all great players for us, but they possessed something even greater, which was outstanding character.

Another great Penn State team was our 1973 squad. We had some great players, but what really carried us was our great chemistry. We had players like Ed O'Neil, Mark Markovich, Chuck Herd and Randy Crowder. Chuck and Randy were like brothers, and they exemplified the feelings of togetherness on the team. They were very bright and responsible to the tradition of football that they represented. And probably the most recognizable name on that roster was John Cappelletti, who was an All-American running back and remains Penn State's only Heisman Trophy winner.

One of the greatest teams I will always remember will be our 1978 squad. Not only did we have an outstanding defensive unit, they were complemented by an offense that seemed to always find ways to get the job done throughout the regular season. Physically, I have always felt this was the best defensive unit I had ever been around. Larry Kubin, Tony Petruccio, and Greg Jones joined Bruce Clark and Matt Millen to form a dominant front line. Lance Mehl was one of the greatest linebackers ever to play at Penn State, and he eventually became an All-Pro with the New York Jets. He had tremendous instincts, and he played so many great games as our inside middle linebacker. Lance was great because he was totally oblivious to pressure.

Paul Suhey was our other inside linebacker. He was a great leader and a very smart football player. He was also a great wrestler, which was just another testament to his great athletic ability. Rick Donaldson, who was also an exceptional athlete, started the season at outside linebacker, but he suffered a season-ending injury three games into the season, and we were left with a minor problem of how to replace such a tremendous athlete.

We had a player named Rich Milot who seemed to have a hard time finding a position where he was comfortable and we were comfortable with him playing. He was a senior that year, and he had previously played running back, but he had a problem fumbling the football. We had also tried him in the secondary, but he didn't backpedal very well. He also just didn't seem to work out when we put him at defensive end. Rich came to me during the preseason and said he would like to try linebacker. My first reaction was that I really didn't want to be the last person to let him down in his career. I didn't know if it would work, but we were looking for a backup to Rick Donaldson at the outside position, so I told Rich I would talk to Coach Paterno about it.

So, we talked, and we decided we would give him a go at it and see how he did. As time went along, we still weren't sure how well Rich was going to do if he ever got into a game, but he did well enough to earn the backup role. One day, after about three weeks of the season, I came into one of the coaches meetings and said: "You know, I think Rich Milot is turning into a pretty good linebacker." And wouldn't you know that the next day, Rick Donaldson got hurt. Now I had to feel like Rich Milot was looking like a great linebacker. That turned out to be a true statement, because Rich and Karl McCoy, who supplanted another injured starter in the secondary, took us to another level. In fact, Penn State fans might remember that Rich Milot went onto a tremendous NFL career with the Washington Redskins as a linebacker.

I was very proud of that team because of its desire and ability. It was a team that led the nation in overall defense that season.

We also had an outstanding offense featuring players like Chuck Fusina, who was a very intelligent quarterback, wide receiver Scott Fitzkee, fullback Matt Suhey and tailback Mike Guman, and our special teams was captained by Tom Bradley, who was, and still is, known as "Scrap" because of the scrappy way he played. Tom got into coaching right after that 1978 season as a graduate assistant, and he has been on the Penn State coaching staff ever since.

This team was highly touted going into the season, but they lived up to the challenge to post an undefeated regular season. Probably our toughest win came in the last game when we needed every ounce of defensive effort to hold off Pitt. We scored on a gutsy fourth-and-goal call from the two-yard line on a pitchout to Mike Guman late in the game to seal a 17-10 victory.

Our first game was no piece of cake either. The season started—and almost ended—at Temple. The Owls were not a great football team, but their coach, Wayne Hardin, had done a fantastic job of preparing them. They punted at least seven or eight times on third down, which successfully kept our offense backed into a hole for much of the game. The score was tied, 7-7, with less than two minutes to play, and Temple had the ball with a first down in our territory, very close to field goal range. They needed probably one more first down to be in range to win the game.

We called a little twist play, defensively, and Bruce Clark came around to the inside and just about destroyed the running back. I had never seen anybody get hit like that. The back flew to one side, while one of his shoes flew to the other. The football went in the direction of the shoe as well. It rolled into Temple territory, and we recovered it. Now, with very little time left, we executed our two-minute offense with great poise. We moved into field goal range, and Matt Bahr kicked the game-winner with less than 10 seconds left.

I'll never forget a game we were playing against N.C. State in November. We played a solid football game from start to finish and won the game handily, but there was a roar from the crowd somewhere in the fourth quarter, and I heard something to the effect of a score from Oklahoma's game. We were ranked second in the nation going into that day's game, and the crowd in Beaver Stadium began cheering like crazy when it was revealed that the number-one ranked Sooners had lost. At that moment, everyone who supported the Nittany Lions realized we would more than likely be vaulted to the top spot for the first time in Penn

State's long, storied history. Even though we had been through four previously undefeated seasons, we never held a No. 1 ranking, let alone a national championship.

The bull's-eye was on us now for the rest of the regular season, but we held strong and set up a national championship showdown with Alabama, which had moved to No. 2 in the polls, in the Sugar Bowl. We had our legendary head coach, and Alabama had theirs in Paul "Bear" Bryant. They had a great defensive football team, but we felt we could do what we had to do, and we certainly knew what was at stake.

We, as coaches, knew it would be a tremendously tough game, and I'm sure our players were aware of that too. Despite all of our talent, and all the fire power we had, there was something missing in that game. We didn't seem to have the perfect chemistry to win the national championship. Whether it was just related to that day, or something with the whole season, I'm not sure. But we just didn't do the things we needed to do. Even when we made a big play, the little intangibles were not present.

It just seemed like it wasn't meant to be our day. We were penalized on offense on the very first play of the game, which put us in an immediate hole. Throughout the entire first half, we played great defense with our backs to the wall for much of the time. We didn't let them score, and things looked great for us when Rich Milot intercepted a pass and took off down the sidelines. It was that one play, however, that really pointed out to those who look for such things what the difference is between winning and losing a national championship. As Rich moved down the sideline with the interception cradled in his arms, he ran out of blockers. If a couple more people would have been hustling, Rich probably would have taken it into the end zone. Instead, he was caught, and although we were in Alabama territory, our offense wasn't able to take advantage of the turnover.

We had punted, and we managed to stuff Alabama for no gain on first down. With time running low in the first half and the ball fairly deep in Alabama territory, we decided to call time-out with thoughts of maybe getting the ball back. On the next play, one of our linebackers decided to cut down the wide receiver while Alabama had a running play going. As our player was picking himself off the ground, the ball carrier ran by him and gained 30 or 40 yards. I expected them to run again to try and set up a field-goal attempt, but they threw a crossing pass. To this day, our players probably still feel the ball wasn't caught, and video replays appeared to show they were right, but Bruce Bolton, the Alabama receiver, made a fantastic play and caught the 30-yard pass from Jeff Rutledge. Whether we agreed with the ruling or not, the play resulted in a touchdown and a 7-0 Alabama lead at halftime.

I was extremely frustrated and upset over a number of things. Some of it had to with our breakdown, but most of it was me being upset with myself. Even getting to the locker room for halftime was difficult because normally the elevators are held for the coaches in the press box to get downstairs quickly, but when we got to the elevator, the door opened, and there was a man and a woman inside. I explained that we were in a hurry and needed to go down, but the lady said rather rudely: "We're going up!"

"Look lady," I said as nice as I could possibly be. "How about giving me a break here. I have to get down there in a hurry."

She insisted that I was going up, just like they were, and I couldn't believe I was involved in such a conversation at this point. Now I was demanding that we go down, and she proceeded to call me an animal. Finally, the guy standing there, who had kept quiet up to now, explained that the button had already been pushed, and we would have to go up anyway. So, I let it go and went up with the rest of the elevator. It turned out the lady was a sports reporter, and I don't know where she was from, but I'm sure I was written about in a negative way somewhere in the country.

That was only one example of the kind of day it was for all of us. We got an interception from Pete Harris at Alabama's 48-yard line, and our offense capitalized when Chuck Fusina hit Scott Fitzkee with a 17-yard touchdown pass to tie it, 7-7. But Alabama got its own spark by running a punt 62 yards to set up deep in our territory. Major Ogilvie ran it in from eight yards out to put Alabama ahead again, 14-7, late in the third quarter. We had two more chances in the fourth quarter.

We got the ball to the one-yard line, but the Alabama defense made a great goal-line stand on two running plays in a row to snuff that chance. We held on defense and forced a punt, which went out of bounds at the Alabama 26-yard line. There were situations where we were playing an extra linebacker defensively, but on the punt return setup, one of them didn't come out. We were flagged for having 12 men on the field, and Alabama was given a first down as a result of the penalty.

We lost the game and the national championship, 14-7, and I remember seeing one of our linebackers, Lance Mehl, and the hurt and tears on his face. He never showed so much emotion as he did after that game. It was a sad, sad moment. Probably the worst loss I had ever experienced. I will always remember that locker room—going in there and seeing those players. What a great football team that was that didn't win it all. I saw the tears on all their faces, and I remember seeing Matt Millen walk up to Chuck Fusina, and, as devastated as he was, Matt looked into Chuckie's eyes and said: "You know, I still love you, Chuck."

That Sugar Bowl loss is a game that will always stick in my mind because it is symbolic of a season where we were so close, yet something just wasn't there. It was a very difficult experience; one that took us all a long time to get over. And Coach Paterno probably had the most trouble of anybody getting over that loss as we tried to move forward. He knew what kind of team we had going into 1978 at the end of the 1977 season.

We also had great defensive teams in the early 1980s with players like Chet Parlavecchio, Rich D'Amico, Matt Bradley, Mark Robinson and Leo Wisniewski. They probably weren't as talented as some of our great defenses of the past, but those guys were like blood brothers, and that was one of the things that pulled them through the tough times. They would fight—during practice; during games; before plays; after plays—but they were very close and very sensitive to each other.

Chet Parlavecchio and I had a lot of run-ins early in his career because he held onto the notion that he should be playing, and I didn't agree. I just didn't think he was as good as some of the others we had playing, and I didn't think he could provide the stability we needed. I liked his desire and confidence in himself, but those are decisions that we as coaches had to make all the time. One thing Chet had that impressed me a lot was his loyalty. He got upset once and decided to stage his own walkout. He stayed away from the practice field for a while and just sort of walked around town. But his loyalty and respect for Penn State brought him back. Chet stayed with it and eventually became a captain, and I appreciated the fact that he recognized what we were trying to do as a team. He was a great leader, and he convinced the whole team in the second game of the 1981 season that we were going to win at favored Nebraska. I think he even had Nebraska pretty well convinced because we hung on for a 30-24 win.

The 1981 team was strong defensively, but we also had one of the best offensive lines I had ever seen at Penn State. Mike Munchak, Sean Farrell, Mark Battaglia, Jim Romano, Bill Contz, Vyto Kab and Pete Speros were the anchors of that line, and all but two of them played in the NFL.

That year was the first time we ever played a bowl game against a Heisman Trophy winner. We were facing the University of Southern California and their All-American tailback, Marcus Allen, in the Fiesta Bowl. It was no secret who their leader was, so our defense had to be up to the task. It turned out to be a special day because a defense that didn't have the greatest talent faced Marcus Allen and held him to 85 yards rushing on 30 carries. Our offense played a solid game as well and we beat USC, 26-10.

That was the same team that fell behind Pittsburgh in the last game of the regular season, 14-0. Dan Marino was Pitt's quarterback, and he started out with two quick touchdown strikes to put us in a hole. Once again, our guys stayed together, and in that game, they believed probably even more than me that we could pull it out. Mark Robinson was a fantastic safety at Penn State, and he put a couple of crushing hits on the Pitt wide receivers that literally turned the game in our favor.

The defense became inspired when it looked like Pitt's receivers weren't finishing their routes, and the offense became inspired by the way our defense was playing. One characteristic about Penn State football that I have always loved—and I will sorely miss—was that our teams might bend a little, but they would never break or crack under pressure. I would soon see that aspect again in this team. Besides the crushing blows he was delivering on the field, Mark Robinson also returned an interception something like 75 yards for a touchdown, and, as a team, we got on a roll and scored 48 unanswered points to win, 48-14. Seeing that game turn the way it did—in front of a hostile Pitt crowd—was definitely one of the highlights of my coaching career because it showed a lot of what Penn State football is all about.

The toughness and strength that 1981 team possessed could very well have been the inspiration for what we would experience in 1982. In '81, we finished 10-2 and were ranked third in the nation in both the Associated Press poll and the coaches poll. We started the 1982 season with four straight home wins, including a thrilling last-second victory over a very strong Nebraska team, but we had to go on the road to face Alabama, who always gave us fits. It would be nearing Bear Bryant's last season as head coach, and it seemed like we couldn't do anything right. We lost, 42-21, and in most cases that one loss would wipe out any college football team's hopes for a national championship.

That squad, however, decided to take the rest of the season as a challenge. and we won our last six regular season games to earn an invitation to the Sugar Bowl. If we had to lose at some point in that season, it seemed like we lost early enough that we could work our way back up the ladder. We closed the regular season with a very tough road victory at Notre Dame and an equally stunning win over No. 5 Pittsburgh. When we lost to Alabama, we fell from third to eighth in the polls, but we slowly worked our way back up, and thanks to one or two upsets of teams ahead of us in the polls, we put the Sugar Bowl in position of having a No. 1 vs. No. 2 matchup. We were second, and the University of Georgia was ranked first.

For the second year in a row, our defense would be facing the Heisman Trophy winner. This time, it was Georgia's tremendous running back, Herschel Walker, who would keep us up at night trying to devise ways to hold him down. He was a tremendous athlete who was known for his strict work ethic on the field and exercise regimen off the field. But we had a confident bunch, and our kids never doubted in their ability to get the job done.

In the season before, we were known for a stingy defense that held Marcus Allen way below his regular season totals, and we wanted to duplicate that feat as best we could against Herschel Walker and his Georgia teammates. A very nice complement to our defense in 1982, however, were the strides that our offense had made in a single year. Todd Blackledge had matured into a legitimate quarterback threat despite facing many doubts and uncertainties early in his career. The offensive line was much the same as the year before, and it had matured into an even more solid unit with backups who could step right in to give the starters a breather if need be. We had a good set of receivers in tight end Mike McCloskey; little guys Gregg Garrity and Kevin Baugh; and probably Todd's favorite target, Kenny Jackson.

But while most of the fans and media focused on the great running backs we played against in the 1981 and '82 bowl games, we knew we had a pretty good tailback of our own in the quiet and unassuming Curt Warner. In the Fiesta Bowl, our defense held Marcus Allen to 85 yards rushing, while Curt gained 145 yards on 26 carries and scored two touchdowns. One year later, our offense not only had a more confident passing game, but it continued to be strong on the ground. Todd Blackledge passed for 228 yards and a touchdown, while Curt Warner rushed for 117 yards and two touchdowns on 18 carries.

Todd connected with Gregg Garrity on a sensational 47-yard touchdown pass early in the fourth quarter when we really needed a spark. I'll never forget Gregg stretching his body and making a diving catch in the end zone. That full stretch ended up on the cover of *Sports Illustrated* the following week, and it spoke volumes of the great reach we had to make over those last seven games to win Penn State's first national championship in school history.

It was true, we had a much-improved offense that season, but I was equally proud of our defensive effort in that 27-23 Sugar Bowl victory. For the second straight year, we faced a Heisman Trophy winner, and our defense stood tall. Normally, a coach isn't very excited when his team allows a running back to rush for 100 yards, but considering this was Herschel Walker, I was more than impressed that our defense held him to 103 yards and a touchdown on 28 carries.

One of the brightest spots of that Penn State defense was linebacker Scott Radecic, who was a captain and an outstanding player for us all season long. He took his studies in architectural engineering just as seriously as football, and he worked hard to excel both on the field and in the classroom, which is the thing that Penn State has always stressed to its student athletes in any sport. The same was true of linebacker Harry Hamilton, who took notes in every meeting. Harry was the greatest perfectionist I had ever coached. He wanted to please, and he wanted to do everything exactly right. That's probably why he is a great attorney today.

Scott Radecic became the heart and soul of our defense, and it really upset me when he sprained his ankle during the week leading up to the Sugar Bowl. I had watched him improve over the years, and playing for the national championship was to be the ultimate accomplishment for him, as well as every other member of the team. It would be Scott's last chance, and I didn't want to think about the possibility of him not being able to play in the most anticipated game of his life.

Scott put all the pain aside, however, and showed us what a tough, tough competitor he was. I was sick when he sprained his ankle, but he played hurt and did an outstanding job under a great amount of adversity. Today, Scott Radecic is a well-respected architect, and he is involved in the designing and planning to add private boxes and extra seating to Penn State's Beaver Stadium.

Other defensive standouts on that 1982 team included Ken Kelley, who was also one of our captains. Ken was versatile because he could play defensive end and outside linebacker. Greg Gattuso, Dave Opfar and Joel Hines played on the inside of the line, while Dave Paffenroth and Rodger Puz alternated at inside linebacker. Steve Sefter was an undersized defensive end, but he was tough and just a great competitor. We also had a young man by the name of Walker Lee Ashley, who gave us everything we had at linebacker, and Roger Jackson, who was Kenny's brother, played a solid defensive back for us, despite not having played much high school football.

I will also forever remember the play of two gritty walk-on players who made their marks in that game. Gregg Garrity was, at one time, someone who didn't believe he could play at Penn State, yet, as I stated earlier, he ended up on the cover of *Sports Illustrated* for his leaping fourth-quarter touchdown catch in the Sugar Bowl. Dan Biondi was a starting defensive back, and despite his lack of size—he was maybe 5' 8" or so— he was as tough as any of the rest of our players on defense.

Some of the teams that we played against gave me inspiration in designing some of the defenses that I drew up. Over the years, we had several close games against some very talented teams. Teams such as Notre Dame, Pittsburgh and Alabama presented us many situations where the game was on the line and our defense was challenged on the goal line.

We stopped Notre Dame at the two-yard line on fourth down late in the fourth quarter to preserve a win in 1987, and there was a similar situation against Alabama in the '80s when we ran into a similar circumstance with the same result. As most philosophies go, sometimes it worked and sometimes it didn't. There was another time in 1992 when we had our backs to the wall at Notre Dame Stadium, trying to hold on to a slim lead as a blizzard swirled in all directions on the field.

Rick Mirer was the Notre Dame quarterback, and he led a drive that was reminiscent of so many great Fighting Irish quarterbacks of the past—most notably a guy named Joe Montana came to mind. Mirer led the Irish the length of the field with his pinpoint passing and got them down inside the five-yard line. Despite the Notre Dame charge, I felt our defense was keeping its composure. It had come down to one crucial play where they needed a touchdown, and we needed a defensive stand. I didn't always make the perfect call down there on the sideline, but on this occasion I did. We had the right personnel on the field, and everyone executed properly, but Rick Mirer proved to be one step better on this day. He dropped back to pass, scrambled to safety and threw an off-balance touchdown pass just over the outstretched arms of one of our defensive linemen. Notre Dame won, and I thought Mirer played one of the best games of his college career. I also thought that game was one of our better efforts defensively throughout the season as well. It was just one of those times where our best effort wasn't quite good enough.

One of our greatest defensive stands came against Pittsburgh back in 1977. We were on the road, and it was, as usual with our intrastate rivalry, the last game of the regular season for both teams. We were ahead, 15-7, late in the fourth quarter, but Pitt got a touchdown and had put themselves in position to possibly pull out a tie. They had just scored, and with a definite two-point conversion attempt looming, Joe Paterno asked me what I thought they were going to do. I told him quite honestly that I had no idea. The field was covered by now with snow, except for the footprints of where the action was taking place. We just called a basic defense, and Joe Diange, our left defensive end, snuffed out the running play and made a great stop. Matt Millen helped bring down the ball carrier too, and I jokingly tell him he was quick to take all the credit for the play, but Joe Diange made the great stop that helped us hold onto a 15-13 win.

I remember Doug Flutie passing for 447 yards against us in 1984 when he played quarterback for Boston College, and Ty Detmer completed 42 of 59 passes for 576 yards against us in the 1989 Holiday Bowl. I often joked that we helped set the stage for Detmer's 1991 Heisman Trophy season.

I speak often of great wins we've had against Pittsburgh, but we were also beaten by them several times in my career. Pitt moved Tony Dorsett to fullback at halftime of our game in 1976 after we had held him in check through the first 30 minutes. The move paid off for them, and the Panthers turned a close game into a 24-7 win. Dorsett won the Heisman that year, and Pitt won the national championship.

We went through a somewhat disappointing season in 1979, I think because we were held in such high regard following our 11-1 finish the season before, losing only to Alabama in the Sugar Bowl. There were high expectations, but we started out 1-2, with ugly losses to Texas A&M at home and at Nebraska. We won four in a row after that but then lost a disappointing game at home to Miami, which featured a young quarterback named Jim Kelly, who went on to a great professional career with the Buffalo Bills. Dan Marino started as a freshman against us for Pitt, and they came to Beaver Stadium and beat us, 29-14. We finished on a positive note by defeating Tulane in the Liberty Bowl, but an 8-4 finish was not what Penn State fans were normally accustomed to.

Our teams over the years also experienced tough road losses against Syracuse in the Carrier Dome and West Virginia in Morgantown. Those games where we struggled always gave me sick feelings — I guess it's just the nature of coaching—but they also provided me with memories of various groups of people who shared a common bond. Not every player has a chance to experience a national championship run during their college career, but as a coach, I've had that opportunity quite a few times. I feel badly for some of those players because they hear so much about the tradition and experiences of past players, but don't get to live it themselves.

I admired players like that just as much, if not more, because they take pride in putting on that Penn State uniform, and they find something inside them to overcome the adversities. They stick together and do what they have to do to pull themselves through the hard times—as teammates.

In all my years of athletics, at any level, in any sport, I had never been involved in a season where my team finished with a losing record. Penn State started what would become an NCAA record for consecutive non-losing seasons in 1939 by going 5-1-2 after posting a 3-4-1 record the season before. The streak lasted 49 years until we finished 5-6 in 1988. I had never even thought about something like that happening to us. It was something you just didn't consider. With hard work and dedication, we felt we would always have teams who would do the necessary things to win.

The season started out well enough as we won by 28 points at Virginia and proceeded to win three of our next four. But out of nowhere, the bottom seemed to have fallen out. We lost five of our last six, including a 21-point setback at West Virginia and a 14-7 loss at home to Pitt. For the first time in my playing and coaching career, we had lost more games than we had won. It was disappointing, but we still had the type of players I admired. These guys never quit; never turned and pointed fingers at one another. They stuck it out and became the nucleus of a team that righted itself to a respectable 8-3-1 record in 1989.

1991 was a unique year for us, because it really confirmed the things I believe in as far as coaching. We had an extremely talented defensive team—probably the most talented since 1977, when we had a group that featured two All-American tackles in Bruce Clark and Matt Millen, plus so many others who were very talented. Talent-wise, the 1991 team had a lot. We had some players on the team who remembered our 50-39 Holiday Bowl win over Brigham Young. It was good to get the victory, but our defensive players remembered the 576 yards Ty Detmer consumed passing the football in that game, and they wanted to show what our true defense was all about when BYU came to Penn State in September of '91. Our players were extremely fired up, and they showed it by holding Detmer to just eight completions and 158 yards passing and limited BYU to just seven points. Those were the lowest numbers Detmer had ever produced as a college player.

As for my beliefs in coaching, I think that talent will only carry any team so far, and when that talent level is equaled on the field, you need something else to carry you through the rest of the game. We most certainly had the talent, but I wasn't quite sure if we had the chemistry or intangibles a team needs. I couldn't shake the feeling that something was missing.

We won our first two games that season with relative ease, including an 81-0 score against Cincinnati, in which our third- and fourth-team tailbacks scored touchdowns, as did our third-string quarterback. The problem with games like that is things tend to come a little bit *too* easily. We were 2-0 and set to travel to Los Angeles to play the University of Southern California. This should be considered a difficult game under any circumstance, but having to travel 3,000 miles and three time zones away should make it all the more difficult in the way a team must prepare.

We should have been humbled enough with the knowledge that we were beaten there the season before, but our early season accomplishments in 1991 seemed to take precedence with most of our players that season. We had people who simply believed they couldn't be beaten. They underestimated the ability of a team like USC and didn't appreciate the gravity of playing in a hostile environment such as what we would face. Our group of players became filled with themselves following the Cincinnati victory without taking into account that USC and Cincinnati—at least that season—were on two completely different levels. Sure enough, we got into the game and made some costly mistakes. Costly turnovers and a couple of missed assignments resulted in a 21-10 USC victory. Our mistakes came from everywhere. Offense; defense; special teams. We were thoroughly outplayed.

It's hard to be critical of a team that finishes with an 11-2 record, but this was the kind of team that had every bit of talent to go 13-0. We had the players, but at a couple of critical junctures, we lacked those intangibles that many coaches notice and value.

It was mid-October, and we traveled to Miami for what I knew would be another tough battle, but one I felt we were certainly capable of winning. We had rebounded after the USC loss and were 5-1 going into Miami. But here again, we lost a game that we really shouldn't have lost. Teamwork seemed to have taken a back seat in that game because we had none of it. We lost because we had players who were being selfish. They thought more of themselves than for the team. We had people who didn't concentrate; people who didn't know how to prepare; people who didn't believe or listen.

After that Miami loss, we made some changes and put together a different team. It was one with a little less talent and ability, but they did what we asked and played together. We told them they would never be a great defensive team until they stopped somebody on the goal line, and they had one of those stands in a late-season win over Notre Dame. We talked about not being a great defensive team until they proved they could hang tough when things weren't going their way; when the other team was hot, and it seemed like everything was going against us.

This revamped team came across that situation twice over the next six games, and both times they proved they were up to the task. We were playing against Pittsburgh on Thanksgiving Day. We had a good lead, but Pitt started a rally which saw them pull within five. They had the ball, but our defense stopped them, and we won, 22-17. The second show of strength we had was in the Fiesta Bowl against a very talented team from Tennessee. We were behind, 17-7, with about three minutes left in the third quarter, but that was when everyone from offense to defense to special teams stepped up and took charge.

Our quarterback, Tony Sacca, hit Chip LaBarca with a three-yard touchdown pass to make it 17-14. On Tennessee's next possession, our defensive tackle, Tyoka Jackson, stripped the ball from Tennessee's quarterback, and Sacca threw a touchdown pass to Kyle Brady to put us ahead. Reggie Givens intercepted a Tennessee pass on the next possession and set up a two-yard touchdown run by Richie Anderson early in the fourth quarter. On the very next play, Derek Bochna hit the quarterback, and Givens ran the ensuing fumble in from 23 yards. Our defense then held Tennessee to three plays and a punt, and Sacca threw a 37-yard TD pass to O.J. McDuffie.

We scored 35 points in less than eight minutes and won, 42-17. What I was most proud of in that game was not so much the final score itself but the *way* our kids did it. They did it in a manner that was more typical of Penn State teams of the past. It was done in a classy way, with people who didn't selfishly go around looking for a way to say how great they were. We did it with people who concentrated; who wanted to do things the way we, as coaches, believed was the right way to get it done. Fortunately, we got the job done and finished as the No. 3 team in the country.

Although I am critical of certain points in that 1991 team, I can honestly say the year was still a very rewarding one in a lot of ways. We had the potential to win a national championship, and the problem might have been that we worried too much about that very aspect. We looked for it so much that we overlooked the little details and discipline it would take to get there. I think we all learned a valuable lesson that talent alone wasn't going to win a national championship. Intangibles go a long way in deciding a team's fate. But unfortunately, we realized that aspect a little too late.

One of my fondest memories at Penn State came from our national championship team of 1986. This was the same team that almost floundered to a losing record early in their careers. We finished 6-5 in 1984, including two disappointing losses to Notre Dame (44-7) and Pitt (31-11) to close out the season. The games weren't even close, and we were again at one of those crossroads where we had to figure out what it would take to turn things around and find the right players to do it.

That group of players worked and worked to get better, and we saw results the very next season. In 1985, we went through an undefeated regular season and played Oklahoma for the national championship in the Orange Bowl. The last time we went into a bowl game as the No. 1

team we were beaten by Alabama in the 1978 Sugar Bowl. We were in that spot again as we prepared to battle Oklahoma, and although there is a lot of pressure that goes with such a ranking, we knew we had the players to get us there. The game was close throughout, and we seemed to have Oklahoma in an unenviable position—deep in their own territory and facing a third-and-24 situation.

I made a dumb defensive call on that play, and it cost us. I called for a blitz, and Jamelle Holieway, Oklahoma's quarterback, hit his tight end, Keith Jackson, with a quick pass over the middle, and Jackson took it 71 yards for a touchdown. Later on, Lydell Carr ran 61 yards for a touchdown against us, and we lost the game, 25-10.

I remember sitting around outside the hotel, long after the game had ended, thinking of how close the game really was and how disappointing it felt to see us lose the national championship because of two big plays. Other than those two long touchdowns, Oklahoma really didn't have that much success against us, but they played a great defensive game and kept us out of the end zone after we had scored on our first possession.

We lost in the same fashion to Alabama in 1978, having gone into the game undefeated, but seeing our dream disappear in the game that counted. We went into 1979 with a lot of high expectations—both from ourselves and from the fans who followed us—and although we had a winning season, 8-4 isn't exactly the type of record people wanted to see from us. I felt good about the group of players we had coming back, and it was easy to see that they would never forget that moment when the game ended in Miami and how much it hurt. Instead of pouting, however, the players collected themselves and vowed to stay together with a determination to come back and win it all the next year.

It was a veteran group we would have coming back with players like Shane Conlan, Ray Isom, Tim Johnson, Bob White, Trey Bauer, Matt Johnson, Pete Curkendall, Don Graham, Duffy Cobbs and Eddie Johnson returning on defense. They were a special group of people extremely committed to their goals. Over a period of two years, those guys had been through so many close games. Eleven times they faced a situation where the last play of the game would have significance in the outcome, and that group of players won all of them. We almost lost to a bad Cincinnati team in 1986, but we stopped them late on a short yardage play, and then our special teams blocked a punt to help us win, 23-17.

We traveled to South Bend that season to play Notre Dame, who was not having a very good season, but they were always tough at home. On the plane to South Bend, I wrote a letter to the kids from our Second

Mile program. It was a very positive letter about the group of people on our team and how much I cared about them and the way they carried themselves. Notre Dame was playing very well, and I remember Tim Johnson, one of our defensive tackles, coming up to me on the sidelines and saying: "Let's quit trying to trick them, Jerry, and just start stopping them. Let us play!"

We were in a goal line defense once, and I noticed we had mis-aligned. But our guys made a good quick decision, and Ray Isom got through and stopped their option for a loss. My mind always replays Bobby White sacking the quarterback from his defensive end position on the goal line in a most critical situation. Bobby was a winner. He was always in great condition—a leader who knew what it meant to pay the price. He epitomized the "we" and "us" type of person we liked to have on the field at Penn State. We fought through a lot of close plays in a big 24-19 win over Notre Dame that day, but there was a time on the sidelines when the thought actually entered my mind of having to change that letter to the Second Mile kids.

We had another close game at home against Maryland. We were ahead, 17-9, but they scored late in the game and were in position to tie us with a two-point conversion. But our defense rose to the challenge once again, and we held on.

There were a few easy wins that seasons as well as the nail-biters where we rose to the challenge. What it all amounted to was another 11-0 regular season and a Fiesta Bowl matchup with Miami, who was also undefeated. This time, we would enter the game ranked second in the country, and although I think we were considered the underdog, we appeared to be the favorite when it came to fan approval. That was just another testament to the desire and pride our players showed in themselves.

Miami came to Tempe, Arizona, amid all the hoopla of wearing battle fatigues and just generally doing a lot of talking. But underneath all of that, they were an outstanding football team with loads of talent both offensively and defensively. The Hurricanes had players like Jerome Brown, Bennie Blades, Michael Irvin, Melvin Bratton, Alonzo Highsmith and Brett Perriman. And it was very well publicized that we would be facing another Heisman Trophy winner in Miami quarterback Vinny Testaverde. Looking at their drop back pass reel of film was like watching a clinic in action. They were indeed as good as everyone said they were.

In a way, I felt bad for them, however, because they felt they had to put on such an act to try to intimidate us. When they arrived at the stadium for the game, they were led off the buses by Jerome Brown, and most all of them had cigars in their mouths, as they were celebrating a victory they hadn't won yet. They had a lot to say when they saw our players, and one of them even said something to me.

"I'm not going to be the one doing the hitting," I said to him. I then told our defensive players to stay focused on the job at hand and not to worry about what was being said. During warm ups, it looked as though even Vinny Testaverde and Miami's coach, Jimmy Johnson, were having a chuckle as they watched our "little" defensive backs warm up.

There was a Penn State pep rally at our hotel a couple days before the game, and I made some comment to the effect that their battle fatigues were appropriate: "They came dressed in their battle uniforms because they know that in order to beat our group of people they'll have to kill them," I said to the cheering crowd. "That's what it's going to take because we're going to be relentless." Thank goodness our players backed me up.

I look at that game as kind of a starting point for what would eventually become the Bowl Championship Series many years later simply because the network that covered the game hyped it to a level I had never seen before because of its No. 1 versus No. 2 status. They moved it to January 2, which had never been the case before. Usually, the Fiesta Bowl had been played on New Year's Day in the afternoon. With so much at stake, whomever had control of the game decided to put it in the national spotlight where no other game would be going on at the same time. All the other bowl games had been played, and there was just one left to decide the national champion.

Our defense was eager to play simply because they knew it would be another challenge against a Heisman Trophy winner. We had become known as a bend-but-don't-break defense that season because of our ability to come up big inside the red zone, which is the area from the goal lines to the 20-yard line. This group of defenders had heard about our previous accomplishments against Heisman Trophy winners, and they didn't want to be known as players who couldn't live up to a similar challenge.

For the game, we finished with eight first downs and 162 yards on offense, while Miami had 22 first downs and 445 yards of total offense. That would appear to indicate a Miami rout, but once again, our players —both offensively and defensively—did their jobs when it counted. Testaverde threw 50 passes against us and completed 26 of them for 285 yards. But I was proud of our defenders because we didn't allow them to turn those yards into points.

Miami scored a touchdown midway through the second quarter after they recovered a fumble at our 23-yard line. Our quarterback, John Shaffer, responded immediately by leading our team 74 yards for the tying touchdown with a little over minute left before halftime. John faced a tremendous amount of pressure all evening, but he kept his cool and even completed a 23-yard pass to Eric Hamilton on third-and-12 to keep the drive alive.

The score stayed that way until early in the fourth quarter, when Miami converted a 38-yard field goal to take a 10-7 lead. Miami was blessed with a great group of receivers, and they played a very important role in the success that Vinny Testaverde had that season. Irvin, Blades, and Perriman all had excellent hands and breakaway speed that we would have to contain every single play. We told our players going in that the best way to keep their receivers in check was to put it in their minds that they wouldn't *want* to catch the ball. Hopefully, they wouldn't even want it thrown their way.

Testaverde completed some passes early, but our defensive players were making them pay. With each completion came a crushing tackle. We were hitting hard every snap of the ball, and you could see the looks of frustration and soreness in the eyes of the Miami receivers. As the game went on, passes that were being caught early in the game slowly became drops. Eyes that were fixed solely on the Miami quarterback were now feeling the strain of looking over their shoulders, wondering where the next hit was coming from. Concentration that was so abundant on the Miami side during the early stages of the game had now been taken over by hesitation. And that was exactly the way we wanted it.

Our defense was giving everything it had with every play. We were looking for one opportunity where the game could turn our way when Shane Conlan made it happen. He had an interception in the third quarter that gave strength to our defense, and although he was hurting tremendously from ankle and knee injuries, Shane stepped in front of a Testaverde pass and returned it 39 yards to the Miami five-yard line. Two plays later, D.J. Dozier, who was our leading tailback all season, carried it into the end zone to give us the lead, 14-10.

Shane's interception was one of five that our defense pulled in from Testaverde that evening. I had said all season how special that group was, and they looked into the eyes of an All-American quarterback and met him challenge for challenge. There were around eight minutes left, and we knew we would need at least two more stops from our defense. We got one when linebacker Trey Bauer forced a Miami fumble that we recovered, but that was just a prelude to what we would have to endure down the stretch.

Miami took possession for a final drive at its own 23-yard line with 3:07 remaining in the game. We forced them into a fourth-down situation, but Testaverde calmly hit Bennie Blades for a 31-yard completion to push the Hurricanes into our territory. At that point, I thought we might finally be running out of luck. I thought of all the times we had faced these crucial situations the previous two seasons and how we had survived. But now it seemed like Miami was cruising down the field with the idea of taking away a title that we had lost to Oklahoma a year earlier.

Miami had moved to the six-yard line and was facing second down. Shane Conlan was out of the game now because of his injuries, and Trey Bauer came over to the sidelines during a time-out to discuss our strategy. "It's pretty rough out there, isn't it?" I asked him, trying hard to force a smile.

"Yeah, it sure is," Trey smiled back.

I was really loose all day long because we had been through so much preparation. I was confident we were ready to put all of our hard work to the test, and I just wanted to enjoy the day. But now, I had become extremely tight. Our defensive unit was exhausted, and they had played their hearts out. As I looked into Trey's eye, I could see the concern, and I knew there were probably 10 other sets of eyes out on that field that had the same looks of concern. I suspected Miami would come right out with no huddle, so I made sure Trey knew which play to call. "Tell me you know the play!" I screamed at him. Trey nodded and said he did. But when the no-huddle appeared for Miami, nothing came out of Trey's mouth. And to this day, knowing the situation, I couldn't blame him. The defensive coverage wasn't what we wanted, but fortunately, Tim Johnson got to Testaverde and sacked him for a loss.

A lot of people thought that call was a great strategic decision, but it wasn't. It was a group of committed people who would not give in; who would not relinquish their efforts. They had put too much time and energy into the season to give in so easily. Somehow, they found a way to get it done. That play just really taught me a lot about our team. The next play was an incomplete pass, and that set the stage for the drama that every college football fan in the country had hoped to see.

It was everything those players had lived for and what committed them to Penn State in the first place. There wasn't anything I wanted more than to see that group of people win a national championship. I had always prided myself on being cool under pressure, but right at that moment, there was nothing coming out of my mouth. I turned to Jim Williams, one of our defensive coaches who signaled the plays in to Trey, and said: "Same defense, Jim."

The Penn State contingent of fans was screaming for one more stop. It was fourth down, and Miami had to get it in the end zone. There were 18 seconds left and they were on our 13-yard line. Testaverde took the snap, dropped back and looked all around for an open receiver. He threw one final time in the direction of Brett Perriman, but Pete Giftopoulos, our linebacker who had an interception earlier in the game, stepped in front of the pass at the goal line and settled it into his arms. Pete ran it back to the 10-yard line before he simply fell to the ground in a combined state of celebration and exhaustion.

They had done it again—this gifted and talented group. All I could do was sit down on the bench and cry. And that's what was going on in the locker room—everybody just hugging and crying. It was pure happiness. It was love based on respect and admiration that had developed over years of hard work. It was an experience that none of us will ever forget.

I've heard it said: "What you give you will have forever, and what you keep is lost." Well, this was a group that certainly gave its all.

That following summer, I figured if there was ever a time when I could motivate young people, this would be it. I prepared a talk for the kids at the Second Mile camp in which I tied in goal-setting, the Fiesta Bowl experience, and the caring the team shared. I gave my speech with my usual fire and gusto, and I came to what I considered to be a fantastic conclusion. Just as I finished, one of the young campers raised his hand. *Questions*, I thought to myself. *The master orator has his audience wrapped around his little finger. They are eating up every word.*

"Were you *at* the Fiesta Bowl?" the young man asked. I stared back at him with a look of mocking disbelief, knowing I had been humbled once again. I was amused, as was everyone else who had heard his question, so I decided to see how tough I could get with him. "Come here, kid," I said as I looked him square in the eyes. "I want to talk to you outside."

Obviously, the boy didn't know greatness. Then again, maybe he did.

A record of 8-4 would be a successful season for lots of teams, but finish 8-4 at Penn State, and you find a lot of fans asking what went wrong. That's how we followed our second national championship when the 1987 season came around. It seemed to be up and down all season for us. We had some impressive wins over Boston College, West Virginia and Maryland, but we also had some disappointing losses against Alabama, Syracuse and Pittsburgh. And the season came to one of the worst finishes

I had ever experienced when we lost to Clemson in the Citrus Bowl, 35-10.

When we began our preparation, we debated about whether we should stay with the things we had been doing the past few weeks—even though they weren't totally sound—or put some changes into our package. We decided to stay with what we had, and it turned out to be the wrong decision. To top it all off, the Citrus Bowl had more functions for the athletes than any of the other bowls, and it became extremely difficult to prepare at the bowl site.

The game was a disaster from the opening kickoff and just got worse as it went along. Our concerns were accurate as Clemson took some big splits in the line and took advantage of things we were trying to do. When Ron Dickerson, who was our secondary coach at the time, became defensive coordinator at Clemson a short while later, their former coach, Frank Howard, called him into his office and said: "Young man, you aren't gonna use that defense here that you all used at Penn State, are you?" I'm sure Ron left that particular defense somewhere back in State College.

The one memory of that 1987 season I will always carry with me is a dream I had near the end of the season. We had just suffered a tough 10-0 loss at Pitt, and we had one more regular season game left. It was against Notre Dame at Beaver Stadium, and they would be bringing an outstanding team with future Heisman Trophy winner Tim Brown included. Even though we were at home, we were the underdogs, and we prepared our team that way.

It was early Thursday morning, just two days before the game, and I was awakened from a dream about our opponent. I looked at the clock, and it was 3 a.m., and I remembered seeing Notre Dame in my dream going for two points. I stayed awake and started thinking about what we should do defensively if that situation came about. Through the years, I had watched Lou Holtz's teams, and I knew that he was very unpredictable in that situation. I had always had tremendous respect for his play calling. As I thought, it occurred to me that it might be a good idea to call a defense and then have our players call time-out after Notre Dame showed their formation. Then we could decide how we wanted to approach things during the time-out.

Saturday came, and it was an extremely cold day, but we played them tough throughout. Our fans were behind us all the way, and I'm sure that gave our players adrenaline. Unbelievably, the game came down to a two-point conversion. Notre Dame scored late in the fourth quarter and trailed by one. Lou Holtz was one who rarely settled for a tie, and that was at a time when overtime in college football was still a long way off. As the Irish lined up for the play, I could see the replay of my dream in front of me. I woke up before the dream ended, so I didn't know the outcome, but I was hoping it would have been kind to us. We carried it out the way I had planned during those early-morning hours by lining up and then calling the time-out. Fortunately, most of the Notre Dame offense couldn't hear to change the play at the line of scrimmage—thanks to our exuberant student section in the south end zone—and we were able to stop them and hang on to a 21-20 win.

I can probably tell stories about every one of my 32 seasons at Penn State, but two other seasons stand out in my mind because they involved such a radical change in the history of Penn State football.

The 1992 season was our last chance to win a national championship as an independent school. The decision had been made a few years earlier for Penn State to become the 11th school to join the Big Ten Conference, and 1993 would be the beginning of this new era. We started the '92 season 5-0, but a tough home loss to Miami in October put a dent in the team's championship hopes and also seemed to deflate the focus that we had started out so strongly with.

We lost four of our last six games after the Miami loss, including a terrible display of football in the Blockbuster Bowl, where we lost to Stanford, 24-3. The 1993 season became a time to recommit ourselves. Not only were we about to display our program in front of arguably the most revered and respected football conference in the country, we would have to do it with the hopes of reestablishing our purpose and focus. On a personal level, I once again took on the title of linebackers coach, as well as defensive coordinator.

A quarterback controversy seemed to surface in the early part of the preseason between Kerry Collins and John Sacca. Coach Paterno knew he would have to make a tough decision because both were capable of leading us. Joe named John as the starter in the early going, but he also met with Kerry and told him he would receive playing time. Kerry told Joe that if John was his starter, he should probably stick with him for the best interest of the team, and he also said he wouldn't want to have to look over his shoulder if he were the starter.

We had a wide receiver in Bobby Engram who could help either of our quarterbacks through a difficult situation, and Bobby would certainly do just that through the next couple of seasons. Our defensive front was good, too, with Tyoka Jackson, Eric Clair, Lou Benfatti and Eric Ravotti. Brian Gelzheiser, Brian Monaghan and Rob Holmberg were the linebackers, while Shelly Hammonds, Marlin Forbes, Derek Bochna and Lee Rubin started in the secondary.

We won our opener against Minnesota, 38-20, and we had a tough nonconference game the next week against Southern California. We hoped to play better than we did in our two previous games against USC that were played in Los Angeles. We were ahead late, but their quarterback, Rob Johnson, brought them back and had them poised for an upset if they could convert a two-point try after a touchdown had made it 21-20. There was no overtime in college football then, and USC coach John Robinson had no intention of settling for a tie. Fortunately, our defense snuffed out the play, and we were able to hang on, albeit just barely.

We traveled to Iowa for our first Big Ten road game and handled the Hawkeyes easier than probably any of us expected, 31-0. Despite that lopsided score, we were a bit sluggish offensively in the early part of the game, and Coach Paterno decided to make a change at quarterback. From that point on, Kerry Collins played himself into a starting role, and eventually, John Sacca would take a leave of absence before he ultimately transferred at the end of the season. Those kind of scenarios are never easy to witness, but they are a part of the game sometimes.

We defeated Rutgers at home the following week, and in our final nonconference game, we caught a couple of fortunate breaks—along with an excellent game plan—to post an easier-than-expected 70-7 win at Maryland. I knew it wasn't going to be their night when they aligned in a shotgun formation near the goal line. When the quarterback started calling an audible, the center snapped the ball over his head for a safety.

Our biggest test was yet to come. We returned home to face the University of Michigan, which was one of the schools that repeatedly made a point of knocking Penn State's presence in the Big Ten. For several years, the conference had been dominated by either Michigan or Ohio State, and players from both schools made it their mission to let us know through the media that we weren't just going to come in and dominate their territory.

On the morning of the game, I had some Second Mile kids with me as I headed into the locker room. I suddenly realized that I had left my defensive call sheets in the car, so I went back to retrieve them. As I did this, I was walking back to the locker room with my head down, looking over my notes to make sure I had everything I needed. I looked up just in time to ram my forehead directly into a truck that had its back rear window opened. I thought maybe one of the Second Mile kids was playing games and hit me accidentally or something, but it was just me not paying attention to where I was going. My forehead was cut, and I needed five stitches to close it, but I'll always remember a young recruit who was standing nearby trying to hold back his laughter as this all had transpired.

That recruit was Curtis Enis, who would go on to have an outstanding career as a tailback at Penn State.

As much as my head hurt, however, the game turned out a lot worse for us because we couldn't quite make the big play against Michigan when we needed to. They made a great call on a passing down against us. They had a punt return for a touchdown and Tyrone Wheatley, their outstanding tailback, ran for a touchdown. And finally, the Michigan defense came up big by stopping us on four plays from the one-yard line. We lost, 21-13, and it seemed like we would have a similar test as the year before when we started out 5-0, only to lose our sixth game.

Two weeks later, we traveled to Ohio State and had to play in a wet snowstorm. The field was a mess, and our quickness became a moot point. It was a battle in the trenches, but we were easily handled by the Buckeyes, 24-6. I saw a couple of good friends after the game, including Bob Stock, my old high school teammate who played at Ohio State, and a young man named Steve Quellhorst, whom I had gotten to know at one our camps and had spent a lot of time at our home. They consoled me over our loss as we shivered outside the locker room.

We were 5-2, and it was tough to forget what had transpired the season before. We could either take control of the rest of our season and make a statement that we belonged in the Big Ten, or we could give up and squabble over reasons why we couldn't get it done. Coach Paterno calmly went over those thoughts in the Ohio Stadium locker room after the game, and the players also discussed where they would like to be when the season reached its end.

I was impressed with that team from there on. We faced adversity at times, but we found the will and courage to overcome it again and again. We defeated Indiana and Illinois at home in the following weeks as well as Northwestern on the road. Our last regular season game was at Michigan State, and it would prove to be an emotional roller coaster. I had made up my mind I was going to stay calm and take things as they came, but as much as I tried, that just didn't seem to work.

For the better part of three quarters, we were outplayed in just about every aspect of the game. We weren't stopping anyone on defense and our offense couldn't get things going. We were down, 37-17, going into the fourth quarter, but we scored three times and pulled it out, 38-37. The feeling in the locker room was unbelievable and it was amazing to think that one point was the difference between us going to the Citrus Bowl as opposed to the Sun Bowl.

We played Tennessee in the Citrus Bowl, and this was our first time of what would become a regular routine of traveling to the bowl site early to get better prepared as a team. Tennessee was on a roll, and we had just snuck in thanks to our comeback against Michigan State. But despite an early lead by Tennessee, we came roaring back to win, 31-13. I'll always remember that game because it was Matt's first bowl game with us as our son. It was a fun trip and a successful finale to our first season in the Big Ten.

There was a lot of hope for 1994. Our goal, as always, was a national championship, but we also had the Rose Bowl in our sights, because it would indicate a Big Ten championship for us as well. We had been to all the major bowl games over the years, and going to the Rose Bowl would complete the cycle. Also, just having the opportunity to participate in the "granddaddy" of all bowl games would be an experience that we could all remember and cherish very much.

This Penn State squad would feature a special offense. Kerry Collins had taken a firm hold on the quarterback position, while Ki-Jana Carter, Jon Witman and Brian Milne would make up the backfield. Bobby Engram and Freddie Scott were the wide outs, and Kyle Brady was the tight end. Andre Johnson, Marco Rivera, Bucky Greeley, Jeff Hartings and Keith Conlin formed an outstanding offensive line. There were probably more pro prospects on our offensive football team than I can ever remember.

We struggled some defensively and had injury problems. Brian Gelzheiser, Willie Smith and Phil Yeboah-Kodie were the linebackers. Tony Pitman and Brian Miller were the corners, and Kim Herring and Jason Collins played most of the season as safeties. Todd Atkins and Jeff Perry played at the defensive end positions, while Chris Maczyk, Vinnie Stewart, Eric Clair and Brandon Noble found playing time inside the defensive line.

Our offense put on quite a display in a 56-3 opening-game win at Minnesota. Defensively, we surprised them with a lot of nickel defense, and I felt pretty good about the way we played. We continued to roll over our next four opponents, including a convincing 38-14 home win against Southern California. Our offense was beginning to get noticed around the country because we scored 48 points against Temple, 55 against Rutgers and 61 against Iowa.

Our first big test was at Michigan, and I'm not sure that I can remember a game with so many great offensive players on the field. Michigan had Todd Collins at quarterback, Tyrone Wheatley at running back and Amani Toomer at wide receiver. Plus, they had a solid line and a couple of outstanding tight ends.

We started off well and seemed to have control of the tempo until we took a 15-yard penalty in the second quarter. That seemed to give

Michigan the momentum, and, at least for a time, they seemed to take over the game. Wheatley broke a long touchdown run early in the third quarter by beating our blitz and turning it outside. The teams battled back and forth, and we regained our composure to take the lead on a great touchdown catch by Engram in the fourth quarter.

We always liked to have a defense in our hip pocket for a critical situation, and as Michigan started a drive down the field, we felt things had come to that critical stage. We got a sack and eventually forced a fourth-down pass, which we intercepted to seal a 31-24 hard-fought victory. This time, that defense we had tucked away came through for us.

The next week, we had a bye, and that gave us extra time to prepare for a rematch with the only other Big Ten school to defeat us in 1993. Ohio State had lost some players from the previous season, but we knew they would come to Beaver Stadium with that same "you don't belong with us" attitude they had a year ago. I didn't worry about things like that, but I knew our players took those two losses to heart the previous season. Our players competed hard and won in a tough Michigan environment to avenge one of the 1993 losses, and now they had their sights set on the second one.

I felt we could win the game, but I was shocked, as I'm sure a lot of people were, by the ease with which we did so. Our offense worked on all cylinders to build a big lead, and even the second-, third- and fourth-team players got into the scoring column. We formed a lopsided 63-14 victory over the Buckeyes and had catapulted into the No. 1 spot in the national rankings at 7-0.

As happy as we were to be undefeated at this point in the season, and with two major hurdles behind us, we would eventually learn that our next two games probably cost us the national championship. We traveled to Indiana and again had built a big lead. It was late in the game, and we were ahead, 35-14. Through a strange set of circumstances, Indiana was able to score a late touchdown. They got the ball back, but we had an interception that was returned for a touchdown. Instead of regaining our three-touchdown lead, however, the play was called back because of a penalty, and Indiana retained possession. As the seconds ticked off, the Hoosiers scored on a Hail Mary pass and converted a two-point try to make the final score, 35-29.

Some of the voters around the country felt the final score of our game wasn't convincing enough, even though they probably didn't see how it had transpired, and we fell to No. 2 behind Nebraska. The next week at Illinois, it seemed like everything was going wrong. The power went out in our hotel that morning, and since that affected the elevators, we couldn't use the meeting and dining rooms we had on the top floor because we didn't want the players climbing 25 flights of stairs. The whole day became an improvisation as we had our pregame meal in the lounge on the main floor. Since the kitchen could not fully function without power, our pre-game meal consisted of pizza and sodas.

We played the game in a cold mist which seemed to have the wind against us most of the time. We put together a horrible game plan defensively, and Illinois, with the crowd definitely behind them, staked itself to a 21-0 first-quarter lead and had scored 28 points by halftime. We rebounded with 14 points of our own in the first half, and we somehow overcame all the adversity to win on a late touchdown, 35-31. The pollsters might not have been impressed with the score, but that team showed a tremendous amount of character by not folding when it seemed like everything was going wrong.

Northwestern came to our place next, and although I thought our defense had been doing a decent job under the circumstances, Coach Paterno didn't agree, and he expressed his displeasure with me. It was easy to see he was frustrated and wanted to be number one. At the same time, Northwestern was beginning to put together a special team, and they showed flashes of it against us that day. We won, 45-17, but Northwestern showed they were a team that was tired of being the Big Ten doormat.

We closed the regular season with another wild one against Michigan State, but our offense once again put up some impressive numbers, and we won 59-31. Our first goal had been met. We were champions of the Big Ten in only our second season in the conference, and we would have our chance to play in the Rose Bowl.

We were successful the previous season by leaving before Christmas for the bowl site, so we did the same for our trip to California. This would be a very important game for us because we still had a definite possibility of winning the national championship. Nebraska was playing Miami in the Orange Bowl the night before we would play, so it seemed we would know our fate long before the Rose Bowl kickoff. We needed a Miami upset, but as hard as they played, Nebraska was just too strong, and they wore the Hurricanes down.

It was important to have our players in the right frame of mind and make it known they still had a definite chance to win the national championship. But any worry about how we would come out soon disappeared when Ki-Jana Carter darted through the line and raced 80 yards for a touchdown on our first offensive play of the game. We played a solid game and closed out an unforgettable 12-0 season with a 38-20 win over a stubborn Oregon team.

The Rose Bowl and its pageantry were a neat experience for all of us: coaches, players, and families. It finished a great run for Penn State as we had now won every major bowl game. Although we didn't officially get voted as national champions—that title, as we had expected, went to Nebraska—we had completed a very successful season, and everyone in that locker room considered themselves the true national champions.

There were many great games I have been involved in during my career at Penn State and many great young men who excelled as athletes as well as gentlemen. During their time at Penn State, these players were taught by some outstanding coaches who preached excellence not only on the field but also in the classroom. During my many years, I worked with these great coaches on a daily basis and saw them in ways the public never gets to see. They are memories I will never forget.

I spoke of J.T. White and his fiery and competitive nature, but I was also capable of showing my competitive side during several heated coaches' meetings. There were many times in that staff meeting room when I thought my competitiveness might get me thrown out the door, but there always seemed to be a mutual respect, and I think that's why we have always had one of the most consistent and successful coaching staffs.

It was my responsibility to draw up the weekly defensive packages with the other defensive coaches, and we then had to present it to Coach Paterno for his approval. At one meeting, we knew he wasn't going to accept anything we gave him because we had all been through a rough week. J.T. White was absent from the meeting and sure enough, Joe gave a thumbs down to our package. When J.T. returned, he asked how Joe liked the package, and I was honest with him and said: "He shot it down cold, J.T."

"What do you mean?" J.T. shot back. "That was a good package."

"You say that now, but you never speak up to the boss," I said, knowing it was pretty easy to get J.T. fired up. J.T. was at the next meeting and he didn't waste any time in speaking his mind.

"Okay, what about that new defensive package?" he asked to no one in particular. "You're too late, J.T.," Joe said without looking up from the table. "I already said I didn't like it. It's a dead issue."

"What do you mean it's a dead issue?" J.T. screamed back at him. "I didn't get to vote on it." Needless to say, that didn't impress Coach Paterno very much. He looked up and there was a nasty scowl on his face. His face was red with anger, and I could tell he had already had enough. He never said a word, but he slammed his fist on the table and stormed out of the meeting room.

We all looked at each other and broke into laughter when we saw the bewildered smirk on J.T.'s face. "Way to go, J," I finally said to him. "You done good. You almost got fired, but you done good."

We also liked to have fun with Joe Sarra because he was always so serious. He always calls Joe Paterno "Coach," and he agrees with everything the boss says. Any time there was a disagreement between Coach Paterno and myself, Joe Sarra sided with Coach Paterno. As I said, Joe Sarra is a workaholic and is very conscientious when it comes to his duties. We were in preseason practice one season, and, as is the custom at Penn State, we had a morning practice and then watched the videotapes of that practice afterward.

Joe Sarra went over to the coaches offices and got involved in some other work, and he forgot all about the video session. Later on I asked him: "Where were you after practice, Joe?" He said, "Aw geez, I forgot all about the meeting."

I knew I could have some fun with this, so I got into him a little further. "This could be interesting, Joe," I told him. "I know you didn't make the meeting, so from now on, who are you going to side with when Coach Paterno and I are arguing?" I told him if he didn't side with me, Coach Paterno would find out about the meeting he missed. At the full coaches meeting that afternoon, I thought I would continue to have some fun.

Joe Paterno was seated to my right, and Joe Sarra to my left. I purposely disagreed with Coach Paterno about something just to get the ball rolling, and after a while, I looked at Joe Sarra and said: "What do you think about it, Coach Sarra? Do you agree with me or Coach Paterno?"

Joe Sarra looked very nervous. He didn't know which way to turn, so finally he jumped up from his chair and put his arms out as though he were asking for forgiveness. "Coach Paterno, I have to confess," he shouted. "I missed a meeting this morning. I don't know how it happened, but I missed it." The other coaches and I were rolling on the floor with laughter, while poor Joe Sarra stood there with a look as though the world had been lifted from his shoulders.

I often went through weight gains and losses with Joe Sarra. He had lost around 25 pounds during the summer of our 1986 season, and when fall practice rolled around, he found he wasn't able to fit into his coaches pants. We were on the practice field throwing a football with some players, and I told Joe to run a deep pass route and if he caught a long bomb from me, practice would be over. He said okay, and off he went.

Joe had to reach, but he made the catch. There were some outsiders watching practice, people like parents and guests, and they watched with amusement as Joe ran his pass pattern. They saw him reach for the ball and catch it. And, although it was probably something they could have done without, the people also saw Joe lose his pants while making the catch. They were the same pants that were too big because he had lost so much weight. The spectacle had everyone in stitches except Coach Paterno, who simply shook his head and turned away.

Joe has been my roommate on the road for years, and we had a trip to Minnesota one season that I'll probably remember forever. They usually give us our room keys on the buses at the airport, and when we arrived in Minnesota, there were three keys waiting for us, one was for me and two had Joe Sarra's name, but one had a different room assignment. I switched his key without him knowing, thinking it would be fun to see his reaction when he realized he wasn't rooming with me.

I went to my own room, and soon there was a knock on the door. I was delivered room service, even though I didn't order it. I asked the waiter what all this was, and he was bringing me an alcohol tray. I didn't know how the mix-up occurred because an alcohol tray was about the furthest thing on the menu I would order. I told the waiter I wouldn't be needing it, but I asked him if he would deliver it to the room that I had sent Joe Sarra to. He agreed, and I realized things were going to get even better.

At about the same time, Joe Sarra was in his room wondering where I was as he sifted through the many pages of defensive notes he had stored in his briefcase. Joe was constantly going over plans with me, making sure we had all the right defensive calls for the next day's game and conjuring up new things we could try. He was probably waiting for me to arrive so he could reveal his latest plan when suddenly, he heard a flushing sound in the bathroom, and then the door opened.

Joe jumped up from the edge of the bed that he was sitting on as a woman stepped out of the bathroom. She was stunned as Joe fumbled for the right words to explain his presence. "I . . . I'm awfully sorry, ma'am," he said. "I must be in the wrong room. I don't know how this could have happened."

Before the woman could say anything, Joe swept his briefcase, his coat and everything else he had into his arms and was on his way out the door. He had just turned the corner when the waiter who had visited me with the alcohol tray stopped at the lady's door and said: "I have a gift for you from your favorite roommate." That was, of course, what I had asked the waiter to say when Joe answered the door. Now, this poor woman thought she had received an alcohol tray from some man in her room whom she had never seen before. It was quite an amusing experience that I'll never forget. Fortunately, Joe Sarra is a very good sport.

Our coaching staff has had many humorous occurrences on the field as well. Some came during practices and others during some of the most critical games of our season. One example was in 1977 when we were involved in one of our customary tough games against North Carolina State. We played them fairly regularly back then, and it seemed like all of the games would be decided in the last few minutes. This one would certainly be no different.

We put together our defensive plan a week or two before the game and presented it to Coach Paterno. He told us he liked everything in the plan but the all-out blitz with straight man-to-man pass coverage. "Well, Joe, I'm not crazy about it either, but we want to have something in there where we know we can get to the quarterback, and it won't be halfway."

"All right," he said. "But only if they're going to pass."

We scripted the plays and worked on everything in practice that week. At one point, I decided to go with a running play against that defense, and it went for a long gain. Joe walked beside me as we left the practice field and spoke with a rather stern voice: "What was that defense, Jerry?" he asked. I told him, and he reminded me that we had agreed it would be used only in a passing situation.

"Relax, Joe," I told him. "We just wanted to see what it looked like against the run."

We were in a tight game with N.C. State throughout the first half, which was fortunate considering that we hadn't played very well up to then. We started out much better in the second half by stopping them on their first three offensive series. We had a slight lead and during their fourth series, we had them third-and-10. I felt the time was right to go after the quarterback, so I called the all-out blitz that Joe didn't very much care for. Sure enough, N.C. State ran the same play we ran in practice. Ted Brown was their outstanding running back at the time, and he didn't disappoint the hometown fans as he ran 76 yards for a touchdown. I missed the last 20 yards of it because I had my head ducked down in the press box.

I was hooked up to Jim Williams' headset from up there, and when I looked down at the field, I saw Coach Paterno charging hard in Jim's direction. "Don't you tell him what that play was," I said to Jim, but I already knew he didn't have to. The N.C. State crowd was going crazy and so was Joe.

Fortunately for us, Chuck Fusina, our junior quarterback, threw a touchdown pass to Scott Fitzkee with 40 seconds left and we won. I ran straight down to the field when it was over and grabbed Chuck Fusina. "Chuck, that was a great game," I yelled to him. "You may think you won it for your teammates, but you won it for me!" Chuck gave me a strange look, but he shrugged off my babbling as though it was something he was used to, which he probably was. The Temple game I mentioned earlier was the reason I was hired as defensive coordinator, but Chuck Fusina was the reason I kept my job there.

The very next season, we were undefeated going into our game at West Virginia, and we had the top-ranked defense in the country. West Virginia was 1-6 at the time, and I made a statement to the other coaches that week that we were just going to play our basic defense that game and shut them out. The first time West Virginia had the ball, I called that one defense, and they marched right down the field and scored. I got stubborn at that point and called it again during the Mountaineers' next possession. And once again, they moved down the field with relative ease to make it 14-0.

They were charged up, and after stopping us on offense, West Virginia regained possession with the idea of putting us away. I remained stubborn, and their first play went for a long gain. Now I could hear the boss screaming through Jim Williams' field phone. "Tell Jerry I don't like that defense," he said to Jim, but I didn't need the relay. "Tell him I don't like it either!" I barked right back.

I finally got over my stubbornness and decided to change the defense. We shut them down the rest of the way, and our offense scored 49 unanswered points as we continued our march to that year's Sugar Bowl.

In 1985, we traveled to Syracuse with an undefeated team. The Carrier Dome is always a tough place to play and the crowd can get unbelievably loud in there, especially when Syracuse presents itself as a tough opponent, which was usually the case against Penn State. The Orangemen scored two of their touchdowns in the game on blitzes that I had called, and now that I was stationed down on the sidelines, I could see Joe's fury up close. His mouth was moving after the second touchdown, but he wasn't saying anything. We rallied to win that game also, and afterwards, I tried to get an idea of Coach Paterno's mood.

"You didn't like those defensive calls, did you?" I asked him. "No," he answered. "I wanted to punch you right in the nose."

"You know, Joe, of all the people around here to punch me in the nose, you'd be the one I'd want to do it. You'd probably be the only one I can handle in this room." It took about three-and-a-half hours, but I finally got a smile out of him.

At the end of that season, we were playing at Pittsburgh, and it was a nervous day for Joe Paterno because he always got keyed up for games against Pitt. We were playing well and had built a 24-0 lead or so by the end of the third quarter. Ron Dickerson was our secondary coach at the time, and he decided to send in our second-team secondary to give them some playing time. Joe saw this and started screaming at Jim Williams because he felt our lead might not be safe enough, and he didn't want to give Pitt any momentum.

Jim got a little bit flustered with Joe's anger, and he signaled in the wrong defensive play. I went over to him and pointed out the error and asked what he was doing. In the meantime, Joe came rumbling down the sideline screaming: "What's the matter with you guys? Don't you want to win this game?"

"Yes, we want to win this game," I hollered back. "What do you think we're here for?"

While all this was going on, there were no defenses being called from the sidelines, and Pitt was moving the ball down the field. Matt Johnson, one of our defensive linemen on the sidelines, casually walked over to me and said, "Oh, so this is how grown-ups are supposed to act?" Trey Bauer was our starting inside linebacker, and he came over to me, handed me his helmet and asked if I would like to try using it.

"Yeah," I shouted rather smartly. "And I can probably do a better job with it than you did."

Life on the sidelines is always an adventure. We try to concentrate and keep our poise, but there are definitely times when it doesn't always work out that way. Sometimes, even the best laid plans can end in sheer chaos. With me around, they often did.

But the bottom line is, we tried to make drills as competitive as possible while trying to make football a fun experience. Not that there wasn't any hard work or tough conditions, but we, as coaches, had a lot of give-and-take with the players. I always felt if it isn't fun, then it really isn't worth doing.

I have spoken quite often of the high-profile names who have played in the Penn State football program at one time or another, and I remember those times with great affection. But there are people associated with any football team who share an equally important role with the team's success, even though their efforts are often overlooked. These unknown heroes are the not-so-gifted athletes who wear their hearts on their sleeves. They are the individuals who play such instrumental roles in making the stars what they are, while at the same time helping the Penn State program to stay at such a high level of success year in and year out.

They are the walk-ons—the young men who audition for football tryouts every year with very little hope of ever obtaining a scholarship. They aspire to earn one, but if it doesn't happen, they still very often leave the program with an equal amount of pride in their efforts and the assurance they did their part for us. I remember these young men as much anyone I've ever been associated with at Penn State.

One player who has always stuck in my mind is a young man named Carlos Quirch. Carlos was a hard worker and a feisty competitor from the South Florida area, and he always had a smile on his face. I called him "The Hammer," which was the nickname Jack Ham had during his playing days. One day I said to him: "Carlos, you're the *real* 'Hammer.'"

Carlos' best friend on the team, and another walk-on, was Jim Restauri. Jim was a boxer and worked on his skills whenever he could. Carlos referred to Jimmy as "The Champ" and their friendship was inseparable. Those two mixed well together as friends and teammates, and they are still close friends today. It has been over 20 years since they played in the Penn State football program, but Carlos and Jimmy still keep in touch with me whenever possible.

It takes a special type of person to be a walk-on football player. There are no crowds watching when they show what they can do. Only a few coaches who are looking for bodies to fill the spaces needed in practice so the starters will have enough opposition to run the plays against. Some walk-ons are young men who were right on the border in the recruiting process. They might have been one or two spots away from a scholarship offer but just not quite what we as a coaching staff were looking for.

Coaches run across this dilemma every year, and the best advice we can give is to let these players know they would be welcomed as walk-ons at Penn State, but they might be better suited either at other Division I schools or even on the Division II level. Some choose those routes, while others elect to seek their initial goal of wearing the blue and white Penn State uniform.

Other walk-ons come to tryouts during spring football practices, and most times, their chances are very, very slim of finding a place on the roster. But they show their grit, and every once in a while, you find that one special person who makes his point that he belongs. One such player was a young man named Brad Pantall, who came to spring practice in 1993 knowing we needed a long-snapper. Brad showed what he could do in snapping the ball back to our punters and holders, and he turned that specialty into an eventual scholarship and himself into a three-year letterman.

The dream of running through that Beaver Stadium tunnel on an autumn Saturday afternoon was on every young Penn State fan's mind as he grew up, but for those who joined the team as walk-on players, it would prove to be doubly gratifying. For the starters and other regulars, stepping onto that field in the dark blue jersey becomes a weekly routine, but a walk-on might get literally one such opportunity in four years.

One player who had such dreams was a young man named Tom Durant. Tom became close to our family—so close in fact, that we considered him to be just that. He joined in quite a few of our family adventures, and I could see in his eyes how much he wanted that opportunity to play in Beaver Stadium.

Tom was a competitor, much like me, and we used to compete against each other all the time in everything. I am a pretty good swimmer, so one time, I challenged Tom to see who could swim from one side of the pool to the other in the fastest time—underwater. With a wink of my eye, I asked someone to stand on the other side to make sure Tom touched the wall and didn't cheat. As Tom got closer, the spotter was counting down the number of strokes Tom had left before he got to the wall. Just as Tom neared the wall, the spotter put his hands to his head in dismay. I had forgotten that Tom wore contact lenses and he couldn't open his eyes underwater. He bumped his head on the wall before anyone could stop him and ended up with a slight concussion. I'm lucky he is still my friend after that experience, but I was even more proud and happy when I got to see Tom run through that tunnel and play on the field he had dreamed about ever since he had started at Penn State.

I had an equal amount of fun with so many of the equipment managers who have come through the Penn State football program. Make no mistake, these guys work just as hard as any of the players and don't receive the notoriety they truly deserve. Tim Shope is the head equipment manager who, as I said much earlier, has to be tough in his position so no one ever thinks about taking advantage of him. Brad Caldwell is Shopey's assistant who started as a student manager with us in 1983 and has been there ever since. They work together about as well as any pair I've ever seen, and they make sure that we are equipped with some of the best student managers around.

I think Shopey will probably be glad about my retirement because he is the one I went to when I needed an extra sideline pass or something that I would absentmindedly leave behind on road trips. And Spider, as we affectionately called Brad Caldwell, was the guy I talked to when no on else wanted to listen. He probably didn't want to either, but he did because he is as loyal as they come.

We once had a student manager named Glenn, who was a dwarf. Glenn was small, but he did so much for everybody. He was a good-natured young man—well capable of putting up with the hard times I often gave him. The managers always used to set up orange juice for the players after practices, and I used to say I always knew when Glenn did it because the juice was set up on the lower part of the lockers.

Glenn also liked to wrestle, and he competed in Penn State's intramural sports program. When he won his first match, I immediately started teasing him in the locker room, saying his opponent was trying to go for a single-leg takedown but got a headlock instead.

My words might look cruel on paper, but Glenn took everything the way it was intended, which was obviously in a good-natured manner. He truly enjoyed the attention. Glenn wanted to be a part of the football team so much, I was very happy to see him enjoy himself. He was a special individual at Penn State, and I was even more happy to see him go on to become a physical therapist.

Another student manager I will always remember is a young man named Rick. He was deaf, but he, like so many others I had come in contact with at Penn State, overcame his disability and lived out his dream. Rick was as good-natured as anyone, and I often teased him to keep him smiling like the others. There were other times, however, where it might have looked like I was teasing him, but in reality I was forgetting the situation. For example, I yelled at him sometimes in practice because I wanted him to move the ball to a different spot, but of course he couldn't hear me, and naturally, I wasn't thinking about his impairment. I often covered my embarrassment with a smile, though, and when I had his attention I would ask him: "What's the matter, can't you hear?" Rick would just smile back and wave his arm at me, as if shooing me away. Rick was a very committed person in whatever he did and I will always remember him.

After 32 years and many unusual occurrences, I will carry many great memories with me. Memories of players; of coaches; of family and friends. Through it all, I've enjoyed myself while trying to be different. I've tried to be human and tough — both at the same time. I've enjoyed being around the young people, and I will have many fond memories of the accomplishments they have achieved.

17

Decisions

THE THOUGHTS RACED THROUGH MY HEAD probably too many times to be counted. It was always one of those occasions where I was forced to weigh the pros and cons, just like anyone else who seemed to have the weight of the world on his shoulders. On one side would be the great home life my family and I had created in State College, while the other side was offering opportunities that every assistant coach ultimately dreams about in almost every sport.

There were a number of times when I had to consider leaving Penn State. From graduate school, right up to a couple of years before my retirement, I struggled with those decisions. At one time, I was a young man who needed to explore the coaching world. I needed to make my mark somewhere else, not really sure whether I would ever come back to my alma mater. Then, after spending more than a quarter of a century at the place I loved to call home, I found myself having to consider leaving for perhaps that one chance to be a head football coach.

I had quite a few interviews when I left Penn State from grad school. I'll always remember the interview at Boston. The man asked me what I could do for Boston University, and I said: "What do you want done?" That's how confident I was in going there, but at the same time, I knew I would be in a whole new world. I was from a small town heading for my first time on my own in the big city. I knew it was going to be a real eye-opener.

The administration that interviewed me took me to Jimmy's Harbor Site, an exclusive seafood restaurant. The menu was written in French, but I didn't want to look stupid. The meals were numbered, so when the waiter looked my way, I cooly pointed at one of the numbers to make my choice. I was squirming in my seat as they brought the food to our table because I really didn't know what I would be getting, never mind that I wasn't even sure *how* to go about eating it.

Finally, I looked at one of the coaches I was with and said: "You know, Coach, I've tried to impress you guys long enough. Could you tell me how to eat this stuff, and better yet, what is it that I'm eating?" The coach laughed and said: "Well, you can take the man out Washington, Pennsylvania, but you can't take the Washington, Pennsylvania, out of the man."

I've already described my coaching career at Boston, along with the experience I had at Juniata College before it. I returned to Penn State as a full-time assistant after Boston University, and I stayed there for the rest of my career. But those years did not go by without difficult choices, not to mention an occasional tug at my heartstrings.

In the early 1970s, I came very close to taking the head coaching position at Marshall University in Huntington, West Virginia. I was in my late-20s, and Joe McMullen, who had coached me at Penn State, asked me to come in for an interview. Penn State was preparing to play in the Cotton Bowl against Baylor at the time, so I pretty much just had the weekend to make a decision. I was on and off the phone all weekend, trying to decide. I went to church on that Sunday and thought some more about it. I had told the people at Marshall I wouldn't be back down there unless I decided to accept the job. Well, that same afternoon, I called Joe McMullen and told him I was coming down. They were happy and said they would start setting things up, such as reservations and announcements.

At the same time, we had a young foster child whose name was Christopher staying with us, and after I had given the news to Joe McMullen, I spotted Christopher at the bottom of the stairs. He had a ball in his hands, and as he looked at me, he said, "P'ay ball! P'ay ball!" He had never really said that to me before, but there he was urging me to join him at that moment.

Christopher threw me the ball, and as I tossed it back, I came to the realization that we wouldn't be able to take him with us. He would eventually return to his home, but at that time, I wasn't feeling very good about myself. I played with him a little more, and then I went outside to where our other kids were sled-riding. They were having a great time with the other kids in our neighborhood, and I suddenly felt that sinking feeling inside me drop just a little bit further. As I studied the neighborhood and my own backyard, I excused myself from a conversation with my neighbor and hurried back inside.

"I'm sorry, Joe," I said to the voice on the other end of the phone. I think Joe McMullen had a feeling I might change my mind because he knew how attached I was to State College. "I'm going to stay at Penn State after all." Seeing Christopher at that moment kind of told me all I needed to know. Maybe the opportunity would present itself again at some point; maybe it wouldn't. But a little boy helped me see that it just wasn't right at that time.

I did get other opportunities throughout the years, including interviews with Boston College and North Carolina. I met with the North Carolina athletic director at the Waldorf-Astoria Hotel in New York City, but it took a lot of effort to get there. I was staying overnight in Hasbrouck Heights, New Jersey, and I wanted to make sure I allowed myself enough time to get to the interview, which was scheduled for 11 a.m. the next day.

I asked a guy at the front desk of the hotel where I was staying how much time he felt I should give myself, and he said about an hour would do it. I decided to leave myself two hours, and it turned out to be a good thing. When I got into New York City, I had little trouble finding the street the hotel was on. I wasn't sure which direction I should go, so I decided to turn right. That was probably my first mistake. I found the number address of the hotel, but there was no hotel there. Driving in New York City is bad enough, but when you don't know where you're going, it's three times worse. I turned down a side street, but I got boxed in by a bunch of taxi cabs.

I was stuck for a while, but I finally got out. I parked for a moment and looked for a telephone. When I finally found one, there was a man and a woman who were arguing right next to the phone and it appeared they were both nurturing a good drunk. I asked if I could use the phone and then they started yelling at me. I argued for a moment and finally thought better of doing such a thing in a strange place. I got to make my call, and the hotel operator confirmed the number on the address. Finally, a passerby—and one of the few helpful people I came across that day in Manhattan—straightened me out with the numbers, and it appeared I was on my way.

I came to a choice of either an up ramp or a down ramp, and, simply put, I chose the down ramp and made the wrong choice. I came to a dead end. It was now either a left or a right, so I decided to follow a taxi that had turned left. I went no more than 30 yards before a policeman came seemingly out of nowhere and pulled me over. He sidled up to my car and said: " You made a left turn back there."

"Yeah, I guess I did," I answered.

"You *can't* turn left there," he continued with a dead stare on his face.

I thought I had a legitimate response. "Why not? I was just following that taxi."

"If you'd just look at the sign, buddy, you would see that it says cabs and busses can turn left—cars can't."

I guess I couldn't argue with what the policeman had to say, but I hoped he would listen to my dilemma. I told him my story of how I was from out of town and how I got lost, and then he said: "Well, buddy, I'm gonna have to give you a ticket."

"For what?" I asked him, finding myself just a little bit more upset with the whole thing.

"For making an illegal left turn," the obnoxious officer answered.

I pleaded with him some more: "But officer, I just told you I'm from out of town and I'm lost. Can't you cut me a break?"

"No, I can't," he said quite calmly and assuredly.

"New York's Finest!" I thought to myself as I watched him write the ticket. Time was running scarce for me by now, but I finally made it to the Waldorf-Astoria parking garage at just 10 minutes before 11. I thought I had made it on time for my interview, but that would have been too easy.

"You can't park your car in this garage," the young, snotty parking attendant said to me.

"Why, is this garage only for cabs and busses?"

I didn't expect him to understand why I was being so sarcastic. He was probably used to far worse. I thought of telling him my true feelings of New York and New Yorkers at that moment, but diplomacy prevailed as I realized I was still not out of the woods. Instead, I tried to appeal to the slim chance that someone in New York would have a heart.

"Look," I continued with a calmer attitude. "I'm late for a very important meeting, and I'm not from around this area. Couldn't you cut me a break and let me park here for a couple hours?"

I was hoping that just maybe I could appeal to this man, but I should have known better.

"You park your car here, buddy, and it'll be towed away." His stare was as cold as his words. "There are public garages all along here. Use one of them."

Right then I wondered how any of these people could have the nerve to call someone, "Buddy."

I drove around a little longer and finally found one of those "public" garages the parking attendant spoke of. It was about five blocks away, and I paid $18 for less than a two-hour stay. I guess everything that happened that day should have served as omen as far as my fortunes for the North Carolina job, which turned out to be bad.

Another opportunity that left me with an extremely difficult decision was the coaching offer I received from Temple University in Philadelphia. A part of me was attracted to Temple from the standpoint that it certainly would have been a challenge due to the school's previous shortcomings on the football field. It was the late 1980s, and Temple hadn't had a winning season for a long, long time. I was also attracted because it was a university that was founded for the common person. That has always been a special interest of mine because of my family background and growing up in the setting that I did. There was a great variety of people around the Temple campus.

I visited Temple and I became very impressed with the people who interviewed me. The university president was a unique individual. He had a good rapport with everyone at the university, including the janitors. I noticed that no matter what someone's position was, this man had a kind word and a good relationship with them. I was a little bit nervous and anxious to meet him, but he immediately made me feel right at home. I became attracted to his personality because he seemed like an eccentric person, and I liked that quality about him.

He did most of the talking while he rocked in his chair. It sounded like they really wanted me for the job. We went to dinner at a restaurant that was very common. It was well-suited for the type of person I was. During the interview, I was talking about how Temple needed something with impact. I felt probably the biggest impact to come out of Temple was Bill Cosby, the great comedian who has been in show business for as long as I can remember. Bill Cosby is a Temple graduate, and no matter where he is or has been, he has always shown a tremendous amount of interest in his alma mater.

I finished my interview and other business with everyone and went home. The very next day, I got a call from the Temple athletic director. He wanted to follow up and let me know that he thought everything went well. Then I talked to the university president, and he kind of said a lot of the same things. But before he let me go, he said: "Wait a minute, Jerry, I have someone else here who wants to talk to you." It was Bill Cosby, himself.

I couldn't believe my ears, but it was really him. We talked for a while about some of the problems at Temple and the possible solutions. He did his best to sell me on the idea of Temple University and Philadelphia, and I told him how my daughter, Kara, had simply idolized him. She watched *The Cosby Show* all the time. It was the No. 1 show on television at that time, and she couldn't get enough of his humor. He asked me if it would be okay to speak with Kara, and she was immediately skeptical that it was really him on the phone.

He told her he would like her to come to New York City and be his guest on the set of the show, and then he would take her out to dinner. Kara was somewhat skeptical whether all of this would actually take place and she just kept nodding her head, saying: "Uh-huh. Uh-huh..." When I got back on the phone, Bill Cosby said to me: "Congratulations. You're really going to enjoy it at Temple University."

I spoke with the athletic director again, and I told him I would have to think everything over and that there would probably be more questions. I vacillated for a number of days, and finally, Dottie accompanied me to Philadelphia with the thoughts and intentions of accepting the position. Then, sometime during the next day, when it was expected I would accept the Temple offer, I turned it down. I just decided I couldn't leave the things that were so near and dear to me: "The Second Mile, Penn State football, and the State College atmosphere that I had thought was so much like my hometown when I had first arrived on campus as a raw freshman.

The Temple athletic director said something to me before I had made my decision that was probably meant to entice me, but instead, it probably deterred me. "There are only two things we want you to accomplish here," he told me. "One is to help Temple get to the Sugar Bowl, and the other is to help us beat Penn State."

When he said those words, they echoed in my ears like something I had never possibly imagined thinking about. Somehow, that notion just didn't register in my mind. *"Beat Penn State."* The place that I loved; the place that I had grown so close to, with so many people over so many years. I was flattered that the university president had so much faith in me and that the athletic director wanted me for the job, but fate had somehow intervened again. The thought of leaving Penn State died when he uttered those words.

One of the other reasons I stayed at Penn State over the years is the community. It's a small community with a large, state university in a small-town atmosphere. It's a very natural area in the Nittany Valley surrounded by the beautiful, scenic mountains. More than anything, it was the people. Being a small town, you would think everyone knew everyone else.

In 1991, before the Notre Dame game, I took my family and one of the Second Mile kids to the local Wendy's. I was paying at the counter when the young gentleman at the cash register asked me if I was "up for the game?" I figured he knew I was a coach, and he was just trying to talk shop with me. "Well, it's really not that important if *I'm* up for the game," I told him, "but I guess I am."

The kid seemed confused as he wondered what the heck I was talking about. "Where did you come from?" he asked.

"I'm a local."

I think I lost him more and more as the conversation went on. "Do you get up for all the games?" he asked me.

As usual, I was now having fun. "Well," I said. "I get up for all the games, but I guess I have missed a few. Like the ones we were blown out in." I walked away from the counter with a smile on my face, knowing I had thoroughly confused that kid, and I probably made him wonder whether he should ever converse with the customers again.

I'll always remember the great people I've met in State College. When we came back there to live, I saw a small community come together to help a young person who had been severely burned in an accident. I saw a phenomenal amount of money raised for that child and his family, and that really impressed me.

My family and I have been involved with the same church in State College ever since Nelson Frank, the minister of the church and kind of a pastor for the football team, walked up the three flights of stairs at our apartment house when I was in graduate school. Nelson asked Dottie and me if we would like to join the church, and from that point on, we've developed very significant relationships and made so many friends. Dottie and I have remained very active in the church (Dottie more so than me, I have to admit). We've been youth group leaders and have had picnics with other families.

We, as a family, have also enjoyed outings with kids from the Second Mile' and we've joined all of our neighbors every year in going around the area to sing Christmas carols. We've also had an occasional July 4th parade in our neighborhood, complete with costumes and the whole works, including me carrying a baton around as though I were the best drum major in existence.

In State College, it is easy to make great friendships, and that's exactly what I have done over the years. I like to have fun, as has already been stated, and I often go to some great extremes with certain people in order to have that fun. One man in particular is Jim Thompson. Jim was an outstanding athlete at the University of Buffalo in basketball and track and field. He and I played a lot of racquetball together, and he taught sports history at Penn State. I used to tell him the reason he majored in sports history was because he lived in the past all the time, relative to his athletic career.

I read in the local newspaper once that Jim was on the search committee for the women's basketball coaching position at Penn State. I told my wife to place a person-to-person call to Dr. Jim Thompson. She said it was a call from Dr. Ken Bell. I got on the phone and told Jim I was the head basketball coach at Furman University in Greenville, South Carolina. He seemed excited as he fumbled for a pen and some paper, and he asked me if I could spell the name for him. I looked into the receiver of my phone rather quizzically and finally said: "B-E-L-L." I almost called him a stooge at the end of that spelling lesson, but I held it back.

He then asked me if I could tell him about the women's program at Furman and I said, "Well, Dr. Thompson, I'm appalled because I can't believe you don't know of the success that we've enjoyed in women's basketball here at Furman. I'm really disappointed in you."

Jim was very quick to apologize. "I'm sorry," he said in a somewhat shaken voice. "But I spend most of my time in academia and doing research." That one almost made me crack up with laughter.

"Well, Dr. Thompson," I continued. "I want you to know I've followed your athletic career, and I know that you played basketball at the University of Buffalo."

"Yes, yes, I did," Jim replied. I could just picture his chest sticking out with pride. I decided to carry it a little further. "In fact, I went to Canisius College in New York, and I used to see you play in person. I was amazed at your abilities."

He was beaming at this point, I just knew it. Finally, I couldn't take it anymore, so I decided to slowly let him in on my prank. "Didn't you play on the 1919 team?"

"No, no," he said rather dejectedly. "I'm afraid I'm not that old." I almost burst into laughter as I thought of his Jim's bubble bursting around him. Finally, I revealed my true identity. "Yes, you are that old, and you've been had by old Jer, buddy." Jim took the gag in a good-natured manner, as both of us often do in such situations, but I knew it would be just a matter of time before he would make his attempt at retribution.

It took Jim only about three months to put his own plan into works. I got a phone call from Ron Pavlechko, the head football coach at State College High School. He said there was an English teacher at the school who wanted me to show her class around Recreation Hall and the other athletic facilities. I told him it would be fine, but I would have to wait until later in the spring and so we set it up for then.

On the day before this tour was scheduled, a lady called me and said: "May I speak to Professor Sandusky, please?" I ate up the "professor" part, as I'm sure Jim would have known, and said: "This is Professor Sandusky."

"I want you to know that we no longer want you to show our English class around the facilities," the woman said. "We want someone with a more reputable character." With that, the lady hung up rather briskly.

It startled me, but I actually suspected Jim Thompson might have put this lady up to the phone call because he might have been at the school evaluating the student teachers. Therefore, I figured the tour was still on. I prepared everything in a well-organized fashion for the next day, and I bragged to the other football coaches that this class wanted *me* to show them around—not just anyone. I walked out to the bleachers of the basketball arena where I was supposed to meet the class, and I waited about 10 minutes. No one came, but I didn't panic. Perhaps they got tied up, I surmised. Ten more minutes went by and still no class.

Finally, Jim Thompson strolled around the corner, and I beamed with pride. "Jim, it's great that you showed up because you're going to be witness to the greatest lecture ever. You might even learn something."

"Oh, really?" he said. His face was like a stone pillar. "That'll be great. I can't wait to hear it." We sat and talked for a while and the longer this went on without interruption, the more I realized how sweet payback must have been for him. I finally spoke the inevitable.

"Jim, there is no English class, is there?"

His look of sheer delight gave me my answer. "Jer, my friend," he said with a gloating look on his face. "You're right, there is no English class, and the score is now one to one."

Jim and I went on and on trying to one-up each other over the years, always thinking we had successfully put in the last shot, but knowing the other guy would no doubt have some kind of answer.

The community of State College is a place where people have class and a place where I have always been able to be myself. I've been around great athletic programs that have a certain charisma. People like Gene

Wettstone, the Penn State men's gymnastics coach. The great Penn State wrestling programs with Charlie Speidel, Bill Koll and Rich Lorenzo.

The bottom line is, when you're associated with a community, a university and an athletic program that exemplifies class, it all adds up to a tremendous amount of reasons why it is so very difficult to leave that kind of situation.

18

A Dream

My career in football had gone far beyond what I had ever believed possible. I can say that now, as I ponder what follows after my retirement from the coaching ranks at Penn State. But I had those feelings long ago—long before I ever had thoughts of retirement. I loved football as much as ever, but I also knew I wanted to do more with my life than just coach football. I was happy beyond my wildest dreams to be known as a Penn State football coach, but I wanted my life to be remembered for something else. I wanted to do something similar to what my parents did in that recreation center when I was a kid; how they reached out and extended themselves to so many people.

I never understood why some of the kids that I saw pass through those doors of the rec center never really had a chance. They never had the same opportunities as people who came from stable, loving families. I didn't understand why everyone didn't have the same opportunities that I did, and it bothered me.

I enjoyed young people—being around their enthusiasm, their love of life as well as their honesty and openness. While in State College, I became involved in a program called an "attention home." My involvement included fund-raising, but philosophically, I differed with this program's approach because I thought they were providing a lot of theory, but they left out a lot of substance in terms of discipline, true love and caring. I didn't think they gave the guidance that was necessary for the young people to change. Not that my answer was any better than theirs, but that was just my feeling at the time.

I also sponsored a Puerto Rican youngster from a home for boys at our football camp. I thought my yearning to help children could be fulfilled in that manner. The boy stayed in the dorm with some of the other campers, and I learned later on that he had been through a pretty rough time there. He put up with a lot of teasing and embarrassment from some of the other kids, but I never knew it or realized it. When he went back to the home, he became very emotional and cried quite a bit about getting teased. The man in charge of the home called me and was really kind of tough on me. I was hurt and disappointed with myself for not noticing this boy's difficult moments at camp, but I was also disappointed that this guy who called me would show me such hostile feelings, when all I was trying to do was help an unfortunate youngster.

I still wanted to do more. I had another dream —a dream to write about linebackers, which was my specialty when it came to coaching football. I wanted to see this idea through and dedicate the project to my parents. As I began my writing, I thought of the idea of building a home for kids; a program where we could provide the home and a family for kids who don't have families. I was very eager to get that program started, and the linebacker book initiated the idea. It would have been difficult to do such a thing at another university, but Penn State football was secure enough that the program was willing to put up with what I was trying to do.

I wrote the linebackers book, and after it was turned down by one publishing company, we decided to print it and publish it ourselves. The publishing company turned the idea down because they said it was "too narrow in scope." But I went forward with my writing efforts more determined than ever, while Dottie and my mother addressed and mailed fliers. We promoted the book in the beginning and sold it on our own. Our goal was to raise enough money to maybe hire an executive director to start the fledgling program we had dreamed about, then let them run with it until we could build the home we had dreamed of for kids.

Needless to say, I was naive about such things, and, I guess if I had really thought about things and analyzed them, there would have been little hope of ever getting things started. But we did get it going, and as naive as we were, we were determined to keep things going.

19

The Second Mile

THE NAME CAME TO ME while I was talking with some of our football players in the locker room. I had shared my dream with them along with some of my ideas, and I had just heard a sermon in church about going the extra mile; doing a little bit extra. I said: "You know, this is what we're trying to do for these kids. We're not going to *give* them anything, but our goal is to provide them with another chance; another start; an extra mile." And that's when the name came to me.

We discussed it there in the locker room, and that's when it stuck. I had a bit of a start, at least as far as the name was concerned, and my next step was to become incorporated as a nonprofit organization. With some legal assistance, that step was somewhat easy. Now we had the linebacker book, and I learned about getting a tax exemption for mailing the fliers at a very reasonable rate with a bulk mailing permit.

I checked on getting a tax exemption by contacting the Internal Revenue Service, and they sent me a number of forms to fill out. They wanted information such as: board of directors, budgets, projected budgets, the number of kids we were serving, and programs. We were just starting out, so we had answers for practically none of those questions. All we knew was that we wanted to move forward. I started to hand write some of the answers to the questions the IRS was seeking, and I told some of my friends and neighbors: "In case you're asked, you *are* on the board of directors for the Second Mile."

The IRS wrote back with more questions, I answered them, and eventually, a guy from the IRS called me at the football office. I'll never forget the way he first came across to me. I realized he was just doing his job, but I was becoming very impatient with the way they were dealing with us—question after question, which seemed to lead to nothing but doubt in their collective eyes.

"What are you trying to do?" this man asked in what seemed like the rudest manner possible. Needless to say, I wasn't in a very good mood at the time, and his cockiness seemed to only make that mood worse.

"What do you mean?" I shot back in an instant. I didn't give him a chance to say anything further. "All we're trying to do is help some young people. We're just starting; we're just learning the things we have to do. We don't have budgets. We don't have all these things you're asking for. Why don't you just give us the tax exemption?"

The man who tried to do the intimidating in the beginning now seemed taken aback by my words of challenge and, perhaps, desperation. I did not intend to be so terse with him, but in reality, whatever I said seemed to get us better results. The man became very helpful and polite. He suggested that we at least get an accountant to help with some of the procedures we had been going through. I agreed to that, and it wasn't long after until we were allowed to send out a few fliers for the word to start getting around.

We were able to raise some money, but we knew we still had a long way to go. Things were being taken care of one step at a time, and the next thing we had to do was put together a board of directors. In the first official meeting that we held, Dr. John Reidell, a local surgeon in State College, volunteered through one of his friends to become involved. John was one of the board members, and he was president of the Second Mile for close to 10 years. Bruce Heim, a real estate person in State College, was another early member, and Bob Poole is the current president.

There were friends from church, and Charlie Lupton, who was in charge of development at Penn State, also came up with some ideas about raising money. Charlie was another person who got involved at the very beginning, when opportunity for success for the Second Mile seemed at its lowest. John Reidell gave us an early contribution of $1,000 to help get things started. That, along with the money from the sale of the linebackers book, helped us get the project at least partially off the ground.

This newly formed board of directors and I developed a three-year plan with a goal to build a home for kids. We hired an executive director, whose name was Ron Coder. Ron was a retired serviceman who was a good friend of Penn State football and a great person. Working together, we bonded well as a group, and we were able to develop some interesting times. We also met up with a man named Cal Zimmerman, who was a construction person in State College. Cal, along with Fred Fernsler, who was a local architect, became early leaders in the building of the home.

Others came together to help as the days and weeks transpired. There was Dave Wilson, from the college of business, and Earl Strong, who was associate dean of the college of business. Many other very influential people from the university and the community joined us, and my dream slowly started to transpire right before my very eyes.

It wasn't always smooth sailing, but we had fun. We pecked away through the seemingly impossible days, and we muddled through many fund-raising efforts. I remember once visiting a very wealthy person from State College. It wasn't something I enjoyed doing, canvassing for money, but it was one of the only ways we would be able to get our dream off the ground. I was so nervous as I gave my sales pitch to this man, and I felt as though I did such a lousy job. I think that was the *only* reason he gave me a small donation, something like $50. Maybe he felt sorry for me and not for our efforts, I don't know. I'm convinced, though, that if I hadn't done such a lousy job in my approach, the man probably would never have donated a penny. So, I had to hope I could do as many lousy jobs as possible.

There were many times of watching very influential people turn their heads away, and listening to people make promises that were never fulfilled. We also had to make several difficult decisions on whether to accept certain donations. A Penn State fraternity hosts an annual event called The Phi Psi 500. It is a traditional race through the streets of State College, and the students always have a lot of fun with it. The down side to us, however, was the fact that beer and drinking played an important role to the participants and volunteers involved in the race. We had qualms about accepting a donation from the event because I didn't want the same kids we were reaching out to, as well as the others who were supporting our efforts, to feel that we would condone the consumption of alcohol that was related to this event. I personally rejected the money one year, but after that, we began to accept it because we looked at every donation as the start of our dream home. We realized that those students were genuine people who simply wanted to do something for our organization. Their donations came at a very significant time for us.

I remember meeting with Bob Kirby, the president of Westinghouse Corporation at the time. Bob came forward and helped us raise over $10,000 toward the beginning of the home. Some other fund-raising experiences included selling programs for a prison run-a-thon with a man named John Sheridan, a Penn State guidance counselor. John and I started at about the same level in terms of knowledge and organization of fund-raising activities. We had hoped to raise money by selling programs from the back of his truck at the Big 33 football game in Altoona, Pennsylvania, but in the long run, it cost us more money than we made getting involved with that program. It was just one part of the old adage "live and learn."

One of my own brainstorms was a notion I called "Kids for Kids," where we had the kids go out and canvas from door to door to try and raise money, but that flopped. People are always apprehensive to literally open their front doors to charity, no matter how genuine the cause might be.

Then came the idea of a golf outing. We thought something like that could work because we had the unique situation of being involved with Penn State football, which could attract celebrities. We put together an outstanding group of celebrities that first year in 1981, including Dick Vermeil, who had coached the Philadelphia Eagles to the Super Bowl the previous season and would later return to the pro football coaching ranks to lead the St. Louis Rams to a Super Bowl championship in 1999.

We also had Matt Millen, who played for the victorious Oakland Raiders in that 1981 Super Bowl against the Eagles and was a former Penn State defensive star. We had several former players and coaches join us for the outing. We had the golf outing in the spring of 1981 after putting it together with very short notice that winter. It became a struggle, and we were about ready to drop the whole idea because we hadn't secured enough participants to join the celebrities.

Then came a call from a friend of the Second Mile, Harry Sickler. Harry paid enough money to bring about 10 to 15 of the local high school golfers—and himself—and as a result of his generosity, we were able to go through with our first Second Mile golf outing. The outing grew from that point on and got a little bit better each year.

So many fun times developed every year, and we had one particular occasion in the spring of 1984 when the great comedian, Bob Hope, visited the Penn State campus to do a special show for the benefit of the Second Mile. That was a great honor and a special thrill for everyone in attendance at Recreation Hall. A man named Tom Nardozzo became chairman of our annual golf outing, and he eventually got the chance to play in Bob Hope's Pro-Am Desert Classic in Palm Springs.

Tom put together a committee that worked year-round to make the outing a huge annual success. Willie Mays, Bill Mazeroski and so many other sports figures took part throughout the years. The late Bob

Prince, former voice of the Pittsburgh Pirates, brought many of the former players with him, and he often took part in the organization of the outings.

The multitude of athletes that participated was always so genuine, and they made The Second Mile golf outing the success it has become. The outing continued to grow over the years, and as we began to move forward, there were more lectures and fund-raising events. I went out and spoke quite often to business groups, not really sure of what I was doing but trying to raise money for the Second Mile. Quite simply, we just plugged away and plugged away.

Earl Strong had lectured all over the world on management, but we never seemed to reach the level that I think he hoped we would in our early stages. He lectured us and taught us that our success would be E-Z, as in easy. The E would stand for "Efficiency"—organizing and focusing our attention on the most important points; channeling our energies in the right direction.

Earl used to always say: "In order for the Second Mile to be a success, it needs 'Zigarnic.'" It was a German term that, according to Earl, meant "the compulsion to succeed; the will to keep trying; a driving force to move forward." I don't really think we were very efficient or well- organized in those early years, but I know that we had that zigarnic.

We learned through many trials and tribulations in those early days. There was some dissension within the board of directors, and I had to ask someone to step down from a voluntary position because of that dissension. We were criticized in the newspapers for our "million-dollar budget to serve a handful of kids." At that time, our budget was only $46,000. The article was written by a young lady from the student newspaper, and I asked her to visit with me in person so we could discuss her article. She did, and I said to her: "I can appreciate your opinions on child care, and I can understand your terms of handling children, even if I don't agree with them. But when you write as a matter of fact that we have a million-dollar budget when our budget is under $50,000, then we have a problem."

I asked the young lady to print a retraction, but she wouldn't do it. She had ultimately misinterpreted our *goal* to *raise* a million dollars. That hurt our organization because people thought we were some sort of Taj Majal builders, when, in reality, we were scratching our heads and clawing to keep our heads above water.

In those early stages, when we realized our dream to build the facility, we purchased 20 acres of land, hoping to keep moving forward. But the tough times and the dissension continued. There were people who disagreed with what we were trying to do. Some argued that we should rent a place; others said we should buy; and still others said we should build. Those were the types of conflicts we had early on within the organization. There were a lot of negative feelings, and it all kind of came to a head when, at one of the board meetings, one of the most influential members of the board stood up and said: "I've had it, I quit!"

And he was probably right. We *didn't* know what we were doing. But, thank goodness, we had that zigarnic. I always remember that moment because if I were to give an emotional or motivational speech, I could never have touched what that man said when he quit. A couple of board members said: "Hey, we'll get this thing done. Hang in there and stay with us." It was my dream, and those people showed me they weren't going to let it die.

We had a board member named Bill Jeffries. He was retired from his work at the university, and he was a loving and caring individual. Our organization was flat broke at one point, unable to make the next payroll, but Bill came forward and loaned us the money that we needed. That point was probably the lowest we had ever hit in the history of our organization. Dissension; division within the board; lack of funds. Fortunately, we had some people who came aboard to help us keep going. A man named Harold Schaub, who was a retired president of Campbell's Soups, came forward and contributed a condominium. It wasn't successful, but we were able to raise some money as a result of the effort there.

There were other ventures that helped us get a little bit of money here and there, and we were able to keep climbing. My son, Ray, was somewhat creative in an artistic way, so I asked him if he could draw us of a picture of a road that traveled to a home. "The road should wind through hills and valleys," I told him. "I want the picture to depict the struggle to get to that home. I want it to be the Second Mile home."

Ray went to work on the picture and began by drawing a simple road with rocks, mountains, a water crossing and even a snake pit. He also had a picture of footprints with holes in each shoe. As each shoe moved forward, and the journey became longer, the holes grew bigger and bigger. I joked with him, saying I knew the road would be tough, but I never realized exactly *how* tough. His picture really told the story of the struggles we had been through as well as the road that awaited us.

There eventually came a day when we would arrive at our goal. Through the help of the Zimmerman Construction Company and volunteer labor, the home we had put so much effort in had finally become a reality. With it, so did our dream. The picture that Ray drew still hangs in the house as a reminder of the struggles along our seemingly impossible path.

We thought we had arrived when the house took shape, but in reality, it was just the beginning. The beginning of many more rough times and struggles. Now we had to find kids for this home, and we had to hire houseparents to get the program started. We needed more money to become tangible. John Sheridan called me and said he had received a phone call from a lady who wondered if we could hook up one of the football players with her son, who needed a male role model in his life. Todd Blackledge, Penn State's quarterback at the time, became what we called a "friend" to that youngster and that was the beginning of what we called the Friends Program, where some of our athletes volunteered to spend time with local kids. Todd became involved with that child to the point where he was like a member of the family. He was a big brother to both the boy and his sister, and they all came through some tough times together.

That was our first program, and we considered it an excellent start. The next step was to hire the houseparents so we could get the house in operation. There was a man named Fred Von Dracek who was in the College of Human Development at Penn State. He was a brilliant person; extremely well-organized when it came to programs for kids. He played a big role in helping us find the right houseparents.

I was very particular in my hopes for the right people because this was one area I felt we simply could not make a mistake in. For instance, there was one couple who applied, but I refused them, because the man smoked. We had a lot of arguments within the board of directors as to which person or persons we would hire. We finally decided on a couple from North Carolina.

Eventually, this decision resulted in more dissension because we ended up hiring the wrong people. On paper, and in the initial stages, this couple seemed perfect for the job, but they ended up disappointing us with their commitment to the responsibilities. Fred Von Dracek was especially upset with that episode. He didn't agree with the board's decision, but he stayed with us to help keep the Second Mile afloat, and I'll always appreciate that.

We encountered more problems within our staff in this never-ending struggle. It became apparent that we needed a stronger manager in the position of executive director; someone who had much more experience in handling children's needs and who had an awareness of the total picture of running an organization whose aim was to simply help children.

It was a difficult decision because we had really cared about the person who was in the executive director's spot at the time. I'd rather not mention him in this book, but he had done an outstanding job of getting us to that stage, but we knew we weren't going to move further until we had someone who was more of a professional in the child-care area. It was a decision we struggled greatly with, and we wondered how we could handle it in the most diplomatic manner. Whether it was in a diplomatic manner or not, Earl Strong put the ball under his arm at one of our executive member meetings and carried it the rest of the way.

We were mostly quiet for a while, unsure of who might speak up first, or what would be said. Finally, Earl spoke: "I know what's wrong with this organization," he said. "It's like the story of the farmer who had a huge container of milk. He tested the milk and found it to be sour. He did everything he could to see what the problem was. He ran tests; he brought in experts, but the milk remained sour. So, there was only one thing the farmer could do. He decided to drain the container, and when he reached the bottom, he found a rat..."

No sooner did Earl reach the end of his story when the executive director stood up and said: "Yes, and I am the rat."

A dead silence fell over the room as some sat with their heads down, while others stared at the wall or the table in front of them. Earl's manner wasn't the most diplomatic, but I guess it hit the point. It was, and remains, one of the hardest things we ever had to do because the person in question had been with us from the very beginning.

The Second Mile was incorporated in 1977, and four years later, we had seen the completion of our dream house. In the early days of the house, we started out with three kids, whose names were Tom, Steve and Bobby. At that stage, we really weren't organized well enough to handle those kids. Tom was a real con artist. The first time I saw him he was bullying around some little kids. When he saw me, he approached me and said:, "Oh, Mr. Sandusky, what a great guy you are. I thank you for everything." But I had already seen his true colors a few minutes earlier.

Steve was a different person. He really didn't care where he lived, and nothing mattered that much to him. Not even living in a detention center later in his life. It was sad because regardless of where he ended up, it didn't matter.

Then there was Bobby. He was there during the period where we went through some problems and had to dismiss the first set of houseparents. On a Thursday night prior to a home football game against Notre Dame that Saturday, I was at the Second Mile home telling the kids we were going to have to get new houseparents. I stayed until about 11 that night trying to settle the situation, but it seemed as though Bobby didn't know how to accept it. Whether he cared or not, I wasn't really sure. A few months later, a couple named Elliott and Kathy came in and solved the houseparent situation. They were good people, and I was excited to see them working with the kids.

One night, at around three in the morning, I was awakened by a phone call from the State College Police Department. They wanted to inform me that "my kids had run away from home," and they had them in their custody. I kept thinking to myself: *"What kids? Which one of my kids would want to run away from home?"*

"What do you mean?" I said to the officer as I cleared my head. "Your *kids,"* he answered quickly.

Finally, he expanded on his answer and told me it was a couple of the kids from the Second Mile home—Steve and Bobby to be exact. Actually, I had expected something like this at some point, so I went to the police station to claim them. I asked them why they did it, why they would want to run away, and they explained their troubles with Elliott and Kathy.

"The houseparents were mean," Bobby said as he sulked with his big blue eyes. "They made us eat all the food on our plate, and they made us clean our room."

"Boy, that's pretty terrible," I said with my best mock sympathy. "You guys are really having it rough out there."

"The guy (Elliott) grabbed me around the back of my shoulders," Bobby continued. "And he made me do something when I didn't want to do it. Do you ever grab your kids like that?"

I didn't want this running away thing to become a habit, so I thought of a possible solution —at least an experiment to make them think twice about doing it again. "No, Bobby, I don't grab my kids like that. I grab them like this."

With that, I put my hands gently around his throat. By now, I could tell they were totally confused. Both boys had a scared look in their eyes. Bobby didn't want to go back to the Second Mile home, and Steve didn't want to go to my house, so I sat at a red light at 4:30 in the morning debating with myself on where to go. Finally, I told them we would compromise. We would go to the Second Mile home that night, and another night they could come to my house. That was just an example of the organizational structure we had in the early days of the Second Mile.

There were plenty of kids who came through the Second Mile program and did very well with their lives. A boy named Rick was probably the first child to succeed in the way we had hoped. He graduated from high school and ended up a fine serviceman. Another boy named Mark went to college and is now working in England. C.B. went on to be another serviceman. He was always special, as was a boy named Ross. They used to come to my house and stay, or go to my parents after they had moved to State College.

C.B. went to football camp and always complained about so many things with the Second Mile, and when we played in the 1990 Blockbuster Bowl, he was in the service around Miami, so he and a friend came to the game. We were up real late after the game, and it was so interesting for me to listen to him talk about all of his experiences at the Second Mile. He had forgotten about all the discipline and supposed rough times he had complained about as a youth. His memories instead were nothing but fond ones of the Second Mile.

There was also Stanley and David. Both were special youngsters who did well during their stay at the Second Mile. They both made their way into foster homes eventually and have done very well. These were the beginnings of the Second Mile, and although the road was often rocky, it was indeed time and effort well spent.

We've had lots of houseparents that helped along the way, but it was always difficult to keep the good ones. We couldn't establish the home and family environment that we had liked, and we didn't want to get away from that. It became apparent that adjustments had to be made.

20

A New Era

JACK RAYKOVITZ WAS OUR NEW EXECUTIVE DIRECTOR, and he deserved a lot of the credit for leading us into this new era. He inherited an organization that was serving close to 20 children in two different programs—the Friends program and the foster home. Jack also had to often rectify the almost constant problems with the houseparents. To summarize what Jack meant to the Second Mile is to say that he was our "E" from which I spoke of the E-Z logic earlier. He gave us the efficiency and organization. He analyzed the situation, dotted every "I" and crossed every "T." He took a program that once served 20 kids and turned it into an organization that currently affects the lives of approximately 150,000 young people.

Jack started new programs and worked with Katherine Genovese and David Shirk. Katherine, as I said in the very first few pages of this work, is our program director, and David is a former house parent who also works in the area of programs. With people like this, we have grown to 10 different programs that cover a wide range of areas. There are prevention programs to help kids avoid the early problems. There is also an early intervention program to help kids at a stage where they have begun to experience problems, and we also have community-based programs.

The foster home has grown and gone through some changes. It is still a home that serves foster children, but we are now licensed as a foster placement agency, which means we have the opportunity to hopefully place children in *our* home in foster homes in State College. We also work with foster programs throughout the state of Pennsylvania. We do public service announcements all over the state trying to convince families to take in foster children.

The Friend program has continued to grow and serve numerous kids throughout central Pennsylvania. Those children attend various events throughout the school year where they meet lots of Penn State students, some of whom are athletes. Various social organizations provide transportation and programming for the children. Most of the activities are recreational in nature, and the children are encouraged to do service projects.

If a youngster and a college student develop a closer relationship, they can go on and join the Big Brother/Big Sister program in Centre County. Here they are able to establish a more intense, long-lasting relationship that began and grew through the Friend program.

We've converted our foster home and tied in with a national organization called A Better Chance (ABC). ABC takes on inner-city kids who are deprived because of their environment. They come from areas that aren't conducive to proper development academically. These children are highly motivated, fairly intelligent, and they have very lofty goals set for their lives. They're very committed to studying three hours a night, and they must maintain a very high grade point average to stay in this program. By coming from their inner-city backgrounds to our small community, they live and learn in a new environment, and hopefully, they end up going on to college.

We have summer camps in three different locations, including one right in State College, which was the first one. Initially, the camp was for kids ages 8 to 13 with most coming from Pennsylvania, although we did have a few come in from outlying states. They come to State College to enjoy an atmosphere of recreation and enjoyable activities, but they are also counseled in human and family relations.

The theme of the camp is cooperation and teamwork. It's about learning to work with each other and growing together. Hopefully, self-confidence also grows within the children, and they find they have the ability to succeed in doing something, while at the same time, it is our hope for the kids to have fun. There are low-level confidence courses, tours of the university, scavenger hunts, canoeing, hiking and swimming.

We also lecture the kids in groups, and we talk to them as individuals, hoping to encourage them to do well. We talk about being *somebody* and what that takes. We talk about happiness; about reaching out and extending themselves to others. We encourage the kids to go back to their communities and get involved with some sort of service project. We made such an act a reward for a return trip to the camp.

We work strongly with the kids in helping them set goals for their lives and to succeed academically. There are games, songs, and challenges and, overall, just a lot of genuine fun. We want them to know they can earn their way back to camp by showing good behavior in school and by simply performing up to their level of capability.

We stay in touch with the kids year-round. I personally write letters to them at least four times a year. They are letters of encouragement, with memories of the camp and reminders of what it means to be a Second Mile person. We let them know how important they are to us, as well as how much we care about them and who they are as people. We send out a newsletter where we ask the kids to respond and send back information to us. They do so with poems they've written and even letters to me.

Our summer camps have been very successful, and many lives have been touched by them. We have made tremendous progress in working with the kids; however, I can recall some challenging beginnings. The first camp we ever had was an interesting experience and a good example of a challenge.

There was a young man named Jason who had emotional problems. It seemed like every ten minutes he would scream, "That does it, I'm going home!" I was not around him that much, but it even got on my nerves. On a Wednesday evening, I showed up at the camp for a softball game in which Jason was playing. He wanted to pitch, but neither his team nor the other one wanted him to. Jason complained enough until his team finally relented and, as expected, he could not get the ball over the plate from the mound. To resolve this problem, he decided to move forward. I could see a line drive coming his way, and sure enough, that's what happened. The ball hit Jason right on the arm, and after the initial scare was over, the first words out of his mouth were, "That does it, I'm going home!" After a bit of calming, Jason managed to get through the rest of the game.

The next day was the last full day of camp, and the staff made some interesting decisions. The first was to end the camp with a picnic and invite the Second Mile board of directors to meet these "wonderful kids." I thought it was a fantastic idea, and I made sure I was there early for the picnic. The staff's second decision was to allow the kids some free time prior to the picnic. That was probably a bad choice. I soon found I was in for some interesting experiences that evening, the first of which was taking a simple walk with three inner-city kids from the Philadelphia area.

We came across some ducks along our path and these kids decided to pick up some stones and use the ducks as living targets. "I'm sorry, but we don't throw stones at the ducks," I said. They stopped for all of three seconds, and it was time to throw another stone.

"Maybe you didn't hear me, but we don't throw stones at the ducks," I said, this in a slightly more stern voice. When the kids felt compelled to repeat their actions only a few steps later, I lost my patience and began chasing them through the woods. Fortunately for them, I didn't catch them.

As I returned to the picnic, I noticed the board members beginning to arrive. I was about to greet them when I noticed a fight breaking out just over the hill from where we were. A young man named Kevin was about to destroy another boy, so I sprinted down the hill and dived into the pile to separate them. After a real tussle, I managed to pull Kevin away. I had become distraught over this episode as well as the one with the ducks, and I now found myself having to greet our visitors. It was then that I heard the voice trailing behind me.

"That does it, I'm going home!" It was Jason—that I was sure of. I quickly turned and with a sigh of relief I said, "You're right, Jason, tomorrow, you're going home." That was my brightest thought of the night.

On the last day of camp, I always tried to see the kids before they left. When it's all over, I really miss them—even the Jasons of this world. Standing outside the dorm I heard someone bouncing down the stairs. Sure enough, it was Jason. He was shouting at the top of his lungs again, but this time he was saying, "That does it, I'm *not* going home!" I offered one of the counselors the opportunity to stay, but we lost the counselor and Jason finally went home.

There continue to be ups and downs, but it has always been very rewarding to see many young people cherish the memories of their camp experience.

There is a more intensive camping experience we call SMILE, which means "Second Mile Intensive Living Experience." It is an extension of the younger program where some of the kids who have been through the program go into the woods to camp out, to work and to learn to live with each other. SMILE is a continuing effort to try to improve their self-confidence and self-image. Other kids move on to become junior counselors at our camps and work with the younger kids in leadership capacities. This, in turn, helps them to become the kind of leaders we had hoped they could be.

We have a camp in Philadelphia made possible by a man named Dom Toscani. Philadelphia has always been an area of strong interest for the Second Mile. Jack Udell is a person who has been a constant supporter—always going beyond the call of duty. He provided us with our first van a long time ago.

The Second Mile now has an office in Harrisburg and a camp for children at Fort Indian Town Gap, a U. S. Army reserve training area in central Pennsylvania. At the Harrisburg office, we have a program called PEAKS, where they made a video featuring Jim Martin, a former national championship wrestler at Penn State; Bob White, who was captain of our 1986 national championship football team; and Suzie McConnell-Serio, a former All-American on the Penn State women's basketball team and a member of the 1988 gold-medal winning U.S. Olympic team. In the video, we talk to the children about peer pressure and staying strong. We preach to them about standing up for what they believed in and showing their ability to handle the difficult situations.

We also have cards that feature our football players and our winter athletes at Penn State, both men and women. The athlete's picture is on the front of the card, and on the back is a special message of encouragement to young people. The messages push for the youngsters to do well in school; to stay away from drugs, alcohol and tobacco; and also to attend school and be respectful to others. The messages on the cards come directly from the athlete that is featured. It is our hope the messages help the child to become a responsible and sensible human being. The cards are circulated to guidance counselors throughout the commonwealth of Pennsylvania, and they use them as a method of reward for some students as well as a chance to get to know them or talk about some specific problem.

We also have a counseling service for families and children who have special needs. A children's fund provides financial assistance to families in times of crisis. Additionally, many young people who have been involved in our programs have been supported as they have attended college or other post-high school institutions.

Bruce Heim started and franchised a Friend Fitness Program that provides mentoring through a vigorous exercise program. Mentors work with children to improve their strength, endurance, and self-esteem. Strong academic effort is also emphasized, and some of these young people are already going on to college and speaking for The Second Mile.

The Bob Burgess Memorial Golf Tournament has enabled us to start a Leadership Institute for high school students. They come to Penn State to learn leadership skills, discuss issues and develop programs to be implemented in their communities.

All of this has been made possible by generous people. We've gone to several fund-raising banquets and had the golf outings. We've contacted corporations, individuals and foundations. Through the efforts of our community development people: Hank Lesch and his staff, who spent hours trying to raise the money so we could have those programs for young people, and so we can see the results of all the effort put forth.

We have camps in Reading, Pennsylvania, made possible by a friend named Dom Toscani; Jack Udell bought the first van for us at The Second Mile; Verne Willaman came forward to pay for a camp; Bob Mayer, a friend of John Sheridan, helped start another; Fred Nicholas and Bruce Heim gave us an office building, while Martha Hostetter has become a strong director of our programs in south central Pennsylvania and oversees the Lancster, Berks and York chapters.

People have come forward over the years to provide tremendous leadership. Kim Ortenzio became involved because she knew our son, Ray, when he was very young. Marty DeRose is the father-in-law of former Penn State quarterback John Shaffer. Ken Ewing and Chuck Chubb are leaders. Bob Poole had led our state board to a new level of performance, and finally, Bob Hill oversees our annual golf tournament, which has become a huge attraction and our most significant fund-raising event. People too numerous to mention have volunteered thousands of hours to make it possible for us to increase our budget to over 1.3 million dollars per year.

Joe Paterno always had a saying in regard to the football season: "You either get better or get worse through each day of your life." As an organization, I can honestly say we've constantly tried to get better. We've continually tried to reach out to thousands of young people and tried to do more for them. As much as we can. To make it even better, the reaching out has always been a lot of fun. Especially at the summer camps, where I've enjoyed wrestling and swimming with the kids. I even had to have knee surgery in the summer of 1991 because of my fooling around. I like to play games with the kids. Games on the playing fields as well as games of wit. I used to pick out a kid and challenge him to repeat the word "silk" as fast as he could. After several repetitions, I would ask, "What does a cow drink?" And the answer would almost always be milk instead of water.

There were many other challenging things to the childrens' minds where I used simple rhyming games to fool them into saying a wrong answer, or I would ask them several questions to get them into a rhythm and then throw something totally off the wall at them. Something like me saying: "Repeat after me, pink." They would answer: "Pink."

"Green," I continued.

And they repeated my words obediently through a series of colors. Then I would say: "What color is the sky?"

A resounding, "BLUE!" could be heard all around, but soon they realize they should have been saying: "What color is the sky?"

As silly as those games sound, the kids enjoyed them, and they certainly had their times of redemption when they fooled me. The kids also enjoyed songs—many that they made up with different words from popular songs such as, "SHOUT" and the one that goes: *"Doo-wa-diddy-diddy-dum-diddy-doo."* They even made up a rap song with me as the subject, and it went something like:

> *"His name is Jer,*
> *You better beware,*
> *He has gray hair,*
> *But he has no flair."*

Again, it was something simple, but they were kids just being kids, and they loved to have fun like that. But there were also plenty of serious times. They would often talk about being *somebody* and not just a *nobody*. They talked about being a special person—a Second Mile person. They talked about reaching for the end of the rainbow.

Any time you deal with young people, there will be extreme highs and lows. There have been moments of frustration, despair and heartache. And times that we felt so bad because we weren't able to reach out to some of the young people we were involved with.

I've had some interesting experiences taking kids to Hershey Park, which is an amusement park in Hershey, Pennsylvania, near Harrisburg. The first time I did it, I took eight or nine of the kids. Three of them came from a community near State College, and when they showed up at my house, I knew right away there would be some problems. One on one, the kids were fine, and they were not a problem to anyone. But together, they summed up the terms "defiance and arrogance." they started the day by ignoring me when I asked them to do something. I got pretty upset and had just about changed my mind about taking them. But Dottie talked me into finishing what I had started.

I decided to set guidelines for everyone to follow the rest of the day, but sure enough, some of the kids didn't show up at the first designated meeting place. They did this several times throughout the day, and by now, I had become extremely upset. One of the boys had grown close to our family since we had met him, but by the end of the day, he was acting up like some of the other kids—talking back and acting rather smart about it. I took him by his arm and told him how disappointed I was with him. I had expected this treatment from the others but not from him.

That night, after we had come home, I stood outside under the streetlight with this young man until around one in the morning. I explained to him that I only set those rules and expressed my disappointment *because* I cared so much for them. He eventually expressed his sorrow as well as his care for me. He really showed he had an air of sensitivity about him, and it shined over him far brighter than the false sense of bravado he had hid behind earlier in the day.

I planned a similar trip for next summer, but I was extra careful about the chemistry of the kids I would be taking. It started out pretty well or so I thought. I picked up the last of the eight kids in Harrisburg, but there were two more kids there whose mother sort of convinced me to take them along. After five minutes, I knew why their mother smiled at the thought of me taking her kids off her hands for the day. As soon as we were on our way, those kids had everyone in the van climbing all over the seats and carrying on. The perfect chemistry that I had carefully put together was ruined. The new kids had definitely contributed to the others' decision not to follow the rules. Somehow, though, it seemed the kids always won me over. They always have, and always will, get to my soft side, and I guess that was why it was pretty easy for me to stick with them.

A lot of the kids I grew close to and spent a lot of time with spent some time in psychiatric clinics. I tried to visit them, and there was one young boy who had a lot of problems at home but still had so much good in him. When he got away from home, he was fine, but when he was at home, his problems magnified. Another youngster was very warm and receptive to one of my visits, but the next time, he became very cold and seemingly unresponsive to me. He became upset because I wouldn't take him away for a weekend to let him run with his friends. He completely ignored me for a long time, so I got up as though I were going to leave. But I knew I couldn't leave with what looked like a grudge against him.

"You know, it's not right to treat people like this," I told him. "You should talk to me." The boy laid into me, screaming from the top of his lungs. "Get out of here! Get out of here!" His voice echoed into the hallway and staff people came rushing into the room. I looked at him with sincere tears in my eyes. "I can't believe you're doing this to me," I said quietly as I walked out of the room. It was one of the most difficult episodes I ever had with a child who had as much troubles as he did.

My family and I have become personally involved with many of the kids. A young man named Chad stayed with us quite often. He ended up doing very well in school, and he went to college and became involved in sports. Our family swells with pride from relationships like that with young people.

Some people take odd turns in their lives. I have personally seen two kids from the Second Mile past grow oddly apart and come together again in the most unusual way. One took a very disappointing path that led to crime and eventually prison. The other did very well for himself. He kept his head on straight and made a nice career for himself in the service. One commendable trait he learned was leadership, and because of that, he was eventually hired as a guard at the same prison where the first young man ended up as an inmate.

And there have been many others who have made great examples of themselves. Troy cried during his first visit to camp because he was homesick. He was ready to leave, but we got him through that rough time, and it pleased me greatly to see the change in him. He eventually became a leader at the camp, and he even wrote a skit about smoking being bad for a person's health, which his group also acted out at the camp. Troy had a great way with people, and once he got over that initial hump, he developed a tremendous amount of self-confidence.

There was a time when I considered leaving Penn State to accept a head coaching position at the University of Maryland. My consideration for this position was in the newspaper, and one youngster named Josh, whom I had gotten close to, saw the story and called me right away. "What would we do?" he asked me with all the sincerity a child could muster. "Without you there won't be any more summer camps."

I assured him the camps would go on with or without me, but his plea struck a chord in my heart. Just to think that our camps meant so much to Josh and so many of the other youngsters, and seeing the kids give me gifts at Christmas time, I knew where my heart would stay. The gifts were never large or expensive, but they were filled with love and care and had a tremendous amount of meaning behind them. One child whom I had known since he was very young, cut out a piece of board in wood shop class and inscribed a tribute to Penn State football on it. That was his way of telling me how much he cared about me, and that I meant something to him. That woodwork will always be a part of me.

There are a lot of letters from the kids, and they all carry a significant meaning. I recall two in particular that I can share in this manuscript. The first one was written by a young girl to one of the camp counselors:

"I am considering going to college very much, so I'd like to attend Shippensburg University for a degree in Counseling and Spanish. I love both areas, and I hear there are a lot of openings for counselors at the grade-school

level who speak fluent Spanish because they're having problems communicat-
ing with kids through translators.

"My confidence has been boosted knowing I can handle almost any-
thing that comes my way. I really have to give most of the credit to the Second
Mile camp though. If it weren't for that camp when I first moved to Halifax
after my parents' divorce when I was in seventh grade, I probably wouldn't be
the person I am today. The camp taught me how to deal with my problems;
how to talk to people positively; how to deal with different situations; and,
most importantly, how to cooperate and work with anyone. I do a lot better in
school because of this."

That letter was written in the early 1990s, and it has since rung
true for countless young people who have come through the summer camp
programs the Second Mile has to offer.

There was a child I visited a lot named Charles. I always knew that
the Second Mile camp was something he looked forward to with great
anticipation and enthusiasm every year. He talked about the camp constantly as a place where he gained acceptance and love. We exchanged
letters during the winter months, and I could see Charles' anticipation for
summer and the camp through each and every letter.

In the summer of 1991, we got a phone call at the Second Mile
office from Charles. He was calling to tell me he had joined the Navy. He
had kept all the newsletters from the Second Mile over the years, and he
wanted everyone to know he had been accepted into the training program
for the Navy Seals. He also wanted to credit the Second Mile for developing the self-esteem that carried him that far. He felt very good about his
accomplishments, and he wanted to share it with us.

I spoke of Chad earlier, and there was also an African American
young man named Kevin who attended our summer camp. A guidance
counselor named Bill Lee took an interest in Kevin, and today Kevin is a
graduate of Holy Cross College, where he played football and now works
as an accountant. Kevin paid his own way to come and speak at a fund-
raiser for The Second Mile in Hershey, Pennsylvania. He and Chad both
did a tremendous job.

A little girl named Janelle who came to our camp lost her mother at
a very young age. I was fortunate to get to know her, as she and her dad
would occasionally attend some Penn State football games. I would ask
her how she was doing in school, and she would answer, "All right," with
a shy little smile. With a response like that, I thought she might be an
average student, but later, when Janelle was a senior in high school, I
received a wonderful letter from her aunt. She talked about how well

Janelle had done in high school, being in the top five in her class, what The Second Mile had meant to her, and how she wanted to attend Susquehanna University. I am proud to say that The Second Mile made that possible. Janelle has done extremely well and is a great young lady.

I try to stay in touch with the kids as much as possible. One year I was preparing for the holidays and a bowl game with the football team. Sitting in my office, I was kind of worn out, but I decided to call a boy named Billy. Billy was always upbeat and he would surely help me recover. I asked him how he was doing.

"Great!" he said excitedly.

"And how are you doing in school?" I continued.

"Fantastic!" Billy answered. "I only had two detentions this week." I held back my laughter as I thought about his response. "That's really good, Billy, but you might be interested in knowing that this is only Tuesday."

Another special young man was Jamie. He struggled through special education and graduated from high school. He always attended our summer camps and really lived for those days. Through great effort, Jamie graduated from high school and got a minimum wage job. Later in his life, he sent a $100 contribution to The Second Mile so that other kids could enjoy what he had.

There was another youngster who lived in our foster home. I always told him that he should be a teacher and a coach. Later, he was placed in permanent foster care. I hadn't seen him in a while until I ran into him at a high school graduation. He was now a junior in high school, and as we talked, he told me that he still planned on being a teacher and a coach. He also told me he would be applying to colleges the following year, and he might need me to write him some letters of "reconciliation." When I heard him say that word, knowing he meant recommendation, I thought to myself, "Kid, you're going to have to be a coach." Speaking of coaching, I started football camps for young kids and had ten or so kids who attended and who had also been in The Second Mile program.

One young man had gone through a difficult year and I was genuinely concerned for him. Everything was going well for him at the football camp until we had a game session and not one pass was thrown in his direction. He wanted to be a wide receiver, and he became very upset. I talked to his coach and asked if I could draw up a couple plays so that he might get a reception. The coach invited me to run the team.

We had some practice time before the next game, and I decided the best chance to get the young man a reception would be to put him at tight end and run a little delay. He resisted my decision, insisting he was a wide receiver. I asked him to go along with me on this decision, and he said he didn't even know where the tight end aligned. "Just do it for the coach," I pleaded with him. When he refused again, I told him what just about any coach would say to an uncooperative player. "Okay, then," I said. "You can go to the sideline and try sitting down."

As most players would react, the young man sat down for a while, and later he decided to cooperate. Our team went ahead, so now my mission was to get him a catch. I showed him the diagram of the play, but he didn't run it correctly. When he returned to the huddle, I took him aside and tried to walk him through it.

"You're embarrassing me!" he exclaimed rather loudly. I responded by saying that I was only trying to help. The next time, he ran the play a little better and it looked like he was open. "Throw it!" I shouted to the quarterback. He did, and the young man made the catch. I let out a shriek of jubilance for him as he took one step with his reception before he was tagged, and as this happened, I noticed the ball pop out of his hands, into the air, and into the hands of an opposing defensive player who ran it back for a touchdown.

"That does it," he said dejectedly. "They'll never throw me another pass." He kept repeating this over and over, and I went to him and said he should go and play defense for the extra point. He was once again upset and refused, and I looked to the sky with my arms raised high and shouted, "Did you ever think I might be trying to help you? Where is Courtney Brown? Where is LaVar Arrington?"

Thinking about the kids and what we may have done for them, we have become involved and haven't just sat on the sidelines. There have been times when we have fought with kids, and often, we have fought for them, knowing that kids like Peter and Jason can make it all worthwhile. Seeing another Jason grow into a special young man is very rewarding. Watching Frankie and Allan become outstanding students and seeing them become involved in sports feels like my own personal championship.

We throw out the rope and hopefully, the kids will take hold. We try to motivate, mentor, and provide memories. If nothing else, there will always be memories. I will remember jet skiing with a young man named Brett. Dolphins jumped out of the water less than ten yards away from us, and as I looked out over this vast body of water, I thought of how there was so much out there for Brett and the others. I wanted all of them to know how much I care.

My office, as well as my walls at home, are adorned with pictures of kids whom I have grown close to over the years who have come through the Second Mile program. They are kids that have touched my life and have been a part of me for a long, long time. They are people that I could never leave, and they are people whom I want to see reach their development all the way to the end.

Whenever I'm asked to recall what the Second Mile means to me, I'll always remember a group of people who came together. We were naive, and we certainly had a lot more courage than brains. We tried to stay organized and we were able to pick up a first down here and there to move in a positive direction. We came through some awfully tough times, and thankfully, people stayed with us. We began operations, and one program led to another and another.

Once, I was asked to talk about The Second Mile during a speech I was giving, so I decided to see if I could find some element of meaning out of the first letter of each of those words. The following is what I came up with:

T = TRUST: What you need to develop a relationship with children. Trust has been the foundation of the Second Mile from the early people who believed in us when we were just dreaming.

H = HUMOR: The many experiences we've had with the kids over the years, also
HONESTY: The method we use to make people feel confident and secure about themselves.

E = EMOTION: The feelings kids get when they succeed and when they fail.

S = SPECIAL: The feelings we, as a staff, get around the kids and what they mean to us.

E = EXCELLENCE: We're not just looking for immediate success. We strive to instill values and principles in the lives of these children. We're looking for long-term results.

C = COMMITMENT: It's what we make to the kids and our efforts to see it through.

O = ORGANIZATION: We try to get the children to be efficient, to set goals and to plan and work daily on reaching those goals.

N = NATURAL: We love the kids because they say what they think, and it comes out naturally. We, in turn, don't try to put on any airs. We just try to be ourselves with them.

D = DISCIPLINE: Hopefully, this is instilled in their lives so they know how to carry themselves with respect, consideration and dignity. We follow a saying: "If you treat a person the way they are, they'll stay that way. If you treat them the way they can become, they will *become* that person."

M = MOTIVATION: We hope to get a child to extend themselves; to reach out. One child comes to mind who wrote us a letter which said he was inspired by the athletes' cards for good grades and for helping around the house. He said his greatest wish was to play at Penn State and to be able to give Nittany Lion Tips to other kids.

I = INDIVIDUAL: Each child is important, and it comes down to each one making the decisions that will lead to a productive and positive life. We've received many letters and evaluations from counselors who have seen and helped the kids in the program. I also like to use **INVOLVE-MENT** for all the many kids and programs that have been a part of the programs we offer.

L = LOVE: The Second Mile has been a complete act of love since its inception. It is summarized by a young girl's letter that told us she had changed residency, but she was still very interested in going to camp again. She said she learned what it feels like to be loved and respected. She said it was an experience she would like to repeat.

E = EFFORT: The whole organization has received tremendous effort from so many people. They have come from all walks of life; all levels of income; all levels of interest. We have expended our efforts to help so many children, but there are still so many more, and there is much, much more that needs to be done.

Many of the kids who have come through the Second Mile program have gone on to college. We had a big year in 1991 as four children from our ABC program made it to college, including three who attended Penn State. Numerous kids from the summer camps have also gone on to college. One young man named Kevin earned a football scholarship to Holy Cross and another earned one to Akron University.

Success is a very relative thing to the Second Mile. For some, it might be going on to college; for others, it might be staying out of jail. The experience has instilled self-confidence in so many youngsters, and they can go on to live productive and wholesome lives.

The Second Mile has been a positive influence on children, but it has also had a positive effect on adults. So many of us have experienced the warm feelings, the caring, and the oneness that a group of board members has shared. So many committed people have come forward and developed lasting relationships. These special people worked together and continued to persevere through so many trials and tribulations.

One person who was a counselor at one time for the Second Mile went on to finish his education, then started his own program for children in Lewisburg, Pennsylvania. It is similar in that it reaches out and touches the lives of children in much the same manner that he had seen so many lives touched during his time with the Second Mile.

Earlier, I had discussed two letters that I wanted to share that really said a lot about the meaning and existence of the Second Mile. One was from the young lady who told us how much our camps meant to her, and how she was inspired to go to college and how she had gained confidence and self-assurance that she could accomplish anything in her life.

There was another youngster who came to us at a very young age. He came to our football camps, and I spent hours and hours with him. I decided to include the following short excerpt from a very meaningful letter he wrote to me when he was in the service:

"I will never forget what you have done for me. The Second Mile was 'The Wind Beneath My Wings.'"

When I read that sentence, I truly felt we had met our purpose. We're there to give a little boost. Some people might not get off the ground, while others might, as the song says, "fly higher than an eagle."

Hopefully, we are the wind beneath many kids' wings.

21

The Great Pretenders

WE FORMED A SINGING GROUP AT THE SECOND MILE CAMPS, and we called ourselves The Great Pretenders because it seemed like that's what we were doing when we would sing. The two most prominent people in this group were Joe Sarra and myself.

As I've stated before, Joe is an assistant coach at Penn State and a good friend to me as well as the Second Mile. Over the years, Joe had received numerous tickets for his driving habits. Once, he lost his Pennsylvania driver's license over some of his incidents, but he went to Harrisburg to appeal the decision. He won the appeal, and on his trip back to State College on the same day, he got pulled over for speeding.

I mentioned before his penchant for calling everyone, "Buddy." One time, he was in New York City, and he stopped to get gas in his car. The gas station attendant didn't speak English, so Joe kept calling him "Buddy." It was Buddy this and Buddy that, as Joe is known to do, but all the attendant could do was shake his head and look very confused.

It got to the point that by the time Joe was filled up, the attendant took his payment and forgot to pull the nozzle out of Joe's car. The whole tank toppled over when Joe pulled away from the island. The attendant came running out screaming at him, and they eventually had a huge argument over responsibility for the incident. It's a pretty good guess that Joe, at least for a time, had to go without driving privileges in New York as well.

There were those who came and went in our singing group, but Joe Sarra and I were the mainstays throughout the years. We started out as The Bobbin' Robins, and we performed for The Second Mile Camp. It was at about the same time when break dancing was very popular. We sang *"When the red, red robin comes bob-bob-bobbin' along"* and *"Rockin' Robin"*, and we did our own dancing, calling it the 1940s version of break dancing.

The kids didn't understand the way we signed pieces of paper as The Bobbin' Robins and handed them out at performances. They interpreted that as us thinking we were good. One youngster rolled up his autograph and threw it at us during a performance. This touched off a chorus of boos, and everyone began throwing their papers at us. But we continued and made a rule that nothing would stop us from performing. One youngster at one of our camps told us not to hesitate to take the "Great" out of Great Pretenders. And I was inclined to believe he was right.

Other fun times back then were our football games between the Old-Timers (coaches) and the Jelly Donuts (the kids) as well as Brad Caldwell, Penn State's assistant equipment manager, acting as Brad the Bull with myself being Humbo Jericho, the matador. I used a broken golf club for my sword, and I wore a cape to look the part as best I could.

The plan was for Brad to ram me with his horns, and I would go down. Then, I would come to life and eventually finish him off in swashbuckling style. This represented the Old-Timer's victory over the Jelly Donuts. I was supposed to stick the sword under Brad's arm, but I accidentally stuck him. Fortunately, he didn't get hurt, and he was, I might add, a very good sport about the whole thing.

We staged interviews between kids from the Second Mile and Penn State football players, and we had Second Mile fight songs, parades, floats and other forms of entertainment. All of this took place either at halftime or after the Old-Timers vs. Jelly Donuts game.

The kids loved Brad Caldwell. He did a perfect imitation of the Heisman Trophy pose with one knee held high in the air, and one arm poised in a stiff-arm position while the ball was tucked firmly under the other arm. Brad entertained the kids with imitations of other football players, and they loved having him at the camps.

I believe I live a good part of my life in a make-believe world. I enjoyed pretending as a kid, and I love doing the same as an adult with these kids. Pretending has always been a part of me. I've loved trying to do the right things to hopefully make a difference in kids lives' and maybe make things better off for them. I am tough and competitive with the kids, but the one thing that has never been pretend or make-believe about me is my genuine love and care for the kids. I've always wanted to be accountable and trustworthy to them. Whether it is my family, the football players or the kids at the Second Mile, I love being with them to share my life and experiences.

Once, Dottie said to me: "Jer, you're probably the only one who really enjoys the things that you do." That's probably true, but that's okay with me. I enjoy the life that I have had, and I'll never regret being called a "great" pretender.

22

Tough Times

WE'VE WON OUR SHARE OF VICTORIES, but life hasn't always been a rose garden. I had a friend who, along with me, was going through some tough times with illness and family. He once said to me: "You know, I grew up watching the show, *Father Knows Best,* and everything always seemed to end on a positive note. But in reality, life just doesn't seem to always work out that way."

As far as the Second Mile is concerned, there have been a number of disappointments. One youngster that I was very close to and spent many hours with got involved with the wrong crowd and turned completely away from the Second Mile and all the programs. He became a lost person in so many ways. He was another child who couldn't seem to find himself. I could see that deep down he cared, but he became very unreliable. He didn't have the necessary discipline and direction to do what was right on his own.

Another young man once told me he had been on drugs since he was eight years old. He said he was introduced to drugs and alcohol by a babysitter. He revealed this information to me when we were in the midst of a one-on-one discussion. He had even spent time already in Alcoholics Anonymous. I worried about that boy a great deal because there are some children who act upon others in a violent manner, and I truly felt he had such potential. But more than that, I also thought he was capable of hurting himself, period. This young man had bounced from one situation to another. Every time I thought he was headed in a positive direction, something happened to take him a few steps back.

Some kids ended up in prison, and many others were never able to turn the corner. And there were many tough decisions within the Second

Mile home. There was a boy there who had the potential to do a lot of positive things with his life, but he got into stealing and turned into a chronic liar. We had to dismiss him from the home, and while this was not an easy decision, we had to do it for the sake of the entire group.

Probably the most difficult period of my life came to a head in 1991. The trials and tribulations of that year were the result of decisions and risks that began around 1985. At that time, I was talking to a friend who was a very prominent board member of the Second Mile and also doing quite well in the construction business. My parents were in the process of retiring at the time and they didn't have much in terms of retirement income (other than what they had set aside in savings for these years) because they had worked for a non-profit organization.

I was concerned for my parents financially, and I was also looking for a way to get a quick return on a possible investment. This friend told me he was thinking of building a restaurant, and it looked like a good deal. He had already owned one, and seeing how it seemed to be doing well, I became excited at the possibilities. I told him I even had a name for the new place if he would let my dad and me become small investors. He agreed, and I told him we should call it "The Training Table."

I wasn't particularly interested in jumping right into the restaurant business, and I was certainly no expert. But I liked this idea, and I felt it could be a place that would do substantial business with family food in a family atmosphere, while the name would help maintain that atmosphere as well as tie into my sports background.

My friend liked the idea, and we went in together as investors to buy the land he was looking at. We had a decent return on our investment initially, and my dad was able to secure some extra money that was helpful to him in his retirement. It started out as probably the best investment I had ever made.

The group that bought the restaurant was called "Training Table Associates." I was only an investor in the land, but the people in the association asked me if I would like to be a partner in the group. I thought the other investment was easy to deal with, and I thought one of our children might need help financially some day or maybe there would come a day when I couldn't coach anymore—for health reasons or whatever. I felt it would be nice to be financially secure, and I also looked at the opportunity to donate more money to the Second Mile.

I had never entertained thoughts of becoming wealthy, but those thoughts helped me decide to accept their invitation. So, I ventured into an initial agreement assuming that, like the land deal I was involved in, it would be a limited partnership. I had my usual tasks to keep me quite busy—football; the Second Mile—and without realizing what I had done, I had signed a general partnership. I went into the experience on blind faith. I knew how much money I could provide, and I really didn't think I was at tremendous risk.

I was paying on one of several loans as a part of 10 people. Eventually, some problems developed with the restaurant, and my construction friend and the architect entered into a dispute. Costs escalated, and suddenly there were threats of lawsuits all around, which was something I wanted nothing to do with. Construction of the restaurant was delayed, things were moving at a very slow pace, and eventually, we missed our projected opening date.

The restaurant did finally open under difficult circumstances and after numerous delays. My friend began experiencing problems in the construction business, and he lost a substantial amount of money. It was a time in his life when everything seemed to be falling apart, and the restaurant just added to his worries. Combined with all his other problems, the restaurant was the last thing he wanted to deal with.

I don't think the restaurant was ever given a chance because of all the difficulties involved. Life continued its ugly fall for my friend, and the restaurant struggled until it eventually closed.

Through everything, we remained hopeful that something good would result from it. But times seemed to only get worse. A deal to sell the restaurant fell through, and tensions soon mounted. The financial problems continued for my friend, and soon he was not able to make the rent payments on the restaurant. It was a very substantial loan we were committed to, and we were definitely to be held accountable for it. The banks did give us a little bit of time, but as much as we tried to resolve the problem, nothing seemed to work.

Eventually, the debts grew, and I was responsible for a much larger payment than I could afford. The only thing I could pay was what I had committed to in my own original analysis. This created more tension in the Training Table Association, and it turned into a real crisis. Fortunately, I was touched by some good friends. They came through for me in the clutch. I've always said you can tell who your true friends are because they are the ones who stand beside you. They find ways to help instead of looking for ways to escape.

With help from great friends, I was able to obtain legal assistance I wouldn't have been able to afford otherwise, along with business advice I knew nothing about. The problems didn't go away completely, however. I had to meet with bankruptcy attorneys, and it was a sickening experience to face. Eventually, the issue was settled, and I had to pay a lofty financial price. It was probably more money than I made in my first six or seven years of coaching football.

The most difficult thing about the whole experience was that more people than just myself were involved. I was fearful for my family and what might happen to them. But people—friends—assured me that everything and everybody involved would stay together, one way or another. They, along with my father, supported me through a very tough time. I'll always be grateful to the people who were there when I needed them. I'll always cherish those relationships.

Even though there was a great financial loss, I couldn't help but think of the words of one of my fellow coaches. As I stated before, Bob Phillips told me when times get difficult: "It's not what *happened* to you that's important. It's how you *react* to what happened."

The important things I needed to remember through the whole experience were to stay positive; remain beyond bitterness; to try to salvage a friendship. People might wonder why I would still support a man who helped guide me into such a financial quandary, but this man, my friend, was a man who stood by me during the early struggles of the Second Mile. I believe in my heart that he never intended to hurt me or my family. He could probably have provided better advice, and he could have taken more time to consider some of the things he was doing, but I know he didn't mean for it to go down the way it did. So in the aftermath, I always looked at it as anticipating the day when we could stand together again and move forward.

At a time when this crisis was bad enough, I was faced with dealing with another unfortunate occurrence. My father retired and moved to State College from Washington, Pennsylvania, and that seemed to set off a string of health problems.

He had experienced an irregular heartbeat and seizures over the years resulting from a fall from the stands at a high school basketball game in State College. He was fortunate to have survived it under the circumstances. The fall resulted in back and hip problems, while at the same time he was diagnosed with prostate cancer. He underwent radiation treatments and suffered through many difficult days. He found out he needed a hip replacement and when the doctors were planning for that, they also found my dad had some internal bleeding. He had to go back to the hospital, but he refused, and I remember seeing what a struggle it was for him to move from one side of the house to the other. He crawled and pulled himself up by the furniture.

I looked at him and remembered a man who was so strong; so full of life and love. I wasn't seeing the dad I remembered at that very moment, but that image resurfaced when I saw him pull through all those particular troubles with nothing but simple perseverance. At that time, my father wouldn't quit in the battle for life, and that was the man I knew and loved so well.

The greatest thing I remember about visiting Dad in the hospital was an orderly named Ramon. He was of Spanish or Mexican descent, and my dad's face lit up every time Ramon came into the room. They sang and had a lot of fun together. When my dad was having surgery, it was Ramon who wheeled him down the hallway, and you could hear both of them singing as they traveled to the elevators.

When I talk to the Second Mile children about prestige and power, I tell them about Ramon. He didn't hold an influential position in the community, but he approached his job with a positive attitude. He made his position significant by making people feel better. Ramon never complained about having to help people when they were hurting and suffering. He was the patient's light in what is often a very dark situation. His enthusiasm, as well as his love for his work, was contagious. I tell the children that doctors save lives but so do janitors, orderlies and others who might have jobs with less stature or prestige. It is people like Ramon who give me the inspiration to share my stories with others.

As I've said before, I've been very fortunate to have been surrounded by some outstanding people in my life. I've always tried to learn; to sit back and observe; and to benefit from my association with these people. I have thoughts and beliefs relative to what it takes to be a champion. Everything is related. What it takes to put together a great family; a great athletic team; a great business. If you want to be a champion, there are certain choices you have to make.

My feelings are that one must prioritize his life physically, spiritually and mentally. You must also decide the important things: family, friends, times to work and times to play. For the most part, people I've been around have made positive choices. They have enjoyed positive outlets from their tensions and anxieties, and they've been able to go beyond themselves in reaching out. They are thankful for what they have received and are willing to give to others.

There are seven C words in relation to becoming a champion in my mind. The first one is **COMMUNICATION**. Whether it is with family, a team or an organization, it is important for everyone to be on the same page. Everyone should understand their role with constant feedback in terms of everyone reaching their intended goals.

COOPERATION: We talk about "we" and "us" people. They are willing to share or give up a little bit of their individual pride for the good of the team. They are not so much worried about their role, but their contribution to a successful group. It takes people with discipline and people with respect and consideration for others.

COMMITMENT: Knowing what it means to make a true pledge of allegiance. So many times, the pledge of allegiance is just words. It is easy to talk about your beliefs, but the tough part is standing up for them. A commitment can be somewhat scary because, in essence, you're giving in to something that is bigger than yourself. Whether it is family, school, church or anything, you might be forced to make decisions that are not popular or cool. You might be laughed at or criticized, which can hurt greatly.

A commitment means you make no excuses if you fail. I am convinced that those who make the commitments are never the losers. They might run out of time in an athletic contest, or they might not have enough time to prepare for a specific test, but they did not lose. The losers are those who are afraid to fail. They might stand back and experience a lot of things in life, but they miss a few of the things that might bring them more happiness than they would ever know. They miss the opportunity to lose themselves in a cause and lose themselves in reaching out to others.

When I think of commitment, I think of that 1986 national championship team that defeated Miami. The commitment level of that group was so great, they were able to get the job done. There were 11 times during that season when the game's outcome was decided on the last play. We won all 11 times, and one of the biggest reasons was because those players committed themselves to a cause. They refused to give in and fought with everything they had.

CLASS: "What is class?" is a question I used to write on the chalkboard. After that, I wrote the following words: *"Class is not afraid. It takes on challenges and tackles difficult situations with great effort and energy. Class wins without boasting and loses without excuses. Class is not 'I' and 'me,' it is 'we' and 'us.' Class isn't related to wealth and fame. Some of the richest and most powerful people might lack it, while the poorest, most handicapped person might beam with it. Class never tries to build itself up while tearing others down. Class is already up and needs not to strive to look better by trying to make others worse. Class can work with kings, queens and presidents, and still have time for the most common worker. Everyone is comfortable with a person who has class because that person is comfortable with himself. If you have class, you don't need much of anything else. If you don't have it, whatever else you have will not make much of a difference."*

When I think of class, I am again reminded of the former Penn State wrestler I am friends with, Jim Martin. Jim lost in the NCAA semifinals in his senior year, but he came back hard in the next match to finish third. The class inside of him wouldn't let him quit, despite the fluke loss he had suffered earlier. His loss was unexpected, and he could have easily crumbled, but he didn't, and it makes him a better man for the class that he displayed.

COURAGE: Winston Churchill once said: "Success is never final; failure is never fatal. The only thing that counts is courage." It does take courage to put on the football equipment in the heat of summer or cold of winter. To do battle in any sport or athletic event takes the courage to start and follow through on your dream, whether your goals are met or not. It takes courageous people to rise up and be the best in the toughest battle, no matter what that might be.

I always carry the words of Colin McCarty with me: *"If we don't ever take chances, we won't reach the rainbows. If we don't ever search, we will never be able to find. If we don't attempt to get over our doubts and fears, we will never discover how wonderful it is to live without them. If we don't keep our dreams alive, we won't have our dreams any longer. If we take a chance now and then—seek and search; discover and dream; grow and go;—through each day with the knowledge that we can only take as much as we can give, and we can only get as much out of life as we allow ourselves to live, then we can truly be happy. We can realize a dream or two along the way, and we can make a habit of lives with wonderful days."*

CONSISTENCY: It is easy to play football with emotion for one quarter, or to prepare for a couple of days. However, champions work when others are resting, and they find the strength to do it just about every day, without fail.

CARING: It is what all the other Cs lead to. It is an appreciation for others—love based on respect and admiration. I've seen this in Penn State football. I've seen black, white, brown and yellow come together, but the greatest part was that they were all blue and white on the field, and that was all that mattered. You can tell by the looks in their eyes and the determination on their faces that they will be tough to beat.

Some of the most emotional experiences of my life have been in those locker rooms after great wins and very tough losses. Truly, the most significant experience came after the Fiesta Bowl win over Miami. Everything that happened in there—the hugging, the tears, the love—was sincere and genuine. It all came about because a group of people came together that year and showed how much they believed in each other, and how much they cared for each other.

I use these seven Cs when I talk to kids because they are often the ones who can benefit from such lessons and hopefully build a better future for themselves.

23

Touched

BEING A FOOTBALL COACH, I WAS CONSTANTLY DEALING WITH GAME PLANS. Maybe that is why I look at the certain aspects of life and nature as God's own game plan. Because as I look around, I see the complexity of life, and it amazes me how everything interrelates. I'm astonished with the beauty, the still waters, the calm, the differences, the unique people, and the rules and regulations that help us to function and what life would be like without them. There are the peaks and valleys; the sunlight and the shadow of death. I'm not a very complex person; I'm actually quite simple, but I still believe there are moments that are sacred and there are precious things not meant to be touched.

I'm always amazed at God's plan for everyone. No matter how small or insignificant we are, there is something each one of us can contribute— something we all can do. We all have a place in this life. When I think of all these things being related, I think that's why volunteering has been so important to me. We can't stand alone. We need each other. I believe when you volunteer, you're buying into God's plan of giving and sharing and doing unto others as you would have them do unto you. We want to stand for something special; stand a little taller; reach a little higher. We care through action, but when we get wrapped up, we can become vulnerable. We can get hurt.

I remember visiting a cousin who was suffering under the stillness of a coma in the hospital. At the time, I was hurting. I didn't want to see him under those circumstances. I went through with it, however. I talked to him. I touched his hand, and later I was glad I had made that visit. He died right after I left.

I have visited homes of helplessness, filth and despair, and I will always remember the emptiness that comes with doing so. I felt fortunate to have what I had after visiting such homes, and I was touched by the sadness of such a situation. I have also visited the elderly and witnessed the hurt they have suffered. They have so many unpleasant tasks and often, so little reason to live.

I once visited a man named Harry Chapman. He was a great football coach in the high school ranks. He was in the hospital when I saw him, dying of bone cancer. A mere sneeze could crack one of his ribs. The minute I saw Harry, I knew he was hurting, but I could tell by his actions that he was more concerned for the way I felt. He didn't want me to be uncomfortable because of the problems he was having.

When we dare to care; when we reach out and touch someone's hand, trying to make the world a better place, we get back so much more than we can give. To see the gleam in a child's eye when he or she succeeds. To see happiness come across the face of a lonely person sets off a very warm feeling.

I have walked with some of society's so-called best, but I've also been hugged by some of society's least. I know I cherish the latter a lot more. In this plan, we are but one little candle, but when you dare to care, it does make for a better world.

We are given many talents, and God creates great hope for us all. He lifts us to great heights. We have conquered parts of outer space, yet He is always there to humble us by exposing us to great suffering and hurt. God reveals Himself in the outstretched hands of a loved one; in the outstretched hands of a child in need. He reveals Himself through those who are handicapped; those who have the least. He brings love, hope and happiness to those of us who already appear to have so much more. He touches us after a tough loss, but no matter how bad we've done that day, friends and family will still be there.

God reveals Himself in so many strong leaders. He reveals Himself in Jesus Christ; in the commitment of those who followed Him and the people who are human, just like us, with so many of the same doubts and questions. Nobody has touched more lives than God, but how did He do it? He didn't go around waving His crown and boasting of Himself. He did it by example, by standing strong and not wavering, even when His whole world was crumbling. He did it with true toughness, giving the comfort of knowing that He is the person you want around you when times get to be their toughest. We feel His presence when we fail to reach out and touch the lost and heartbroken. When we fall, He is ready to pick us up because He cares. He relishes in helping us to move forward.

I have been touched by a lot of people who have fallen with me. People like Samantha, who wrote the letter telling us what the Second Mile had meant to her. Also by C.B., who told us we had been the wind beneath his wings.

I am touched by Shirley Reynard, who is disabled, but she donates to the Second Mile because she wants to help others. I am touched when Shirley stands up as a leader for the handicapped groups. She stands a lot taller than I ever could. I am touched by the many calls and letters from the young people whom we've had at the football camps.

I wish, sometimes, that I could press a button to bring back the times when life was so much simpler with the kids. The times when they didn't worry about what they were missing with drugs, alcohol and sex. They didn't have to worry about protection from AIDS and HIV. They enjoyed life's simple pleasures in a naive time; a time of make-believe. There were simple activities and worthwhile outlets. People just enjoyed each other simply as people.

The foundation of this book was when we attended a fund-raising mission to a little central Pennsylvania community called Philipsburg. A radio station there was holding a telethon, and we were hoping to raise a substantial amount of money for the Second Mile. We pulled into the station, which was situated just off a mountain road, and we were greeted by a man named Dave.

Dave was the manager of the station. He was also the disc jockey, janitor and everything that kept the station operating. I took some people with me, including Bob White, who was a captain on our 1986 national championship, Bill Kenney, who was, and still is, a Penn State coach, and several other football players and athletes. We all enjoyed that day and its experiences. Dave was my kind of person—not fancy, but willing to work. He told us he had written a ballad about the Persian Gulf war, which was in progress at the time, and he said if we were willing to sing it with him, we could have ten extra minutes of radio time. Well, when Dave mentioned singing, he had hit the right chord with me. "You're on, Dave," I said excitedly. "We'll sing with you."

The show wasn't very organized. There were several lulls in the action, and we kind of jumped from one subject to another. During the course of the show, we received a grand total of two calls. One was from a lady who was very upset because she requested a song and it was held up because of our show. The other call was a $20 contribution, and I think that was just because the person felt sorry for us. It turned out to be a $20 trip, but the enjoyment we all received made it seem worth a million bucks.

The day was utter chaos. No organization, bad singing, everything. But it was fun. And as we came down from the mountain, I felt something. "You know," I said to no one in particular, "I wonder about us, but I really feel I've been touched in a way that makes me want to share all of these experiences with somebody. With everybody."

That was how I came up with the idea for this book. That is what it's all about.

Over the past few years, two of the lives who have touched my own life the most have been taken. During the difficult times, I think of the words Coach Bob Phillips reminded me of about how we react to the bad things that happen in our lives. I also think of my father and the love and respect I have always had for him. I have called him the greatest male role model I could ever have, and now, as I embark on my own retirement, my feelings haven't changed.

Bob was a good friend to me as I learned more and more about what it took to be a successful college football coach. He passed away in April, 2000, from Parkinson's Disease, but he will forever be remembered as a great role model. He showed genuine and sincere interest in all kinds of people, especially children, no matter what level of athletic ability they had. He got to know their names and treated them as special people. Whenever someone was in need, they could always go to Coach Bob for help.

I saw him two weeks prior to his death, and we laughed about past antics with J.T. White, as well as some of the more memorable football camps we had been through. One day, before he died, I witnessed Bob struggle to respond to me. It hurt to see this man who had done so much in his life for others waste away right before my eyes. A young girl who was a daughter of one of Bob's nurses brought him a stuffed lion and, although he couldn't respond the way he would have liked, the smile on his face said it all.

We lost a very special man and very special friend that day. A man who made a positive impact on so many young people.

Ironically, through all the rough physical times my father had endured in the preceding years, he would eventually succumb to the same disease that took Bob Phillip's life three years later.

It was September 14, 1996, and we had started our season with impressive wins over Southern California and a very good Louisville team. We were playing Northern Illinois that day, and it was still early in the morning when Dottie received a call from our daughter, Kara, who said she thought my father was dead. Dottie told me, but I had been sensing it and I knew it was coming. "It was time for it to end," I said very quietly.

I'll never forget that moment. He was so tough, and he battled so hard. But he was suffering and had become very frustrated. I immediately went to my parents' house to be with my mom. She is such a strong-willed person, and I guess I was in some sort of state of shock, even though I sensed his end was nearing.

The coroner was there and he asked me if I wished to see my dad. I walked into his bedroom and there he lay, motionless. The rock of my life was gone. I held him and everything became a flashback. I thought of times when I was a kid until some of the very last days when I had taken my father swimming. As the cycle of life would have it, there I was, holding him up in the water, trying to help him swim; getting him to kick his feet; doing the same things he had done for me over 45 years before.

At one point in our swimming lessons, I was concentrating on his feet, and I accidentally lowered his upper body and head under the water. Fortunately, some people on the side of the pool noticed and as I spied their concerned expressions, I realized what I had done. I quickly pulled his head out of the water and he screamed at me, "What are you doing?!?" When I was sure he was okay, I put a smile on my face and said, "It's payback time, isn't it?"

That day, we raced about five yards in the water and even then, he competed so hard. This was a man I could never defeat in anything. Not long before Dad passed away, I was there for a visit, and my mother was upsetting me. She wouldn't accept any help, and I felt that everything was taking a huge toll on her. She was saying things out of frustration that she thought my dad wouldn't hear, but he did. Even though I knew how much she cared, I yelled at her. She got upset at the whole thing and left the room. Now, my dad and I were alone. What I had just done was never, ever condoned by my dad. I was afraid he would be upset and scream at me. All he did, instead, was look up and say, "Jer, you're 150 percent right." I smiled, somewhat relieved in the fact that he understood, but I would always be concerned that my mother was doing too much, despite the inner strength she possessed.

Now, as my father lay still and lifeless on the bed, I felt a rush of memories surge through me. I wanted to stay with him, to stay with Mom, but I knew I had to leave. Dad would have wanted me at that football game, and he would have wanted me to carry on as always. I drove away from their house and went about my regular pregame rituals, which included picking up some of the Second Mile kids. Man, how my dad loved them, just as he had loved the kids at the Brownson House so many years before.

When I got to the football locker room, I went on with everything as usual, without saying much to anybody. I knew the players and coaches and other team personnel cared, so not much needed to be said. We won the game, and the players presented me with the game ball. I took it as a tribute to my dad, and I remember talking to a Second Mile youngster that night about my dad, telling him stories, and hoping he would understand.

The next week was a very emotional one. We decided to have a service in State College, followed by a final service in Washington, Pennsylvania I had so much I wanted to say, and somehow I managed to get through it. Whatever points I might have missed were expressed in a song that Kara sang in her grandfather's honor.

The experience in Washington was more difficult, because I got to see all of the people who had touched me and made such a difference in my life. There were the mentally and physically handicapped, the poor, the wealthy, the famous, and the unknown. When it was finally over, I stood alone with my family and hugged every one of them. We had all come from various paths, but on that day, we were one.

We won another game the following weekend against Temple, but it left me with a very empty feeling. I would never be able to share the happiness of victory or the sadness of defeat with him again. But I knew he would always be beside me, to comfort me and pick me up, just the same way he did at least a thousand times before in my life.

24

The Final Decision

THE WINTER OF 1999 WAS KIND OF DIFFICULT. I tried to do a lot of things. I came to the realization that I was not destined to become the head football coach at Penn State. I didn't want my experience at Penn State to end with anything but positive feelings. I tried to start football at Penn State's Altoona campus, because I knew I still loved football. I didn't want to leave the Second Mile, and Altoona was close by, but that prospect never worked out. Suddenly, I found myself sitting back and thinking: *What am I going to do with myself?*

There was talk of me going into athletic administration, but I knew that wasn't for me. I was a football coach, and I liked working with kids of all ages. I found myself going around and around, wondering what was next.

The thought of retirement had never really entered my head throughout those many years, but as April came around, I finally considered taking advantage of a 30-year window of opportunity to retire from Penn State football, so I could begin to turn my attention fully toward the Second Mile, the organization that I loved.

I spoke to Coach Paterno, and he turned me over to Tim Curley, Penn State's athletic director, and we began going over the process of negotiating retirement while maintaining some sort of relationship with the place that I loved: Penn State University.

The month of June came around, and I was involved with coaching in the summer camps. Those camps had become such a huge part of me. I had been in charge of the on-field operations, and now I had to decide what I was going to do. I thought of all the young people who had come through those football camps—as well as the Second Mile camps— and how they had touched my life. I wondered what they would think of me no longer being associated with Penn State football.

We were approaching the last week of camp, and shortly I would have to make my decision. One way or another I wanted to make my decision on the afternoon of the day *before* I actually had to make it. I was heading to the practice field, and I tried to call Tim Curley, but I couldn't get hold of him. A couple of days previously, I held another meeting with Coach Paterno, and it was then that I truly felt it was time.

I was out on the practice field, and Brad Caldwell, the man we called Spider, came out and did one of his annual skits with me because the kids always enjoyed the entertainment as much as the football lessons. As we worked together, I realized it was going to be my last time out there. I had tears in my eyes, and the kids didn't understand the emotional stress I was going through. I called Dottie and said: "This stinks, I don't feel good about this decision at all, but I guess I'm going to do it."

When I finally reached Tim Curley, I told him of my plans and he asked me how I felt. "I feel lousy," I told him. "I don't feel good about this at all." He told me to take the rest of that day and think about it some more.

I spent that evening with friends and although I didn't talk much about it, they could sense what a struggle it was for me. After that evening, though, I was more comfortable with my decision, because I came to the realization that, as emotional as I was about that football camp, I would have that same feeling or worse about Second Mile camps, when it would involve leaving kids without being able to spend as much time with them as I would have liked. The tears would come the same way.

I lay in my bed at night thinking that the Second Mile had become extremely important to me and had become a huge part of my life. I knew deep down that during my most difficult moments, when I had times of great decision, times of difficult and sometimes devastating experiences, the people whom I leaned on the most were the Second Mile people. They were always the ones who were there for me when I needed them the most. People like Bruce Heim and John Reidell, who stood by me and helped me through times of crisis.

I had made the decision and it was final. We were going to have a press conference the next day because we knew it had become public information because of the retirement window. We felt it would be better to tell everyone as soon as possible. When camp ended that morning, I had plans to go miniature golfing with my son, Jon, Mac Morrison, one of our linebackers, and Brett from the Second Mile. We made it to the golf complex and all of a sudden, a photographer showed up and asked if he could take some pictures. My first thought was that maybe he was doing a picture story on Mac, but I would soon learn he was there because of my impending retirement announcement. I stopped at my office before I took Brett home, and there were a bunch of phone messages for me. Although I had wanted to wait a day or so, it became apparent that the story had leaked out. Suddenly, the press conference we had planned for the next day had moved up to that evening and had turned into a phone conference with the media. Just like that, my retirement had become official news.

Some of our players, like LaVar Arrington, got mad at me because I had never really talked to any of them about what I had been thinking of. I sat down and wrote a couple of letters to explain my decision. The first was to the players on July 6, 1999. I told them about the retirement window and how sorry I was for the distraction my decision may have caused. I told them I would never have believed I would have taken myself out of coaching at that stage, but it was extremely important for me to end my coaching career at Penn State with a positive feeling. I let them know I wanted to provide athletes at Penn State with what they deserved, but the uncertainty of whether I could have provided that positive feeling for five more years prompted my decision. I ended my letter to the players by telling them, simply, that I cared.

Then I wrote a letter to the supporters of the Second Mile. I told them that change can be challenging; change is inevitable. I let them know with the change I would be going through I would be able to provide more time to the Second Mile. I told the supporters how much needed to be done concerning children who faced hopelessness and despair, and I spoke of the huge challenges we would face together. I reminded them how frowns turn to smiles, and how many children have gone on to bigger and better things. And I asked the supporters to hang with us and stay through this transition, as well as through the future times when children would need us.

The first of many lasts was the annual media day proceedings at our 1999 preseason football camp. It was described as a can't-miss season for Penn State because of the many returning starters we had on defense, as well as an offense. These players would come in with much more experience, especially at quarterback, where we had two guys who were very capable of leading our offense—Kevin Thompson and Rashard Casey.

As the media converged onto the grass field of Beaver Stadium that bright August afternoon, the feeling began to hit me that things were actually coming to an end. It would be the last time I would do this. The last time I would talk to sports journalists with my thoughts of how much talent we had returning, and how best we could utilize that talent. It would also be the last time I would ever have my picture taken with the entire team.

We practiced through the same long two-a-days I had grown accustomed to as a raw freshman back in 1962. We were building for our season-opener, which was an added home game to our schedule. It was the first time Penn State would participate in the annual Pigskin Classic. We were pitted against Arizona, which came into the game ranked as the pre-season No. 4 team in the country.

I was relaxed during most of the pre-season practice sessions. I was having fun and enjoying the time I had left with the kids on the team. Finally, the day came to play Arizona, and as we prepared, I couldn't help but reflect on the fact that this would be the last time I would prepare for a season-opener. As I said, the 1999 season would see the first of many lasts for me.

At Penn State, our setup was for the team to get dressed for games at the practice locker room and then be bussed over to the stadium, which, with the route we took, was roughly a mile-long ride. The weekly motorcade was lined with die-hard Penn State fans, and as the I sat on that bus for the first game of the 1999 season, I had tears in my eyes as I thought of all the people who were there.

Inside the stadium, I looked up at the press box and thought of the many times my mom and dad had made the trip from Washington, Pa., to see me play here and how they had always been there for me. I was disappointed that it was all coming to an end and my dad wasn't there anymore. It was one of those occasions where I didn't know whether to feel happy or sad.

We felt we were in for a battle in that game, but everything seemed to go our way. It was one of those days where even when we made a mistake, it turned out to be a positive play, like a quarterback sack. We were able to take Arizona out of the gimmicks they liked to employ, and we actually won the game quite easily. That got our season off to a fantastic start because expectations were extremely high for Arizona, and we did pretty well.

The first real challenge we had came in a game that not many—other than everyone affiliated with the team—figured would be much of a challenge at all. It was against the University of Pittsburgh and in a game like that, no matter what the records are for either team, or who's up and who's down, the rivalry always seems to be there. It would soon prove to be just such a day.

LaVar Arrington had an interception, but he also dropped two. We misjudged another pass, and they caught a touchdown off of it. Near the end, Pitt was driving down the field with a chance to win the game. Dave Fleischauer, an unheralded athlete at Penn State who worked awfully hard, came up with a big sack to knock Pitt back for a huge loss. LaVar then blocked a long, last-second field-goal attempt, and we were able to hang on for the win. As we had thought, the game was much more difficult than people had expected, but it felt good to get a win in that manner because we needed that kind of experience. Everything had come so easy up to then, and we were about to head into the most difficult stretch of our season. What I didn't realize was how difficult that stretch was going to be.

We had some tough trips coming up with a trip to Miami heading the list. That week, my son, E.J., and his wife, Maureen, had their second child, and they named him Ryan Arthur. Arthur was my dad's name and my middle name. I was talking to Brett, one of the Second Mile kids, and I told him about my son naming his new baby. I said the baby's middle initial and mine were the same. I asked Brett if he knew what the A stood for and he said: "Yes—aggravation." He was probably thinking what I might have been to him and many of the kids from the Second Mile.

When we went to the stadium in Miami, we were greeted by a very hostile crowd. They were really on LaVar Arrington for a very honest mistake he made earlier in the week when he mentioned he didn't know much about one of the Hurricane's great linebackers. He said it in a manner that he was only interested in his team, but it was taken out of context and eaten up by the Miami fans and media. We were leading, 3-0, and we increased it to 10-0 with a touchdown pass. I turned to look for the defense on the sidelines, and I noticed LaVar on the other side of the bench turned toward the crowd.

My first thought was that he was taunting the crowd, and that was the last thing I wanted to see. I wanted him to concentrate on the game and not pay attention to anything else. I didn't want anything distracting him from the huge challenge we had in front of us. I kind of saw red at that moment, and I charged back toward that bench to get LaVar's attention, but I tripped on the chairs in front of the bench. As I was falling, I knocked over the bench, but I continued to scramble to get at

LaVar. "The game is out here!" I screamed at him. "The game is out here! Forget about what's going on in the stands!"

LaVar just looked at me, not sure what was happening. He just saw a crazy man with fire in his eyes screaming at him, and the other players had little clue either. His first inclination was to just laugh, which he did, but I screamed at him again. "Turn around and quit paying attention to the stands!" He looked at me and said: "You're right, Jer." And he went back toward the field and to what he was supposed to be doing.

It was that kind of day, very emotional. It was raining during most of the first half, but not very heavily. When I walked out to the field for the second half, it had started to rain harder. I started to think we might not want to receive the second-half kickoff, because we had been playing pretty good defense. So, when Coach Paterno came out, I told him what I thought and he agreed. He tried to get the attention of our captains, who were on their way to midfield with the officials. Coach Paterno even asked another official to try to catch our captains, but the official was too slow and didn't get there in time. The captains opted to receive, which they were originally instructed to do, and it turned out to be a good thing they didn't hear us, because the rain stopped almost instantly and we ran the kickoff back 40 yards or so.

We had great field position, the rain had stopped, and we went down the field and scored. It was almost another great strategic decision by Jer. Had we decided to kick there, it's quite possible we could have lost the football game. We were in a very emotional game, one that was see-sawing back and forth. We were on defense in a critical fourth-down and short yardage situation late in the game, and if Miami would have made the first down on that play, the game would have been over. We wondered if they would try a field goal, but it would have been a long one, and they had missed an extra point earlier. Miami lined up and tried a running play, but two of our players came through in a very big way.

Maurice (Mo) Daniels and Ron Graham, who were both second-team linebackers, stood the runner up and held him for no gain. Now we got the ball back, and we scored on a long touchdown pass from Kevin Thompson to Chafie Fields. Miami still had time to mount a final drive, but Askari Adams, one of our defensive backs, came up with a big interception and we were able to win the game. Mo had been with us for five years, and he had always come up in the clutch to make big plays, while Ron Graham was an outstanding player also.

When Askari made the interception, I was jumping higher than I had jumped in many years. My son, Jon, ran toward me screaming that the game wasn't over because Miami would get the ball back. I think he will make a great coach some day, because he was right. They did have enough time, but fortunately, we got another interception from Derek Fox to seal it.

We played Indiana at home after Miami, and it was the first time I had found myself disappointed in the team. Indiana had an outstanding young quarterback, and although we played well enough to win the game, there were indications of a lack of discipline and a lack of concentration. We had too many people who were trying to make plays, only to see those efforts turn into big plays for the opposition.

Now we had come to a kind of crisis stage in our season. We traveled to Iowa, and I talked to the team the night before the game. I compared this stage of our season to becoming a foster parent. Any time you're involved in foster care, there is also a honeymoon period where there is enthusiasm, and people are trying to please each other. That's where I felt we were. After I had announced my retirement, there was so much enthusiasm and publicity. Against Pittsburgh, we had chances to make plays and we didn't. Same for Miami and Indiana. Now it seemed like we were having some doubts. The public had come down on the defense, and people were feeling that maybe we weren't as good defensively as we were thought to be. We weren't living up to the fans' expectations, and we probably weren't living up to our own either.

I told the players the night before that Iowa game that I had some thoughts in my own mind. I thought maybe we had some people who were too self-centered. I questioned whether we were really tough; whether we had received too much hype; whether we talked too much. I questioned whether we really had enough fight and whether we really cared enough.

Were we willing to lay it all out there week after week? I let them know that the honeymoon was over and gave them some advice. I told the players they should listen to us (coaches) and forget about everything but us. Forget about recognition and forget about professional football careers. I talked to them about all the great teams and the great athletes. I talked to them about former Super Bowl championship teams and how many of those athletes were unheralded in college, and how many of our own championship teams came from people who hadn't been heavily recruited.

I was concerned with people who were missing appointments and who were missing classes, and not taking care of the things they were supposed to take care of. We played well enough and won at Iowa and then came home to play Ohio State. We were able to stop the run early, which enabled us to turn our linebackers loose. I remember Mac Morrison getting a concussion and having to come out of the game, and Ron Graham playing extremely well in his place. Mac followed me around the entire game, begging and pleading for me to put him back in the game. I told him I couldn't, because the doctors ordered him out, which was true.

We knew we had another big challenge the following week as we headed out to Purdue. They had Drew Brees, a great quarterback, but we talked about that challenge the night before the game. Every person in that room said he was not going to make a mistake. Everyone, including the coaches, had his own responsibility, and that's all he could take care of. The one thing we had to do was fight; to keep our poise no matter what happened.

We had some great plays that day. LaVar had a quarterback sack where he caused a fumble, picked it up and ran it in for a touchdown. Courtney Brown intercepted a pass and returned it for a touchdown also. The goal-line stand where we had put together a kind of unique, crazy defense. Courtney was able to shake himself free and get two sacks in a row. I wasn't sure we could call that defense, but we had no choice at that time.

There were a few times when we did lose our poise, and I was yelling as much as anyone. That was when Brandon Short said to me: "I thought that meant we were *all* supposed to keep our poise out there." We held on for a great win at Purdue, and I will never forget hugging an exhausted Courtney Brown and many of the other players after the game.

We won the next game at Illinois and then followed the three M's: Minnesota, Michigan and Michigan State. We fought hard against Minnesota, and I remember the uneasy feeling I had before the game, like things just not seeming right, and how Minnesota was such a dangerous team. Sure enough, things just didn't go our way, and we found ourselves losing a game we never should have lost. We blew too many assignments, didn't cover the tight end a couple of times, and that cost us for big plays. We didn't cover the back out of the backfield, and we got burnt for it. It seemed like we just flat-out blew the game. There were some disappointing experiences, and we would soon find it just wasn't meant to be.

There should have been an illegal procedure penalty called on a play where they had a large gain. We stopped them three plays in a row, and now it was fourth down. I wanted to use what we call our "preserve" defense, which is a blitz. I felt like we could have sacked the quarterback, but I was talked out of it. It wasn't something a normal person would have attempted in all likelihood, but I've never been known as a normal person. Looking back, I wish I would have made that call because I think it would have worked and we would have gotten to the quarterback. It was one of those agonizing decisions you think about as a coach, long after the game is ended and the results are final. I still think about it today.

We came away from that game feeling like we were still not precise enough to be a big league football team and win a game like that. We didn't make enough plays defensively or offensively and we let Minnesota hang in long enough to gain a chance for a last-second field goal they made it and won by two. Next we had another home game, this one which everyone figured to be much tougher than what was expected from Minnesota.

Frank Rocco, one of our associate athletic directors and administrators at the time, called me during the week of the Michigan game and said the university wanted me to run out of the tunnel with the seniors as part of my last home football game. I wasn't sure I wanted to do that because I had never even done it as a player and I really didn't want to detract from the focus of that game and the focus that the players needed to have. Frank explained that it really wasn't for me, but for the other people involved who wanted to give me a proper send-off. So, I did it.

When I ran out of that tunnel and onto the field, it was kind of like running into a vacuum of people. I ran into the arms of some of our players and hugged them. There were tears as it almost felt like I was hugging every player that I had ever coached. The last one I came to was our son, Jon. He was a player on the football team and I thought of how many fathers in this world who would give anything to share a similar experience.

The game itself was such an emotional roller coaster. One of our biggest mistakes, probably, was not making enough substitutions early in the game to give the defense ample rest. We scored twice on defense and that, in a way, made it worse because the defense ended up being on the field too much.

Toward the end of the football game we went ahead, but we had a couple of critical penalties. One was on third down when a Michigan drive was stopped. Under the right circumstances, we would have gotten the ball back and had a good chance to run out the clock. Instead, the defense was forced to stay on the field, and Michigan capitalized. We weren't as precise as we should have been, once again, and it just seemed like victory wasn't supposed to happen for us. That setback against Michigan was a terrible, terrible loss.

Michigan State was the last of the M games, as I called them. We got off to a horrible start. It was another terribly frustrating day. One where we gave up only 253 yards total offense, but we gave up 35 points. We had a number of injuries, among them LaVar Arrington, who was still feeling the effects from a devastating hit he had put on a Michigan ball carrier the week before. The injuries also affected special teams and went right on down the line.

We started out poorly, as I said, but then we battled back. We started clicking again on both sides of the ball, and it looked like we were going to make a great comeback. I can say we had our chances, but in the end we just didn't have enough to get it done. It was the same old refrain. A fumble here, a couple of dropped passes there. Michigan State made the plays in the clutch to win the game, and once again we were a team that suffered lapses at the most crucial time.

Those were three of the most difficult losses I had ever been through as a coach. Those three losses were comparable to our 1978 Sugar Bowl loss to Alabama. They had the same slamming devastation; the same numbing effect on everyone involved.

Maybe we were trying too hard, because when it reached that stage of the season, where we had everything in our grasp, it just didn't work out or come together. Sometimes, as I look back, I think we might have blitzed too often in those three games. Instead of thinking we had to hold the other team, we often had the pressing thought that we must shut them out. That may have been the wrong thought in terms of saving strength.

It was frustrating and lonely as we walked off the Michigan State field in a slow drizzle. I remember having a sick feeling afterward, and as I sat on the bus, I felt very depressed. I looked out the window and saw a young man with his father who had come all the way from the Harrisburg area. The young man had met LaVar Arrington a couple years earlier at a high school all-star football game in Harrisburg, and LaVar had always been nice to him. Now, as he stood in that same depressing drizzle with his dad, he yelled to me from outside the window.

"Coach Sandusky," the young man said. "Thanks for everything. We're really going to miss you."

I kind of blew him a kiss, then bowed my head and cried. It sort of summarized everything I was feeling during that emotional roller coaster. I had the honor of looking into our son's eyes and sending him into battle in a place where maybe he didn't belong, because he might have lacked the size and speed of others. He went out there, however, because we asked him to. He did what we asked and that is a champion.

I came away from that season with a tremendous appreciation of what it takes to be a champion from a lot of people.

Soon after the regular season ended, there was the Quarterback Club banquet, where I was honored with a Distinguished Alumni award as a part of the Penn State football program. I learned I would have to make a speech in accepting the award, and I can still recall some of the things I had to say:

"I learned on Friday that I was receiving this award," I said to the captive audience. *"Had it been a total surprise, I probably would have made you happy by just talking not longer than a minute. But since then, a lot has crossed my mind, and I will try to compromise and say some things that are important to me.*

"This day started when I was a senior in high school, when I was looking for a place to go to college and hopefully play football. I was looking for a place that was a lot like the one I was leaving. A place that was plain and proud. Those who know me, understand that I am happiest when I am playing games with my family; riding a bus with Second Mile kids; teasing kids; singing songs as part of the Great Pretenders at the Second Mile camps and Penn State football camps.

"I found a plain university with many first-generation college students. Genuine, sincere people who were very similar to what I was. The 'pride' part of me came from my father, who taught me never to do anything halfway; to give it my best shot and do it from my heart and soul; to be proud of my effort in the end. I found that here at Penn State and I found the 'We are, Penn State' pride that goes along with it.

"The first person I met at Penn State was J. T. White, and you could see from the sparkle in his eyes the competitiveness and pride he carried. You could also see that plainness in his way with words. I owe a lot to other coaches such as Jim O'Hora; Bob Phillips; Frank Patrick; 'Tor' Toretti; Dan Radakovich; Earl Bruce, and so many others. They were coaches, yes, but they were so much more than that. They were and are true friends who drove us and pushed us, helping us to reach higher and stand taller. They brought out the best in us and they were there if we ever needed them. They weren't out looking for another job or trying to get ahead. They were there for us and that was their purpose."

I also talked about portions of my playing career during my acceptance speech. I talked about the way I looked up to Dick Anderson and how I wanted to succeed as a graduate assistant, and I talked about how Joe Paterno had hired me, and one of my first assignments from him was to leave the great linebacker, Jack Ham, alone. I talked about the numerous goal-line stands we faced; the come-from-behind victories; and the players who showed the same examples of pride along the way.

I had never wanted a grand exit from Penn State football, but this honor was exactly that. As I stood up there, I shared with the audience as many memories as I could think of. I told them about the young man who stood outside our bus at Michigan state and gave me those emotional and encouraging words.

"I had a great ride with so many fond memories," I said in closing. *"It comes to an end now, because I never wanted to ask for more from those players than anything I was able to give myself. We asked for commitment, they gave it. We asked for loyalty, they stuck with us through the highs and lows. We asked for courage and cooperation, they gave us those, too. We asked them to care, and they cared deeply. I hoped that the players trusted this ending had come because I cared. Because I wanted those who were left to get the kind of commitment they deserved. I wanted to have many great memories of Penn State football.*

"When I ran out of that tunnel at Beaver Stadium before the Michigan game and into the arms of the players, I was hugging every player I had ever coached. When I hugged my son, Jon, I was hugging my family. When I blew a kiss, it was to those who had touched my life and weren't there at that moment in time. When I said thank you, it was to all of you for your support and warmth. And when I cried, it was to say 'I love you.'"

The audience gave me a hand, and I cried once more. It was a very nice honor, and although we still had some unfinished business as a team, the award I received that night let me know that my efforts over those more than 35 years at Penn State did not go unnoticed.

Now, it was time to go on to the Alamo Bowl to coach in the final game of my career. It seemed like we had lost a lot of believers after the results of those last three regular-season games, but we still had a group of players who believed in themselves and a coaching staff who wanted to carry that belief through to the end.

We had a practice on a cold, rainy day, and I remember the defense was practicing on the upper practice field while the offense was on the field down below. Coach Paterno blew his whistle, which meant the defense was to join the offense. Our defense gathered together, and I tried to get Joe Sarra to lead the charge down the hill, but he wouldn't do it. So I led the defensive charge, and I had everyone screaming: "Remember the Alamo Bowl!"

I remember a nice boat ride around the city of San Antonio on Christmas night and a birthday party we had for Matt at Planet Hollywood Hotel. There was also a luncheon where sports commentator and former University of Pittsburgh football coach Mike Gottfried said some very great things about our defense, and he spoke fondly of Brandon Short and Mo Daniels, and I remember the great Christmas eve party we had.

I sat in the bleachers at a pep rally the day before the game, and it was a lot of fun sitting with the fans and signing autographs for people I didn't know. We all felt like we knew each other, because we had a common bond. When the game itself came around, I took great pride from the warm reception I received from the fans, and I appreciated the signs that said, *"Thanks for the Memories."*

When I ran out onto the field before the game, the Texas A&M band was playing their march, which is very inspirational. As the band played, I felt like they were playing their song for me, because I had always sung it ever since we played at Texas A&M for the first time in 1980 or so. There was so much pride and spirit in the Alamo Dome that night, and that's what college football had always been about to me.

I had a relaxed feeling, and I remember telling the players in the meeting before the game to play tough and to hit; to be tough inside the 15-yard line. They did what I asked. They played the way we had wanted them to, and it was simply great.

When the game ended, I felt like we were a team that was so good and talented. We didn't reach our goals, and it seemed like it wasn't meant to be the season we had planned for. But the kids played like champions on a night where they could easily have considered it a lost season and quit. They poured Gatorade all over me and then a couple of the backup players hoisted me onto their shoulders. I once again blew a kiss to the crowd, and I tried to hold back the tears, but a few trickled out.

I went into the locker room, and the players gave me the game ball. I was speechless as I still had the tears in my eyes. When everything was finally over, I was standing there kind of not knowing what to do. Brad "Spider" Caldwell came to me and did his infamous Heisman Trophy pose for me because he had to do it just one last time.

I ended my career the way I wanted it to end. I ended it with the people I wanted to be with. I am happy to be able to share my highs and all my tremendous experiences with the readers of this book. You, as much as anyone, are the people whom I love.

Epilogue

IN A BASEBALL GAME AS A YOUTH, I once told a friend: "I'm gonna hit the long ball." Did I do it? No, I didn't. As a matter of fact, I struck out three times.

I guess there is always some kind of philosophy about everything. Especially when it comes to hitting the long ball. I look at that a lot in the same manner that I look at life and trying to find happiness.

So many times in life we come to bat and we're looking for that home run. We often search for happiness in the same way. So many people go around looking for happiness through parties and big times, or through wealth, power, prestige, and things of that nature. They're looking for that home run, but it really doesn't come. The home runs seem to come more often when you go up there and just try to make contact. If you just try to take care of the basics in life; concentrate on just hitting the ball, and BINGO, there it goes.

So often in life, happiness comes in the same way. It comes more often when you extend yourself and you get involved in something bigger than yourself. You lose yourself in a cause, or some program, or a group of people who are headed in a positive direction.

I believe happiness also comes when you extend yourself and reach out to others. When you reach out with the loving, caring hand of concern to help someone find their way or to give them a little guidance or support along the way.

This is how I have been touched by so many people in my lifetime—and how I hope I can add a little touch to others' lives, as well.